A Boy's Own

MINING

Adventure

by

D1637901

Brian Page

Published in Scotland and the United Kingdom in 2008 by
PlashMill Press

First Edition

Copyright© 2008 Brian Page

Typography and Cover Design Copyright© 2008 PlashMill Press

Brian Page hereby asserts his right to be identified
as the author of this book. Brian Page asserts all
Moral Rights regarding this book in accordance with the
Copyright Designs and Patents Act of 1988. All rights in the design,
typography and layout reside with PlashMill Press.

*All characters in this publication are based on real people but have been modified
and names have been changed to protect the identities of those concerned. All
events described in the book are based on real events. No responsibility or liability
whatsoever will be accepted by the publisher or the author for damage or injury
caused by attempts to replicate them.*

A CIP catalogue record for this book is available
from the British Library.

ISBN-13: 978-0-9554535-3-3

Printed and bound by CPI Antony Rowe, Chippenham, Wiltshire

PlashMill Press
The Plash Mill
Friockheim
Angus DD11 4SH
Scotland.

This learned work is dedicated to my family, Bobbie, Susie, Julie and Martin, without whom I would still be in the dark.

"Life is made up, not of great sacrifices or duties, but of little things, in which smiles and kindness, and small obligations, given habitually, are what win and preserve the heart, and secure comfort".

Sir Humphry Davy FRS (1778 -1829)

Acknowledgements

First and foremost - many thanks to Rod Fleming, my Editor at Plashmill Press, who continues to display an unnerving amount of faith in my literary skills.

Photographs of Bold Colliery - Courtesy of I. Winstanley, Coal Mining History Resource Centre (www. cmhrc.pwp.blueyonder.co.uk)

To Elizabeth Milne– a big hug for the loan of a very precious film.

Extracts in Chapter 25 taken from:
1) The Lancashire Mines Rescue Web site.
(www.colsal.org.uk/sites/lancashireminesrescue/BOOTHSTOWN.asp)

2)Extract from - 'A Report on the cause of, and the circumstances attending, the accident which occurred at Knockshinnoch Castle Colliery, Ayrshire, on the 7th September, 1950.' By: Sir Andrew Bryan, J.P. F.R.S.E. HM Inspector of Mines.

Contents

Illustrations

(Between Pages 114 and 115)

Chapter One

These Boots Were Made for Walking

I was always keen to fit in, even as a green strip of a lad, and I soon realised that my army-surplus boots were a bit out of place in my new surroundings at Bold Colliery in deepest Lancashire. I also noticed that a number of miners wore clogs.

Until then, the only time I'd seen this strange looking footwear was in a film starring Gracie Fields. I forget the name, but I recall it featured smiling mill workers, kindly bosses, Charabancs, Blackpool, terraced houses, wrap-a-round pinnys, flat caps, pulling together and an overwhelming tendency for 'Our Gracie' to burst into song with a voice that could shatter glass.

However, needing to stay abreast of footwear fashion, Lancashire style, and believing that a pair of clogs might make me feel more at home, I asked Charlie, one of our mechanics, where I might get some. This seemed to be a reasonable ploy, as Charlie always wore clogs even when driving his Austin A40 (the car of choice for the discerning mineworker).

"I'll get thee a pair if tha' wants," said Charlie and true to his word, on the following Monday, he duly presented me with a pair of black size tens, neatly tied together with a piece of string. Suddenly, the enormity of the situation started to dawn and, realising that I would be expected to wear them, I undid the string, removed my boots, slid my feet inside, tied the laces and stood up.

It was then that I made a fundamental error of judgement—I tried to walk.

It started off all right; I lifted a leg, pushed it forward, laid it down and tried to follow up with the other leg. Now normally, as you carry out this manoeuvre, you automatically bend the foot which is on the ground. Unfortunately, mine was now encased in a bloody great lump of unyielding wood; the end result was that I was suddenly thrust forward at an angle of about thirty degrees and crashed into Charlie's tool locker. This, for some unaccountable reason, seemed to amuse Charlie.

"I see tha's never worn clogs before, owd lad."

I thought, "Well you can't fault Charlie for perception," but it still left me in something of a quandary—if I couldn't walk two steps without destroying a metal cupboard, how the hell was I going to walk two or three miles underground, without doing serious damage to my body, the walls of the tunnel and anyone else in my path?

Charlie, on seeing my stricken look, said, "It's easy, just remember a clog doesn't bend. You have to roll the sole forward, that's why they're curved underneath. Thar'll soon git the hang of it." And, as if to prove the point, he left me hanging onto his cupboard and clattered off up the workshop—the swine.

So, standing as casually as I could and with a marked reluctance to leave the safety of the locker, I realised a number of things: I should give up on my never-ending search for sartorial elegance; clogs were very stiff and very heavy and had been invented by some madman (probably Dutch) and what's more, had convinced an entire population that they were a good idea. And finally—I realised I would have to learn a whole new way of walking.

Oh, and did I mention that the soles and heels were shod with a curved steel bar running around the perimeter, reminiscent of a designer horse-shoe. Obviously a good idea in order to preserve the life of the wood, but—as I was about to find out—devastating if you stepped onto a metal surface.

So, pretending to be in no hurry, I checked that no one was watching, geared myself up and lurched forward by rolling my feet as instructed and keeping both leg muscles in a state of complete lock-down. Progress can best be described by imagining Boris Karloff, in his favourite role as Frankenstein's monster, clumping off down the hill in search of a friendly virgin. Only in my case I wasn't looking for anyone, virginal or other-wise, and the only person being terrorised was me.

Anyway I finally got to the workshop door and set off across the pit yard. Gaining confidence with every stride and trying to ignore the fact that my calf muscles were now in spasm, I went forth.

Until, that is, I stood on a locomotive rail. At this point, the airborne leg began to emulate the adagio stage of one of Dame Margot Fonteyn's more acrobatic 'pas de deux', whilst the other attempted to screw itself into the ground. Sadly, unlike Dame Margot, I didn't have the benefit of Rudolph Nureyev to catch me, which meant that, having given up being airborne, I landed in a disgusting heap on the ground.

It was quickly becoming obvious that in order to be able to go forwards and avoid breaking my legs, I had lots of new techniques to master. And all to be achieved if possible, without anyone witnessing the sight of a tall idiot, rolling along at an alarming angle, watching for rails, trying to keep upright and stopping at regular intervals to relieve the onset of cramp in both legs.

There was, however, no option but to persevere. After all when you've spent two pounds sixteen shillings and ninepence on state of the art footwear, you can't just pretend they've been stolen.

Later on, whilst on my usual eagle-eyed stroll around the coal face and just as I thought mastery was in sight, the left clog iron came loose. Sadly, as the iron was now fastened to the underside of the clog by one nail at the front, it tipped forward. I now found that instead of putting my foot safely on the floor, I was suddenly suspended on the twin points of a curved iron, intent on digging itself into the ground.

The end result was that one leg made an inadvertent attempt to pole vault over the iron, while at the same time, the rest of my body took to the air once more and I bloody well fell over again.

To my utter amazement, I learned that some people wore a pair for Sunday best. Apparently they were highly polished with a strap fastener over the instep and were known as 'Dandy Clogs'. The other interesting thing was that some misguided folk used to dance in the damn things—well so did I, but not on purpose.

You can see I'd been thinking a good deal about clogs—generally whilst lying on the ground—and I don't believe people were dancing in the footwear from hell at all—I think they were just making gallant attempts to stay upright.

I finally came to the conclusion that if I was to avoid either breaking my legs, or being renowned throughout the pit for falling over, it was definitely time to visit the Army Surplus Stores again. This time I would buy a nice new pair of second-hand boots, preferably a pair having been worn by a Desert Rat. After all, if they were good enough to beat Rommel—they'd be good enough for me.

Chapter Two
Got A Job Mister?

The year was 1958 (for younger readers, this was when Cliff Richard was a lad) and for some unaccountable reason I thought that working in a coal mine would be better than doing a year's National Service in some exciting place called Catterick. I think it's called judgement.

So, with very little understanding of what I was letting myself in for, I cadged a lift from a mate, left the safety of Liverpool and after driving through something called 'the countryside,' found myself standing outside the offices of a place I was to get to know extremely well. This was my first sight of Bold Colliery, a huge NCB coal mine located in deepest Lancashire and the guy I was waiting to see was the Area Chief Engineer whose name was Jack Reynolds.

I hadn't known this until ten minutes earlier when, having bumped into a chap coming out of one of the offices, I asked whether they wanted any help. You can see I had decided to keep my request fairly low key with regard to technicalities. Having stared at me for a minute he shook his head and in a strange accent reminiscent of Norman Evans in 'Over the Garden Wall' (try Google), said, "Aye mebbe lad, but thar'll need to spik to Big Jack."

Having just about understood him, I asked in which office 'Big Jack' could be found.

He then went off again with his strange way of speaking. "Nay lad, he's not in th'office, he's dern pit, thar'd best wit for him ower yon, he'll be coming up soon, thar'll not miss him."

Then, just as he was going on his incomprehensible way, he turned and said, "Aye and if I were thee I widn'e call him Big Jack—it's Mr Reynolds to thee."

So, having gone 'ower yon' I waited to see a man I didn't know, coming from god knows where, at a time known only to him.

Anyway, I whiled away the next half hour by staring in fascination at some huge towers on top of which were mounted what looked like giant bicycle wheels. Every couple of minutes or so they would whirl around in one direction and then, after a small pause, would whirl around the opposite way. Amazing.

Just as my new found pastime was beginning to wear thin, I spotted a stocky chap coming out of a door at the base of one of the towers. He was either walking towards me, or what was perhaps more likely, the office. It's a good job my erstwhile helper hadn't thought to describe what Big Jack looked like, because this guy was covered in coal dust from head to toe. In fact, as he strode along you could see little wisps of the stuff leaving him and disappearing off in the breeze. However, as I couldn't spend all day waiting, I stopped my blackened friend and asked if he was Mr Reynolds.

It turned out he was and with some trepidation, I asked if he could give me a job.

Now, these days, a great deal of emphasis is placed on the correct way to prepare for interview. It involves, among other fatuous issues, a detailed study of body language, behavioural science, response strategies, critical factors, conflict management, childhood accomplishments, stress versus pressure, positive attributes, social attitudes, interactionalist approach, enthusiasm, interpersonal skills, integrity and the ability to lie with impunity.

Happily, in 1958, I hadn't been exposed to this new world order and apparently, neither had Big Jack, because I was then subjected to the most surreal, but sensible, job interview I had before or since.

It took place in the middle of the yard where I found myself staring into the face of a man who bore an uncanny resemblance to Al Jolson. Then without any further preamble, copious notes, a CV or references, he asked how old I was, my background, mechanical experience and whether I was in a Union. I did my best to answer sensibly and made up what I couldn't remember. However, despite the lack of rehearsal, I must have looked confident because, after about ten minutes, he offered me a blackened hand and said, "Right lad, we're just about to begin a big mechanisation programme and we'll need mechanics like you. There's a job underground if you want one. See that guy in the office over there, tell him you're hired and he'll fix everything up. Now, I must go and get clean." This last statement was a bit unsettling—I thought, how the hell will I recognise him again if he's all shiny and a different colour?

A whole series of emotions now began to kick in as I realised I had asked him nothing—what did he mean by 'underground,' how do I get here from home every day, how much will I get paid, when do I start, is it too late to join the army, how will I ever understand a word these people are saying, what the hell are those big wheels for, will I get dirty and do miners wear glasses?

But most of all—would I ever get used to being called 'lad' by everyone?

Before we get carried away with the excitement of me having been given a job of some sort, I need to give you a short lesson in mobility. What you have to understand is that this was the 1950's and the vast majority of people worked within a bus, tram, or bicycle ride away from their place of work. Now, as I lived in Liverpool, (Knotty Ash actually,) this meant that Bold Colliery was a dim and distant place lying some miles beyond the number ten tram terminus at Prescot.

It wasn't that in those days we didn't travel at all, it was just that we tended to go the other way, to places like the Pier Head or, if we were on a proper day out, New Brighton (this latter venue, being a long way on a boat, required butties).

So, trips into deepest Lancashire were uncommon to say the least. I did have a fine racing bike, but for some unaccountable reason, we always cycled into a nearby foreign country called Wales, which consisted largely of steep hills, sheep, water, singing and pubs that closed on Sundays.

What I was also about to discover was, it wasn't just the distance that had to be overcome (which these days would be considered negligible;) it was the fact that culturally we were poles apart.

Don't get me wrong, I'm not talking about a love of Elgar or one-eared painters, it went far deeper than that. You see mining in Lancashire was part of the fabric; they lived in villages, pits were mostly within walking distance, they all knew one another, miners' daughters married miners, they had clubs, banners, parades, beer, whippets, ferrets, rugby, dialect and tragedy.

Whereas in Liverpool, we had football, trams, tonsillitis, the Liver Birds (not the ones off the TV), Chinatown, ferry boats, bomb sites, tunnels, adenoids, an overhead railway, two cathedrals and a well hung statue outside Lewis's.

Having realised I now had a new, but somewhat ill-defined, job and recovering sufficiently to venture back into the offices, I once again encountered my friendly direction keeper and broke the news to him. "Mr Reynolds says I can have a job and he says I'm to see you about what to do next."

Now as an example of erudite conversation, I have to admit this fell somewhat short of perfect, but he didn't seem too put out and began by saying, "Aye lad, I thout he would, he's desperate for big, strong young uns like thee." My new found confidence began to waver—what the Hell did he mean by desperate? I also found out later that he really meant 'daft' instead of 'strong'. I think its called hindsight.

Chapter Three
How did we Manage?

It may be worth remembering that when I started in the mining indus-try, things were somewhat different. Radio 1 for instance, hadn't been invented—which just goes to show that not everything improves with time.

Now I realise that younger readers believe we have always had bagless carpet cleaners, but this is not so. In the late fifties the cleaner of choice was an upright effort generically known as a 'Hoover,' regardless of who the actual manufacturer was. It came in a tasteful brown colour, was made of cast steel, was driven by a rubber belt which regularly snapped and was so heavy it took two people to carry it upstairs.

We didn't have turkey twizzlers, Ally McBeal, IKEA, speed cameras, Ant and Decking, Margaret Thatcher, the Channel tunnel, double glaz-ing, garlic, central heating, Ben and Jerry (whoever they are), PC World, Muesli, latte, Celebrities or Richard and Judy.

We did have milk delivered in glass bottles, lead-based paint, Abbot & Costello, washing lines, Duffel coats, shirts with a spare collar, remould tyres, tweed jackets, flannel trousers, padded headboards, Stirling Moss, Murray Mints, Graham Hill, Doris Day, Jim Clark, Harry Secombe, nylon carpets, shiny shoes, Mike Hawthorn, blue paraffin, muslin food covers, navy blue knickers with pockets (for girls—so I'm told,) Jack Bra-bham, asbestos garages, khaki shorts and Dolly Parton.

It's no wonder nostalgia is so popular.

A word here about measurement, you'll find throughout this learned work that I have used what used to be called the 'imperial' system. This can't be helped, because although I was carried kicking and screaming into the brave new world of metrication, I still have no real grasp of met-ric sizes in relation to me. For instance if someone tells me they have knocked a hole in the wall which is six feet by three feet, I know instinc-tively that I could walk through the gap. If, however, they tell me the hole is 2010 by 900, I don't have a clue whether I can crawl, drive a car or pole-vault through the space.

Fortunately—for me anyway—there'll be no such confusion in what follows. All the time I worked in the pit, we used good old yards, feet, hundredweights, tons (not tonnes), pounds, shillings and pence. For younger readers, this may present a golden opportunity to excel at mathematical conversions, while at the same time, re-living a great period of social history. Or maybe they'll just read something else.

It's interesting to note that despite metrication being implemented some 40 years ago, we still can't quite get used to being told what to do—witness the continuing use of the mile, the pint and the knot. As recently as last year I went to buy some timber and the man in the shop said the piece I wanted was 'a metric six foot'. There's still hope for us Luddites!

In my unstinting search for clarity and accurate information on behalf of loyal readers, I consulted a number of learned documents and while doing so, came across this definition of a colliery:

A *colliery* is a human-engineered mine for the extraction of coal. It may be of outstanding universal value from the point of view of history or technology, either intrinsically or as an exceptional example representative of this category of cultural property. It may be a monumental, or an integral component of a complex cultural landscape.

And then, when I had read it for about the twelfth time, I thought—this doesn't sound anything like the place where I worked; and I just bet that whoever wrote it worked in Brussels.

However, I mustn't start off on a sour note, I can only tell you that we already had a far more succinct and accurate definition of a colliery—if only they'd asked.

Chapter Four
What's What and Who's Who

It's one thing knowing where the coal is, it's quite another trying to extract it (or 'get the damned stuff out,' as we used to say.) Now I don't want to bore you at this early stage, but it may well help if I explain a little bit about the methods we used. I'll also introduce you to some quaint names along the way. So here goes....

As you no doubt remember from your primary school days, most of our coal, for some strange reason, is deep under the ground and lies in a thing called a seam, which could range in height from six feet to a couple of inches. The good part, as far as we were concerned, was that it ran for many miles across a wide area. This meant we had to devise a way of cutting out as much as possible in one location at a time, known as a 'district.' The method we used for cutting the coal was called 'Longwall' mining, probably because it was in the shape of a long wall—you can't fault the logic.

What we did to open up a new area was to drive two tunnels about 250 yards apart to the start of the seam. We then cut our way through the coal at right angles (the longwall) to join the two tunnels together. Now we just need to name all the bits and we're ready to start.

Isn't this fun?

The road along one side of the seam is called the maingate, which will house all the electrical equipment and hopefully, the fitter and electrician—if all is well. The road at the other end is called the tailgate and the block of coal in beween is called the coalface (often just the face to save time.) Fresh air travels up the maingate, along the coalface, and then down the tailgate. Once past the face, the air is no longer fresh, but is known as return air which carries away coal dust and mine gases such as methane and carbon dioxide, depending on how lucky you were.

As mining progresses and the entire longwall travels forward through the seam, the cavity behind the longwall increases and is allowed to slowly collapse under the weight of the overlying strata. (When I say 'allowed' I don't mean to imply that we had any control over the speed of collapse—a thing called geology took over and did its own thing from then on).

As we are beginning to see from the riveting description above, mining occupies a strange, twilight world of its own. For maximum enjoyment, the reader needs to become familiar with a number of hitherto unknown personnel who, between them, are determined to bring the coal to the surface in order to earn money. What follows is a brief description of the main players and you might wish to memorise them to avoid confusion later—or not, as the case may be.

The Mine Manager

In my time, the Manager was probably the nearest thing to God on earth. His word was absolute law, both literally and figuratively. To be fair, his responsibilities were onerous as, in law, he was responsible for the mine even when he was ill, or on holiday. In fact, if he refused to retire or resign, the only way to make him relinquish control was to have him certified as mentally unfit. I have to say there were one or two Managers I came across who should have been—certified that is.

The Manager was regarded with awe by the workforce and was always addressed as Mister (or Mester). His office was large, dark and foreboding and an invitation to visit was akin to being tried for treason.

The Deputy Manager

A man with the same qualifications as his boss—but with a less well developed sense of infallibility. He could be compared to a Cardinal, trying to remain loyal, but just waiting for the chance to be the recipient of white smoke. Fortunately, they were fairly thin on the ground, as only the bigger pits were blessed with their presence.

The Under-Manager

Of these there might be quite a few; they were the visible face of management and generally looked after specific sections of the pit. As well as there being several on day shift, there would always be one lucky individual on the afternoon shift. His job was to oversee repair work in readiness for the night shift. As a consequence these men were often quite lonely and one or two would even resort to chatting to us about their career prospects.

The Overman

We are now narrowing the managerial field, both geographically and intellectually. This chap was in charge of a 'district,' a part of the mine that generally included a coal face, roadways, conveyors and everyone involved in making sure lots of coal was delivered to the main transfer point. Many Overmen operated on the false premise it was they who were in sole charge of the mine, but with the added power of life and death.

The Deputy

This chap was in charge of a particular coal face and was primarily responsible for safety. His original title was 'Fireman' which stemmed from the nineteenth century, when Deputies had the enviable, but short lived job of pushing flaming sticks into pockets of gas. The objective of this lunatic enterprise was to cause an explosion, in order, so the theory went, to dissipate the accumulated gas. As a job with long term career prospects it therefore had certain disadvantages. Deputies were generally concerned with life threatening things such as gas testing, ventilation, filling and packing, roadway supports and disputing yardage calculations.

The Shotfirer

This was a man who was treated with some caution by the rest of the workers. Although he officially occupied a position below that of a Deputy, he was always offered a seat on the manrider, he could cadge water with impunity and snuff or chewing tobacco was made freely available to him. This unusual degree of deference could possibly be due to the fact that at any one time he would be carrying some twenty pounds of high explosive. (Mr Nobel's finest—'We go out with a bang.') His ensemble was completed with a box of detonators and a firing key slung casually on his belt.

Face worker (Collier)

The ultimate success or otherwise of the pit was dependent on the skill and output of these chaps. Unfortunately, this meant they regarded most other workers as parasites and us 'engineers' with barely concealed contempt. That's not to say they were unfriendly, on the contrary, you could have some amazing conversations with the average collier as long as coal was coming off the face in grand style. They were, at the time, a close-knit bunch, living mainly in the many villages around St Helens and Wigan. As such, it was difficult at first to penetrate their parochial demeanour and even more difficult to penetrate their dialect. As I worked on the same coal-face for several years with one particular team, I got to know many of them very well. In all, I found them to be warm-hearted, blunt speaking, hard-working, cynical, contemptuous, funny, helpful and aware of danger. But not necessarily in that order.

Mechanics & Electricians

As far as colliers were concerned we were what were laughingly known as 'skilled men,' of which there were two categories, namely, the 'fitter,' or the 'electrician.' What you soon realised was that the esteem in which you were held was transient and depended entirely on the speed with which you could sort out their problems, having responded to the call, "Fitter (or electrician) wanted on face." Typically the drama would begin with the dreaded call and, as we spent our idle time sitting in the maingate, we would grab a tool bag and dash, whilst bent double, up the coalface to the source of the cry. Obviously, as far as the colliers were concerned, a stoppage of any sort was costing them money, so however quick you were to arrive, they gave the distinct impression that you were far too slow.

Banksman

The Banksman was in charge of the surface shaft at the colliery. He controlled the access of men to the cage. He collected the tallies (brass checks) from the men as they entered the cage. When he was satisfied all was in order he would ring for the cage to be lowered into the mine shaft. At other times, materials would be sent into the pit via the same cage. Coal would also be sent out of the pit by the Onsetter who was in charge of operations at the pit bottom. The Onsetter was the underground equivalent of the Banksman, but not as powerful.

Before we move on to fresh excitement, let me just tell you about the lack of light underground. It's dark in a pit, in fact it's very, very dark and it comes as something of a shock to find just how black it is when first you are completely alone and for some reason or other, decide to turn off your cap lamp.

Let's be clear, when describing how dark it is in a pit, we're not using words like obscure, dim, gloaming, murky, dusky, gloomy, night, shade, pitch dark, unilluminated or crepuscular. On the contrary, pit dark is stygian, sinister and is the total absence of light of any kind. You can put your hand to within an inch of your eyes and see absolutely nothing. A fellow worker can be standing next to you and you wouldn't know it. There is no such thing as 'getting accustomed' to the gloom and then being able to see their eyes glowing. You could paint your mate all over with white gloss and it would make no difference—you still wouldn't see a thing. I guess the best way to describe it is total, physical blackness.

This all sounds rather gloomy (joke) but you soon got used to the fact that you were totally dependent on your cap lamp and of course, when you were on the coalface during the shift, there were plenty of lights up and down.

Here's another interesting thing about coal mines—the deeper you go, the hotter it gets. I think it's to do with something known as the geothermal gradient, which, as everyone knows, is the rate of increase in temperature as you dig deeper in the earth. This averages out at 15 degrees F for every 1000 feet. (For younger readers this is about 25 to 30 degrees C for every kilometre).

Now, as our pit was about 3000 feet deep, the temperature on the coal face would be about 45 degrees to start with. So if, in summer, it was 70 degrees on the surface, all this nice warm air would be dragged down the shaft and the temperature for us would be a nice cool 115 degrees. It must be interesting to work in a South African gold mine where the depth averages about 11,000 feet (3500 metres). Not a lot of people know that.

Perhaps you can now see why it was important to suck an awful lot of air into the pit. Not only did there have to be enough to dissipate the gas, clear away the dust and ensure we could breathe, but it also had to keep us cool. Well, relatively speaking anyway—it was still bloody hot on the face.

Chapter Five

What's He Saying?

A word or two here about dialect. I lived at the time in Knotty Ash, a major Liverpool satellite, where it is generally recognised that 'Scousers' speak with impeccable diction albeit with a tendency to flatten vowels to such an extent that they no longer convey the original meaning. Liverpudlians, however, believe this incomprehension to be the fault of the listener. The only concession to there being a problem with pronunciation is to blame the condition on the draught from the Mersey Tunnel. To be honest, I have seen no objective research to prove that this is the case. It was clear that one of the busiest operating theatres in Alder Hey Children's Hospital was for the removal of Tonsils and Adenoids (or T's & A's as we in the medical profession call them.)

However, when faced for the first time with the Lancashire dialect as practised by the mining community, I realised that Scousers had been unfairly maligned. By comparison, we were the epitome of Received Pronunciation, our words were all in the right order, we used the same ones as those on the Wireless, we could blend in seamlessly with Oxbridge graduates and we were much sought after by the diplomatic service.

On the other hand, English, as spoken by Lancashire miners, was redolent of an Indian amateur dramatic society's gallant attempt to put on a Shakespeare play. Words like 'thee,' 'thy' and 'wilt,' were freely interspersed with less comprehensible phrases such as 'owd skorric,' 'aye-up and si'thee' and 'warrut doin' darn theer then?'

An early illustration of my inability to 'crack the code' came about when Les, a fitter with whom I worked, said he wouldn't be at work tomorrow, as his wife was unwell. Anyway, on his return, I came over all solicitous and asked how Maud was doing.

"Who's Maud?"

"Your wife."

"What?"

"Maud—your wife."

15

"What are you bloody on about? My wife's name's Brenda."

"What?"

"Brenda."

"But you said the other day that your wife's name was Maud."

"No I bloody didn't"

"Yes you did, you were talking about planning a trip to Wales and you said you'd have to ask our Maud."

"Briun, you're a bloody idiot, 'our Maud' is a term we use in Lancashire for a wife, it's not her bloody real name."

"Oh."

It's one thing to try and write this stuff, but you try listening to several people having a conversation in it, or worse still, have someone ask you a question you didn't understand and to which they were expecting an intelligent answer.

What was clearly not an option was to keep repeating 'what?'—As though you were deaf.

In order to keep the narrative flowing (as they say in literary circles) and prevent my computer's dictionary from having a seizure, I've decided to restrict the use of dialect to where it might help with the story. For the rest, you'll just have to remember that everyone (except me) spoke like Wilfred Pickles on speed. In reality of course, I had to learn the language both in order to survive and to avoid being considered as a deaf halfwit. Well, as much as possible anyway.

By the way, if you don't know who Wilfred Pickles was, try Google.

Chapter Six
A Taste of Things to Come

Having been employed by the NCB, as they say, I had first of all to receive some training in the lore of the pit. This took place in a now defunct colliery called Clock Face and, in my growing terror of the unknown; I failed to ask the derivation of the name. There were four of us 'trainees' and having been told to bring overalls, boots, butties and some water, we were issued with a safety helmet, cap lamp and battery—but no canary and no Davy lamp.

We were placed in the tender care of a retired collier, who regarded us with some suspicion and a distinct lack of understanding regarding our future role in the brave new world of 'mechanisation'. He was, despite this technical gulf, a kindly soul and treated us with courtesy. What he did have, of course, was vast experience of pit life and he would answer all of our naive and daft queries with great patience. We, on the other hand held the fond belief we were asking in-depth questions such as, "Why don't you have lights along the tunnels?"and "Does water come down the shaft when it's raining?" Already we were gripped by the white heat of technology, as Harold Wilson once famously said. (If you don't know who Mr Wilson was—it doesn't matter).

What we didn't know at the time was that this little pit bore no resemblance whatsoever to Bold Colliery. For a start it wasn't mechanised, it had a small steam driven winder to lower the cage down the shaft and no underground locomotives. We spent the first week learning useless skills connected with rope haulage, which was the means of transporting tubs of coal, running on narrow railway lines, around the Clock Face pit.

I want to share the experience with you, both from my own nostalgic point of view and to satisfy your desire to understand what went on. On the other hand—you could just ignore the next bit and move on.

My problem is to try and describe in words an old fashioned, lunatic way of working, anyway, let's try............

The tubs were bogies about four feet wide, five feet long and four feet high that held approximately six hundredweight of coal. As the roads were much too narrow for locomotives, the tubs were moved around the pit by a system of endless steel haulage ropes running along the tunnels. In order to move a tub you had to fasten it onto the rope by means of a six foot chain. The objective was to hook one end of the chain on to the front of the tub, then quickly wind the free end of the chain three times around the endlessly moving rope. This acted in the same way as a windlass on a ship, where if you wound a rope around the drum 3 times, it grips and starts to pull itself and whatever is attached to the other end onboard. In our mine, this system was called lashing on.

Now, as the rope was continually moving, lashing on was something of an adventure because, if you weren't quick enough, you would find yourself being dragged along with the tub whist still trying to either lash the chain on, or if you forgot to let go as soon as a connection was made. The next exciting part of the task was unhooking a tub from the rope as it came rattling along the rails towards you. This was known as lashing off'—surprise, surprise,

Lashing off was both simple and death defying. Since the tub was being pulled along the rails, the chain was taking the weight of the tub plus whatever was inside. This meant that the chain was rather tight; but in order to uncouple, you had to get some slack in the chain in order to unhitch it.

The chosen method was both inspirational and suicidal. What you did was to move alongside the tub adjacent to the tight chain, stand on it with one leg whilst trying to keep your balance, move forward in time with the tub and push sharply downwards on the chain. This had the effect of momentarily pulling the tub forward and slackening the chain, so that at the same instant you could unlash it from the rope. If all went well the tub stopped, you could unhook the chain and throw it to one side ready for the next hook-up.

Sadly, by this point you were a complete bag of nerves and physically exhausted, which tended to make you forget there were thirty-nine more tubs still coming towards you.

There was further excitement to be had when we were working at the end of the tunnel. At this point, the rails ended at a big steel plate about eight feet square and as the tub left the rails and crashed onto the steel plate, it had to be unhooked before the chain was dragged into a bloody big iron guide wheel mounted under the roof.

This was sort of critical, because if you failed to unhook the chain, it would try to make its way around the wheel on a return journey. The sight and sound of a 6 foot length of steel chain with a hook at one end and a coupling ring at the other, being whipped into a revolving iron wheel while you gamely tried to hang on and stop it, was disconcerting to say the least.

So, if you were still in one piece, you now had a tub unhooked, with another thirty-nine on the way, all of which had to be turned through ninety degrees and lashed on to another rope travelling down the next tunnel. You were now at the point of no return and realised that the only highly sophisticated method for turning the tubs was to launch yourself at it in the manner of a rugby player and with considerable heaving, straining and panic, pull it around on the steel landing plate to face the desired direction. After which, if you were still alive, you could grab another length of chain and lash it onto yet another overhead rope.

I recall our trainer exhorting me to push harder on one particular tub and to emphasise the point, he said something that once again, I didn't understand.

"Come on Bryun rive it rand, thar't big enough t' bull cers."

Having just about sunk to my knees in exhaustion, I stared at him in bewilderment and he said, "What's up, doesn't thee unnerstan what I'm saying?"

This was putting it mildly, but to his credit he tried again, this time striving for mutual understanding.

"What I'm telling thee is to bodily pull the cart around and it should be no problem to thee because you're big enough to bull (service) cows."

Now, as a compliment this took some getting used to, but I think he meant well and he certainly seemed to enjoy watching our feeble efforts to manhandle rusty iron tubs whilst bent nearly double, slipping around on an iron plate and trying gamely to keep things moving, as they say. I did however, begin to realise I had a lot of language problems ahead.

So all that week we 'lashed on' and 'lashed off' and as a bonus, we also learned how to stop a runaway tub by the simple expedient of throwing a foot long steel pin into the spokes of the cast iron wheel as it hurtled past. I don't know why, but this hair-raising activity was called scotching and I also don't know why, but it became quite enjoyable. Similar I guess, to the way in which Russian roulette must seem thrilling just before you blow your brains out.

It's worth bearing in mind that all this adrenalin raising activity took place while wearing second hand boots, old serge trousers, a shirt, a heavy duty battery swinging from your belt and a borrowed pit helmet. And just to complete the macho ensemble, the helmet had a clip at the front to hold your cap lamp which was connected by a cable to the battery. Elf and Safety—I don't think so.

By the second week we had become dab hands at haulage work, a skill which, as our teacher was keen to tell us, we would never use again. So, thinking desperately for something to occupy us, he kept us on the surface and led us off to a nearby railway line owned by the NCB.

On arriving at a little wooden hut at the side of the line, he issued us with shovels and said, with some embarrassment, that as we were being paid we had to do something and would we mind cleaning up between the rails?

It's funny how the most mundane tasks can sometimes be absorbing, but the weather was good, our friend was a nice chap with a fund of stories about pit life, there was no rush to complete anything, as there were about a thousand miles of rail, and the hut was nearby, where we brewed up on a fairly regular basis.

So at the end of this intensive learning curve, I had an impressive number of newly acquired, albeit useless, haulage skills at my disposal. In addition, I had worked on the railway and now believed I could, if I was so inclined, scare the life out of the average cow. Gosh!

After the third week of training I was issued with a certificate and pronounced 'fit for underground work.' So with some sadness, I said goodbye to my new-found friends, mugs of tea, smashed fingers and bacon baps and made ready to report to the Chief Engineer at seven am on the following Monday.

Chapter Seven
I've nothing to Wear

Well that's not strictly true, I'd been given a safety helmet, but had a feeling there was more to it than that. So before leaving my training friend, I asked what I should do in the way of things sartorial. He said that blue overalls were the uniform of choice for the discerning fitter, but I would also need boots, a water bottle and something to carry my butties in (for some unaccountable reason 'butties'—the grammatically correct term – were referred to as 'snap'—again showing a lack of sophistication when compared to Liverpool.)

The place to go, he said, is an Army Surplus Store, where I would find everything I needed. Brilliant.

Asking around, I was informed that the very emporium was to be found in Byrom Street in Liverpool and what's more, I knew exactly where it was, lying to the right of the entrance to the Mersey Tunnel and opposite the Co-Op stores, where we bought clothes and furniture with a funny utility logo on each item.

Now it is important to understand the accuracy of the store's title; army surplus is what it said—and army surplus is what it sold.

There were, as I remember, three or four floors each tastefully furnished in bare floorboards, green walls so beloved of the more discerning public lavatories, dust covered windows and the odd fifty watt bulb peering hopelessly from the ceiling. However, the 'piece de resistance' was the artfully displayed merchandise. Piled high on trestle tables were boots—some shiny, some with laces and some with great studs underneath. Trousers—some with buttons, some with braces, some with dubious stains and some with name tags. Army jackets (as worn in 'Dads Army')—some with shiny buttons and some with bits of sewing cotton where stripes and insignias had been removed (obviously to foil any spies who might still be practising.)

Then, on the top floor, what one might euphemistically call 'a random assortment' was to be found. This was the most exciting section of the store and we spent many happy hours poring over the goodies on display.

We're talking here about things that form the basis of every self-respecting lad's treasure trove. There were tables and boxes bulging with desirable items—knives, gloves, hats, combat clothing, balaclavas, rucksacks, binoculars, water bottles, jerry cans, compasses, pistol holsters (sadly empty,) webbing belts, tin hats, corporal's and sergeant's stripes, first-aid tins, gas-mask bags, ammunition belts (sadly empty,) assorted badges, boot laces, partly solidified tins of Blanco and, in one box, an empty map case with scribbled notes down the side. Difficult to read, but the writer seemed to be mainly casting aspersions on Montgomery's ability to identify sand dunes.

However, if I was to blend in seamlessly with the sartorial requirements of underground workers, I needed to choose carefully.

Boots, obviously, were a priority; both left and right needed to be of the same size with good soles and heels, lots of studs, leather boot-laces, an unbroken pull-on tab and as an added bonus—highly polished.

Next was a gas-mask bag, necessary for carrying your snap tin, thermos flask, newspaper (a dual use commodity.) and water bottle.

An undented first-aid tin, needed to keep your snap out of the reach of mice.

And finally, an aluminium water bottle—probably self explanatory.

The trouble is that faced with such an excess of goodies, it was very tempting to overdo the 'wow—I definitely need this' mind-set. It's all very well coveting an army greatcoat (complete with regimental buttons) but what kind of impression will you make on arrival at the pit looking like an ex-prisoner of war? And of what use will that compass be when you're three thousand feet underground and nobody cares in which direction the tunnel is running?

No—caution had to be the watchword, what we were after here was casual understatement. And the only way to achieve this was to buy a duffel-coat.

The first time I saw one of these wonder garments, it was being worn by Jack Hawkins in The Cruel Sea and very suave he looked. It was obviously dark blue (this was something of a guess, as the film was in black and white,) but what sold it to me were the rope loops with great lumps of wood at the ends instead of buttons—together with a hood (never worn.) The whole ensemble was made complete by his having a big mug of cocoa, brought to him on the bridge by an able seaman—who didn't have a duffel-coat.

Unfortunately, the Army Surplus Store didn't stock naval gear (the clue is in the name) which meant I had to shop around until I found one in a new-fangled 'outdoor' emporium selling tents. Obviously, on seeing a gap in the market for manly apparel, they were selling duffel coats in a tasteful black, but somehow they didn't seem to be as thick or warm as the one favoured by Jack Hawkins.

Our version looked okay, but it lacked that 'woolly blanket' feeling and we noticed that after several weeks the nap rubbed off, exposing a sort of thin, sack-like material to the elements. Rain had an amazing affinity with this open weave and within seconds the garment became very heavy, as the water was sucked through the material and deposited onto your shirt and vest. Once the garment was saturated, the water meandered down the coat, gathered in the bottom hem, and slowly but steadily deposited itself onto your trousers, socks and shoes. And we weren't even in mid-Atlantic, although it certainly felt like it.

Well there you are, what you now had was a fine picture of a mining mechanic: kitted out in ex-army cast-offs, an ersatz duffel-coat, someone else's boots and a gas-mask bag containing butties in an old first-aid tin. Whilst not claiming to be a slave to fashion, you can see I clearly had my finger on the pulse—whatever that means.

Chapter Eight
Into the Depths

Our pit, one of the biggest in Lancashire, was going through a massive redevelopment programme. New shafts were sunk and modern electrically driven winders to lower and raise the cages were installed. Below ground, it was just as hectic and I soon began to realise what the man meant when he inferred that they were looking for big daft blokes like me.

The fuel we were digging out was known as 'deep mined coal,' as apposed to wimpy, girly 'open-cast coal.' Our endeavours were deeply masculine and could best be compared to Pavarotti; whereas the open-cast stuff was much more comparable to Emily Lighthouse (whoever she is.)

Nature, in my estimation, being somewhat perverse, decided to put our coal about three thousand feet under the ground (don't ask me why; it's probably something to do with geological wotsisname.) Anyway, if we wanted to get at the coal, we had to dig a big hole in the ground, which was technically known as a 'shaft.' In fact, we had to have at least two shafts—one to let the air in and the other to let it out. The downcast shaft was generally used to carry men and materials, while the upcast was used for transporting coal. In our case, the manriding shaft was a slightly smaller diameter than its opposite number and was open to the elements (or, as we in Lancashire called it, the bloody weather.)

We rode up and down the shaft in a 'cage' which was similar to a lift but without proper doors, buttons to press, or nice artificial wood lining on the sides. It's important to understand that we're not talking about the sort of lifts (or, as the Americans have it, elevators) you see in Lewis's here. Our means of transport, in the vertical sense, were great big things made of rusty steel and in fact, looked (and felt) just like cages, hence the clever title.

There were two decks in the manriding side and to get in you stepped in under a folding gate which was held open by the Banksman, using a bit of bent wire. Once aboard, you were pushed into a tight mass of humanity as the Banksman ensured that the cage was what he considered to be 'full.' Funnily enough, we only had to be pushed into the cage when going down; when coming up, the problem was reversed and the Onsetter's main task was to stop the whole shift from cramming into the cage. I wonder why?

Oh, and just to make things more interesting, the floor had a set of rails welded to it so that haulage carts could be rolled in. This situation was obviously good for carts and not so good for ankles.

In some pits, there were separate entries into each deck, each with its own Banksman. In other pits, the system was less sophisticated, so that when the lower deck was full, the Banksman signalled the Winding Engineman and he lowered you under the floor to a level that allowed the next deck to be filled. So there you might be, crammed in like sardines, lowered into the darkness, feeling the cage move alarmingly as another 30 of your comrades clambered into the deck above and knowing there was nothing other than a rusty iron floor between you and three thousand feet of empty shaft.

How, I hear you ask, does the cage go up and down? Well there were two systems. The one used for manriding had a steel rope fixed to the top of the cage, which then went up and over one of those big wheels in the headgear. From there it came down into the winding engine house where it was coiled around a big drum, a bit like a cotton reel. This drum was driven either by steam or, in our case, an electric motor. But that's not all; mounted underneath the cage was another steel rope, which went all the way down the shaft and was attached to the bottom of a big flat counterweight located in steel guides on the side of the shaft. The other end of the winding rope came off the drum and was fastened to the top of the counterweight.

So, to recap, when the winding engine man started the drum, the rope attached to the cage began to unwind and the cage descended the shaft. At the same time, the other end of the winding rope began to wind on the drum and so pulled the counterweight up the side of the shaft. Then when we were in the middle of the descent, the cage and counterweight passed one another at an alarming speed—hopefully.

Why all this complication I hear you ask? Well if you think just how heavy a steel two deck cage, plus men, plus a winding rope is, you can see that a tail rope would balance the winding rope and the counterweight would balance the cage. This is where you'll be glad you paid attention to your physics teacher.

A word about the winding rope, ours was some three thousand feet long and was known as a 'locked coil rope'. It was about two and three-quarters of an inch in diameter and made up of over a hundred single strands of high tensile steel twisted together. It was the nearest thing to a length of solid steel you could get and still be flexible enough to wind around a drum. As you might guess, it was enormously heavy—hence the need to counterbalance its weight. Something that does occasionally occur to the occupant of a cage is that when travelling up and down a shaft at about thirty miles per hour, you're hanging on the end of a single rope. Very reassuring.

The other system used to pull a cage up and down the shaft is known as a 'Koepe Winder.' Gosh, I hear you say, is there no end to this fascinating subject?

The amazing thing is that Koepe winding was invented by a Mr Koepe, who obviously had what's commonly known as a 'slow day' and was stuck for something to pass the time. However, what he came up with was a simple solution to a problem we didn't know we had. It went roughly as follows. I know, it's engineering time again, so pay attention, it gets exciting later.

Mr Koepe's idea was to do away with the big winding drum and replace it with a large wheel known as a sheave; a bit like a bicycle wheel, only bigger. This was mounted directly over the top of the shaft and driven by an electric motor. A clever wheeze because, in doing away with the heavy winding drum, the need for extra power to overcome its inertia was avoided. (Now come on, you know what inertia is—it's what the average teenager suffers from when asked to do the washing up).

Anyway, in this new system, there were two cages side by side in the shaft and connected to the ends of the same rope, which passed around the sheave. The rope was located around the sheave in a groove lined with elm blocks to provide frictional grip. Incidentally, whenever they re-lined the sheave with new wooden blocks, they used a high tech method of bedding the rope in- they simply rotated the sheave and then stopped it quickly. This caused the rope to slip and burn its way into the blocks, thus making a nice tight groove the same size as the rope. And you thought mining was just about a bunch of scruffy Herberts digging coal.

In this set-up, as well as the two cages, we had a balance rope hanging down the shaft and attached to the underside of each cage. So now there was a balanced system—the cages weighed the same, the winding and balance ropes weighed the same, so the only out of balance load was the coal being wound up the shaft and even this could be offset by carrying materials down in the empty cage. I told you it was clever.

Since our pit had a very deep shaft, the cages started off very slowly and then built up speed until they were travelling at about sixty feet per second. If you don't think that's very fast, remember that in mid-wind the cages passed within about a foot of one another at one hundred and twenty feet per second (or about eighty miles per hour). Now, although they wound coal faster than men, there was very little difference in relative speeds as far as you, the cage occupant, were concerned, especially if you stared at the shaft wall whizzing past and began to wonder whether the winding engine man would remember to slow down at the right time.

Being idiots and having learned engineering, we used to play a daft game centred around what we would do if the rope snapped. The theory we developed (but never tested) was based on the completely false premise that as we were travelling downward under the influence of gravity, if we timed it right we could jump upwards just before the cage (and us) landed at the bottom. The lunatic theory postulated that our upward leap would provide sufficient reverse velocity to cancel out the downward force.

Sadly, what this really illustrated was a failure to grasp, in no particular order, Newton's Laws of Motion, the need for split-second timing, the fact that it wouldn't work anyway and that it required an ability to ignore the fact that the cage would flatten itself (and us) on impact. Still, refining the theory whiled away many an idle hour while waiting for a breakdown to occur.

There's an ill-founded rumour going around that bungee jumping was invented by some blokes with a bridge and elastic bands in New Zealand. Well, I can tell you, it wasn't.

Long before there was a thing called leisure activity and holiday travel further than Rhyl, I was involved in a bungee experience the like of which these new world, sheep shearing whipper-snappers could only dream.

I had been working late as usual and on arriving at the pit bottom was told that the man-winding shaft was out of action so, if I wanted to listen to the latest episode of Paul Temple that night, I should make my way to the coal-winding shaft where they would arrange to wind me up. On arrival I found two other maintenance guys also waiting for a ride to the surface. Now, as they wound coal non-stop up this shaft, it was most unusual to hitch a ride in this way. Anyway, after some delay, they left one deck empty so we could enter the cage. Did I mention that the coal cages were massive compared to the manriding cages? Well for a start, the cage weighed nine tons, each was three decks high and each deck was capable of carrying two tubs of coal, each holding three tons. This made a grand total of some twenty-seven tons (for younger readers—you will need to convert this proper weight to tonnes—whatever they are). So here we three were, in a huge cage with six tons of coal above us and six tons below, when off we went. Now, due to the depth and the need to avoid the rope slipping over the sheave, we started off very slowly, and then built up speed until we were flying up the shaft; it was just at that moment when something altogether unexpected happened. Just before we reached mid-wind, the power went off in the winding engine house.

So we now had a rather interesting situation—the cage, which, a millisecond earlier, had been travelling at some sixty feet per second, suddenly realised it wasn't being pulled up any more. However, due to a thing called momentum, (a bit like inertia but the other way round) the cage continued upwards for a short time and then, realising the rope above was slack, thought 'hang on, this isn't right' and decided to fall back down the shaft. The main flaw in this decision was the fact that the cage, weighing some nine tons, with another twelve tons of coal inside, was now under the influence of our old friend gravity.

Now, since this little setback occurred when we were part way up the shaft, the cage found itself on the end of about twelve hundred feet of steel rope which had, for a moment, become slack, but which now found itself being unduly stretched by a downward heap of metal (and us) of some 21 tons mass. Fortunately the rope decided to stretch rather than snap. Until, that is, it went completely tight and the cage, the twelve tons of coal and us (though we hadn't been asked) realising it had stretched the rope as far as it could, decided to change tack and zoom back up again. Then, having defied gravity in its upward flight only as long as Mr Newton would permit—plunged back down, and proceeded to stretch the rope as far as it could once again. Fortunately for us, there is no such thing as a totally efficient system, so this oscillating effect went on for about another ten minutes, until all the momentum was spent and we all, cage, coal and us, came to rest in the middle of the shaft.

Think of the biggest bungee set-up in the world; wait until it's pitch black, then multiply it by a thousand times and you might have some small indication of what we had just gone through. Also, if you have ever heard an amusing sketch by the late Gerard Hoffnung, about some bricks going up and down on a rope, forget it—this was a different category of madness altogether.

Do you recall my saying there were three of us in the cage?

Unfortunately, while the cage was leaping up and down in highly energetic fashion, we were alternately playing at being astronauts, first becoming weightless, then seconds later becoming very heavy as the g-force of the skyward journey pressed down on us. We were flung up to the roof, then dumped on the floor; and about the same time we discovered that our helmets, lamps and tools had taken on lives of their own and were following suit. Surprisingly, none of these involuntary activities gave us the impression that all was well.

People say that swearing is a sign of an inability to express yourself; well let me tell you that as far as we were concerned, there was no adequate substitute for the constant stream of cussing and profanities which emerged from us on this occasion. All it takes for anyone to manage the odd naughty word or two, is to experience, in quick succession, abject fear, an overdose of adrenalin, total blackness, a madly oscillating cage, attacks by flying tools, co-mingled bodies and being convinced you were about to die.

Slowly, however, the cage finally stopped behaving like a demented yo-yo and settled, leaving us hanging in the blackness. All we could hear was quiet sobbing and the sound of air rushing past as the main extract fan continued to suck like mad up above. We tried to stand on rubber legs, dried the sweat on our brows, retrieved our helmets and lamps, and made a life-affirming pact. As soon as we got to the surface we would kill the winding engine man—slowly.

Bungee jumping? Pah, been there, done that and it didn't cost a penny.

Chapter Nine

Its Just the Air That We Breathe

Imagine for a minute that you're in the Lake District and have just climbed Helvellyn, the third highest peak at about three thousand one hundred feet. Now, imagine waiting until it's gone dark and deciding to leap off and plunge straight down to the ground below. This is something very akin to the depth of our shaft and takes about as long to travel the same vertical distance. In other words, three thousand feet is an awfully long way down. However, on reaching the bottom, you would find two main tunnels driven out horizontally for about a mile, along which coal, supplies and men are transported by electric locomotives.

Now let me tell you about the air. It's important to have plenty, for two main reasons, one being the need for the people underground to carry on breathing, the other to reduce the ever present cocktail of gases to a level where they wouldn't either blow us up, or poison everyone.

What we had to do was make sure the air went right around the pit, leaving no corners untouched and making sure it took no shortcuts. So, cleverly, as I explained earlier, we had two shafts (you remember the downcast shaft and the upcast shaft). Now the downcast shaft was so called because this was the direction taken by the air (it had nothing to do with the shaft being unhappy.) The air went down this shaft, along all the tunnels and working faces and back up the upcast shaft. Simple really.

How did we get the air to make this convoluted journey, I hear you ask? Well contrary to popular belief, it was sucked out, not blown in. Just below the top of the upcast shaft there was a sort of slipway tunnel going upwards at about 20 degrees, at the end of which was the most frightening extractor fan you ever set eyes on. It was absolutely enormous and had it been in your kitchen, would have torn the cupboards off the wall, the fridge, cooker and sink off their moorings and would have flung them all, accompanied by the dog, about fifty feet into the road. One thing was for certain, you wouldn't want to get too close to the rotating bits.

This monster was designed to extract all the foul air, laden with nasties, from the mine, which was then exhausted through a short chimney into the atmosphere, where a good old Lancashire breeze blew it all away. Obviously the top of the upcast shaft was sealed off to avoid the air taking a short cut to freedom.

Okay, so now we're sucking air out, but how did we get the damned stuff in? Well, this is where the downcast shaft began to earn its living. The top of this shaft was open to the elements and so, as we sucked air out at one end, the fresh air developed an overwhelming urge to fill the gap and thankfully flowed downwards to make up the difference. This of course is your first real life example of the well known but misunderstood adage 'Nature abhors a vacuum.' There you go—a lesson in thermodynamics without even realising it!

Obviously, lots of technical calculations had to be made, involving exciting things like differential pressure, flow rates, automatic indicators, blade velocities and humidity. I feel clever just thinking about it again, but perhaps it's not quite as high on most people's list of 'must have' information.

What of course, you had to make sure of, was that the air travelled through all of the workings. This meant you had to ensure that it didn't sneak off and take a short cut back to the surface, air being a bit lazy that way. Therefore, the intake air (you remember, from the downcast shaft) had to go all the way around picking up gas, heat, sweat, dust and the odd shirt on its way. This meant that any connections between the intake and return airways had to be sealed. We did this by installing sets of air lock doors in between.

So, if you wanted to take a short cut between tunnels, you had to open and close three air doors in turn. Such was the pressure difference that it was impossible to simply open a door and walk through. What you had to do was open a small door in the middle of the big one to release the pressure in between the first two doors. One amusing consequence of opening the small door was that the air, being suddenly allowed to go where it really wanted to go, blasted through the opening at a supersonic velocity. And, as you recall from your schooldays, this increase in speed lowered the temperature to that approximating a Siberian winter. It was, therefore, fairly important to stand to one side when opening the small door, if you wanted, that is, to hang on to your safety helmet, trousers and teeth.

Now as if being in the dark wasn't enough, we had to constantly remember that coal mines also had an overwhelming tendency to try and gas you as you toiled away. I don't know what we did to deserve this unwarranted attention from Mother Nature, but there you are; another fact of life—or not if you breathed in at the wrong time.

For some obscure reason, miners used to refer to gas as 'damp' and a very old miner told me that the word originally meant 'mist' or 'vapour'. I did consider offering the opinion that anything of an explosive capability isn't really best described as damp, but cowardice prevailed.

I learned there was a delightful cocktail of 'damps', each one bearing a vague prefix to describe its properties. There was black damp, white damp, fire damp and stink damp. I leave you to guess which one most readily described the actual gas.

Now I know that what you really want to hear about is the canary, but before we get into matters ornithological, we need to gently revisit the chemistry lessons that everyone learned (and promptly forgot) in school. So, I'll just refresh your memories with a little revision.

First of all there was our old friend Methane; this is a natural gas given off by coal and all in all— there's plenty of it.

Now for the good news—methane isn't poisonous, it has no colour and it's odourless and tasteless. The bad news is that it is highly flammable, and when mixed with air in certain proportions forms an easily ignited explosive mixture. This means that although it won't poison you (the good news) it will, if given half a chance, blow you to smithereens (the bad news.)

Methane is also a very light gas and tends to rise when the air rushing past fails to carry it away. Consequently, it accumulates near the roof, where it fills cavities and fissures. All in all, you might say it's a sneaky gas and definitely not to be trusted.

The next contender is a suffocating mixture of carbon monoxide and nitrogen. This gas has two party pieces, one is to extinguish flame and the other is to cause death by suffocation. Obviously, we weren't too worried about the flame part, but suffocation could be an issue.

Following closely behind, we have Carbon Monoxide which, as every schoolboy knows, is extremely poisonous and, as an added bonus, can explode.

Then, coming up the rear (no pun intended) is our old friend Hydrogen Sulphide, the one with a smell of rotten eggs (remember - 'stink bombs' when you were a kid? That stuff.) Another major drawback, as well as the stink, is that this gas is extremely poisonous and you can only smell it in low, non life-threatening concentrations. This is because the gas acts on the nervous system and the first thing it knocks out, before it moves on to the rest of you, is your sense of smell. Your dilemma therefore, is—if I can't smell it, is it because there is none? Or—am I just about to die?

I suppose you might by now agree that you could really do without all these 'damps' and that saving money by skipping a maintenance routine on the main fan, might not be one of our better long-term decisions.

Chapter Ten

Nature's Little Helper

Okay, now that we know all about gas, let's talk about the canary. I say this because when I worked underground, people, on finding out, invariably asked me one of two in-depth questions. The first was, "Do you grow giant leeks?" And the second was, "Do you have your own canary?" I guess these highly perceptive queries could either be as a result of my mixing with halfwits, or because the questioners were off ill when their class had mining lessons. Anyway.........

Your average canary is not what you might call an intellectual giant of the bird world. Blue Tits, yes, Ospreys, definitely. Sadly, by comparison, the canary's main claim to fame is to twitter a lot, hop on and off a perch and be largely yellow. And then, many years ago, another disadvantage of being a canary was discovered; this was a tendency to faint in the presence of carbon monoxide.

This dubious talent for keeling over meant that, as an early warning system, the canary beat the mouse, its only rival for the job, every time. With the mouse you constantly had to keep looking to see whether it had quietly gone to the big cheese factory in the sky—by which time you might be well on the way there yourself. Fortunately (for you, anyway) the canary had a back-up system, which was its inability to stop singing. There was only one thing that would shut the brainless bird up, even when covered in dust in a coal mine. This meant you only had to listen to the idiot bird and if it stopped, you knew it was time to beat a retreat.

In the early stages of being asphyxiated, the canary also provided another early warning of impending atmospheric problems. It simply fell off its perch and failed repeatedly to get back on again. These futile attempts to regain the high ground generally took place while it was still trying to sing. Pathetic really.

So, as far as miners were concerned, when it came to the creature of choice for an early warning system, there was no real contest. The canary provided both a visual and an audible early warning, whereas the mouse just fell over, with no fall-back system on offer.

We didn't use the little yellow perils on a regular basis, but one exception was at weekends when large scale maintenance activities took place. I remember an occasion when we were working on some machinery at the main coal loading bunker when a call came out for a stretcher to be brought to a nearby tunnel.

Apparently three road repair men had been given the job of re-surfacing the floor in a return airway, which had heaved up and distorted the rails. Now, as the three of them could only be visited by the duty Deputy once in the shift, they had brought a canary with them in a cage. As they moved forward, clearing, levelling and re-laying the rails, they found they needed some more rail clamps, so one of the men set off to get some at a nearby supply cart.

On his return, he was furious (and jealous) to find his two mates had decided to have a bit of a kip in his absence. So, shouting the necessary obscenities and flinging the clamps in their general direction, he became somewhat disconcerted to find they weren't responding as usual. He then noticed, having given the nearest culprit a hefty kick, that his two mates had actually collapsed, which accounted for their lying in an untidy heap on the floor.

He immediately raised the alarm and started to drag his mates into safer ground. Fortunately, one guy, whether due to being dragged over a pile of loose rails, or being exposed to the fresh air, recovered quickly, but the other one, even when dragged out, remained unconscious. When help arrived from the nearby workings and a Deputy managed to revive the victim he was, on regaining consciousness, disorientated and suffering from a blinding headache.

A quick inspection by the deputy confirmed there had been a build up of carbon monoxide where they were working. What we needed to do was get the patient onto a stretcher and carry him out to the main tunnel and fresh air as soon as possible.

I don't know whether you can picture the situation—but carrying a person over stony ground which had just been dug up, in a tunnel where, for most of the time, you had to duck your head, in return air which was hot, in pitch darkness except for our cap lamps - is not something you would readily look forward to.

Anyway, taking turns at the stretcher and pausing only to allow our patient to lean over and be sick, we stumbled along until we came to the main junction and lots of fresh air. At last we were able to walk upright and began to make better progress, when we became aware that our patient was becoming restless and making strangulated noises. Fearing the worst, we stopped to see what was wrong.

It became evident the largely incoherent noises were being directed at our friend the canary. Apparently, as we entered the main tunnel, one of the rescuers, who was carrying the canary in its cage, had caught us up and was now level with the stretcher. Unfortunately, this meant that the bird and our patient were at eye to eye level. Overcome with emotion and a strong desire to kill, our man leaned over and, facing the cage, let out a stream of invective, culminating in a phrase which has stuck in my mind ever since.

"See thee; you little yellow bastard, thar's a good for nothing bunch of feathers and the biggest, most useless, biggest little liar in the world. If I get me hands on thee, I'll rip out all thee bloody feathers one by one, so I will, you bastard bird."

Then, having made a final, futile attempt to smash the cage, he sagged back on the stretcher, just as the canary, showing a marked lack of sensitivity, started to sing and hop about on its perch as though nothing untoward had happened.

As one of his mates tried to explain, "It's thee that's a daft bugger, you should have had the blasted bird in the workings with thee, not hanging on a girder with your coat."

Funnily enough, this logical explanation did nothing to mollify our friend, who just kept coughing and muttering, "I'll kill the little yellow sod."

Chapter Eleven
You Won't See Me for Dust

We're not talking here about gold dust, cosmic dust, radioactive dust, fairy dust, stardust or dust-ups. What we are talking about is coal and rock dust, an altogether less desirable commodity which, given half a chance, covered both you and your jam butties in a fine coating of grime and when really given its head could make breathing something of an achievement. Unfortunately, we were in what might be called 'a dilemma,' because the main objective in being in such a god-forsaken place, was to cut the coal, which meant producing a large quantity of dust. This was despite the fact that we sprayed water all over the cutting drum as it travelled up and down the face. Then, just to make our day complete, the Shotfirer would detonate about forty one-pound sticks of gelignite in the remaining top coal. If you were really unlucky, he would then complete the dust cocktail and blast the tunnel rock in order to advance the roadway.

What we then had was something akin to one of those sand storms you used to see in films such as *The Four Feathers* where our hero, sitting astride a camel, spots the naughty Arabs approaching just as, with a fine sense of timing and a bad scriptwriter, a sand storm arrives. So, pausing only to wind his burnoose around his face, he vanishes and escapes to fight another day. Gosh.

Sadly, we didn't have burnooses, so all we could do was to crouch down and shove our faces into the front of our overalls in a vain effort to filter the worst of it out. Now, as overalls went, they were not exactly the ideal material to allow unfiltered air in and keep millions of microscopic particles out. This meant that the more you tried to keep out the dust, the more you kept out the equivalent amount of air. What generally happened then was, you found yourself seriously short of oxygen, resulting in an overwhelming urge to gasp for breath. Your head would rapidly emerge from close contact with your chest, a huge gasping lungful would be taken, which was still, unfortunately, liberally filled with dust. The end result

37

was always the same; you hacked, choked, coughed, spat and wheezed before plunging your head back into your overalls once more. Or, if your timing was a little askew, you did all of those things whilst your head was back inside your overalls.

And to think that, today, people get terribly worried about exposure to pollen.

There was another source of dust in the pit, which was the brainchild of some boffin who believed he had hit on a good idea. This was to be his unsung contribution to reducing the impact of coal dust explosions. He believed that hanging long wooden platforms from the roof at regular intervals along the roadways and filling them with crushed limestone (which we called stonedust) would have the effect of reducing the severity of such an explosion.

The ignition of methane gas is serious enough, but if it then caused a coal dust explosion, the consequences could be devastating over a far greater area. So, to reduce the risk of this happening, stonedust was introduced, the idea being that the force of the explosion would blow the dust off the platforms. The suspended particles would then starve the explosion of oxygen, reduce the flame temperature and hence, arrest the explosion. Don't you just love having someone else's theory tested on you, while the theorist is safely tucked up in bed—or am I being a just a tad cynical?

One immediately obvious drawback of this scheme was the fact that every time we set off our own, 'controlled explosions,' as we laughingly referred to them, the increased air pressure would flash over the hanging stonedust and simply add it to the air—which was already laden with coal and rock dust.

As a result, we convinced ourselves that this idea was yet another example of someone with shares in a quarry, coming up with a super wheeze for using up vast quantities of useless limestone, backed up by highly theoretical calculations. As far as we were concerned, the genius had simply provided us with a huge store of ready made dust, designed to asphyxiate us at a moment's notice.

Once, while on a visit to the Safety in Mines Research Establishment in Derbyshire, a remote site high on the moors above the town of Buxton, a lovely place where, even in summer, it generally blows a force-eight gale and is freezing. Despite the conditions, the scientists carried out a thorough programme of testing and certifying flameproof equipment, which manufacturers wanted to sell the NCB for use underground.

I was witnessing a test one day with Jim, one of the Research Engineers when the conversation turned to the difficulty they had in creating a coal dust explosion on purpose. I think what prompted the observation was my looking out of the laboratory window at a windswept hill and noticing a number of tunnels built out of our roadway girders and covered in earth and grass. Some were about fifty feet long and appeared to be open at each end. I asked Jim what they were for and he said, "That's the realistic set up we use to try and set off coal dust explosions.'"

Apparently, the tunnels were of a specific length, so that they could calculate the speed and path of the flame front and then assess damage to the tunnel structure. Displaying what might be termed, a morbid curiosity, I asked him how their experiments were progressing.

"Well," he said, "At first we had no luck at all; we crushed coal into various dust sizes, sprinkled it on the many surfaces along the tunnel and tried to ignite it at one end.

After about fifteen attempts, we found this didn't work, so we decided to introduce more realistic conditions and install a number of fans along the roadway to stir up the dust and let it mingle with the air."

"What happened then?" I asked.

"What bloody happened was that on about the tenth attempt to ignite the mixture, there was an almighty explosion. The flame front travelled the length of the tunnel in about a millisecond and hurled itself out of the far end like a gigantic flame thrower."

"Wow," I said, suitably impressed, whilst at the same time making a note never to witness such fun at close quarters.

"Aye, but that's not all," continued Jim. "The explosion was accompanied by the loudest bang you ever heard and, as this happened in an open ended tunnel, it created a massive shock wave. The end result of which was the wave blasted out of the far end, travelled about half a mile down the valley and blew the glass out of two new home extensions and half a dozen greenhouses on a nearby allotment."

I was going to ask him whether stonedust barriers would have made any difference, but there didn't seem to be any point. "What we'd proved beyond reasonable doubt," said Jim "Was that a coal dust explosion is very difficult to create, but if you do manage one, it'll probably be the last thing you ever do. I guess you could call it going out with a bang"

And with those words of reassurance and comfort from an expert, we went off for a cup of tea.

Chapter Twelve

Just an Average Day on a Coalface

Our coalface was called '2 West,' probably because there was already a '1 West' and we were following a coal seam on the west side. It's unerring logic like this that made the NCB famous. Describing just what the face looked like and how we got there, could be difficult, but I'll give it a try.

Picture the scene; you've arrived at the bottom of the shaft and on stepping out of the cage, find yourself in a well-lit tunnel about twenty feet wide and fifteen feet high at the top of the arch. Waiting for you on the next step in the journey, is a train with twenty open carriages, driven by a six ton battery powered locomotive, a bit like a crude copy of one of those seaside railways beloved of children and train spotters.

You take your place on a wooden seat and with a lurch, off you go into the darkness. There is a lot of air in this tunnel, as it's the main intake and is generally bloody freezing. However, such is the excitement of a free ride, you ignore the cold and turn to converse with your nearest companion, only to find he is fast asleep. After about a mile the train stops and you all alight and start the long trek to your coal face. Here the tunnels are smaller, it's pitch black, it's uphill and the face is about another mile away. Occasionally, it occurs to you that you are now somewhere deep in the bowels of the earth and a hell of a long way from the only way out. However, as you plod on, the coalface is finally reached and, as you are now exhausted; you pray that nothing will go wrong. But just in case, you unearth your tool bag, sit on the floor with your back resting on the switchgear panels and take a swig of water. Meanwhile the colliers are making their way onto the face and Kenny the electrician has arrived in a similarly knackered state.

The entrance to the coalface was about ten yards further along the tunnel and this is where the nightmare really began.

The longwall equipment consisted of a number of hydraulic roof supports and wooden chocks, placed in a long line, in order to support the roof. An individual support weighed about two tons and each unit could hydraulically advance itself about three feet at a time. The coal was cut from the face by a machine officially called a Shearer, which was an invention of the devil and was known affectionally as the 'cutter.' The cutter sat on a chain conveyor which lay in front of the powered roof supports, and its shearing action disintegrated the coal, which fell onto the conveyor.

The face followed the coal seam for about two hundred and twenty yards. In our case the seam was about five feet thick. The cutter travelled along the face cutting the bottom half to a depth of about three feet. Having reached the top, the cutter would come to a stop in an opening in the seam, known as the 'stable.' However, prior to the return journey we would have to remove the top half of the seam, which had been left hanging. To do this, a collier would drill 40 holes at a time about 4 feet deep into the coal. The Shotfirer would insert a stick of gelignite into each hole and pack it with clay. He would then couple all the individual wires together and connect them to a long firing wire, after which, having checked that all was well, he would connect the ends to his firing battery, look around, shout 'fire' and turn the key. Just like they did in The Bridge On the River Kwai.

There would be an almighty bang and the entire top of the seam would fall in great lumps onto the chain conveyor, which was then carried off the face. Oh yes, as I might have mentioned earlier, there would also be a bit of dust floating around after that.

The conveyor was then rammed across into the depth of the cut and the whole exercise was repeated, as the cutter travelled back to the main gate again.

This chain conveyor, the cutter (from hell) and the hydraulic rams used to push the conveyor over, were all part of the huge mechanisation programme for which I was unwittingly recruited. Incidentally, the trade name of the chain conveyor was 'Panzer' and, surprise, surprise, it was made in Germany. (Not a race to let evocative names die away, our Aryan friends.) One thing they could be proud of was the set of ring spanners that came as part of the kit. They were absolutely indestructible. We jumped on them, hit them with ten-pound hammers and stuck pipes on the end to get more torque and we never saw one break or even distort— incredible.

Finally, when the coal arrived at the main gate, it transferred onto another, bigger, Panzer set at right angles to the face. From here, it then went down a chute onto a belt conveyor that travelled down the tunnel, through another chute onto—yes you've guessed it—yet another conveyor. Ever onward, the coal was finally transported to the main return tunnel. Here it was delivered into a huge hopper through which a train load of sixty three-ton tubs were filled, ready for transporting to the pit bottom.

How interesting is that?

So there we would be, sitting comfortably, discussing key issues such as the latest Brylcreem advert and hoping against hope we were in for a quiet shift. Sadly, what invariably happened was we that would hear the awful call—"Fitter and electrician wanted on face!"

The next part of this morale-sapping situation came when we asked "What's wrong?" which evoked the succinct response—"Cutter's bloody stopped, get your arses up here." Now, as a technically informed reply this left something to be desired. As I may have stressed, the cutter was a mechanical monster mounted on skids on top of the Panzer, it weighed about six tons, was about eight feet long and was made up of three separate sections bolted together, an electric motor, a hydraulic unit and a gear box. It was some two feet high and about three feet wide. It powered itself along by means of a steel rope fastened at each end of the conveyor and wound three times around a huge pulley mounted underneath the cutter. So, as the gear box was engaged, the pulley turned, the rope gripped and the cutter wound itself along towards the top or the bottom of the face. At the working end, there was a huge horizontal steel shaft facing into the coal. Mounted on this shaft was a three foot diameter steel drum and fastened around the circumference in a spiral pattern were some fifty steel picks, each with a hardened steel tip. So, as the drum rotated, the picks ripped into the coal and the cutter made its way steadily from one end of the face to the other, flinging coal onto a plough (fastened to the front of the cutter,) which, in turn, pushed the cut coal onto the Panzer. Perhaps you can now see what it was I had unknowingly volunteered for during my cleverly vague interview.

Power to the cutter was provided through an armoured electric cable connected at one end to a flameproof box in the main gate and at the other to a socket on the machine. This meant that the cable was some two hundred yards long and was coiled halfway in a long loop so that going up you uncoiled the doubled half and then stretched out the other half for the second hundred yards. The cable lay in an armadillo-shaped steel track to protect it from falling coal or rock. The electric motor, mounted in the middle of the machine, provided power to a hydraulic unit from which both the drive pulley and the pick drum were driven. Interestingly, there was another, smaller, hose tied to the electric trailing cable; this was the water supply to a spray head mounted on the top of the cutter, the objective of which was to 'kill' the coal dust raised by the flying picks. It has to be said that no matter how many times we re-designed and re-directed the spray, the dust laughed in the face of our puny efforts and proceeded to cover everyone in the vicinity with a fine, black coating, reminiscent of the chaps in the Black and White Minstrels.

Still with me? Good – onward.

As the cutter had 'stopped,' both the electrician and I had to attend the scene, each of us hoping and praying it would be a problem for the other. Generally though, if the cable was in good order, the electrician would beat a hasty retreat, at which point, several pairs of (blackened) eyes would be turned back onto yours truly. Survival now meant that I had to out-bluff the increasingly restless cutter man, the Charge-hand, the Deputy and sundry miners working in the vicinity. The futile attempt to do this began by me saying, "I can't do anything with the cutter in this condition, you need to clean off the top so I can get at the hydraulic cover plate."

Strategically, this had its limitations, as shovels were immediately produced, the cover plate was cleaned, compressed air was blown across the top and very soon thereafter they all sat back with renewed expectations of an early resolution to the problem.

Now, to lift the lid of the hydraulic unit meant undoing about twenty-four counter-sunk bolts. This would not have been a problem, except that the tops had suffered an unremitting barrage of coal and rock, with the result that the edges would be rounded off and the countersunk holes would be full of compacted coal dust. However, progress had to be made and steadily the bolts were withdrawn and handed to the cutter man for safe-keeping. Finally the lid was free and could be lifted out of its recess with a pinch-bar and slid across on top of the adjacent motor unit.

This was the moment when I almost audibly prayed that a peer inside would reveal tangible evidence of utter devastation, thus allowing me to say, in a rather superior, technically correct manner, "There's nothing I can do, the hydraulics are buggered."

Sadly, in most cases, the hydraulics had apparently no idea that my reputation depended on their ability to commit Hari-Kari and consequently a quick look confirmed my worst fears—there was nothing untoward to see. All the pipes were in pristine condition, there were no evident leaks, there was no smell of burning; in other words, not a clue to the problem.

Having your first tremulous peer into the depths, an activity closely shared by four or five other jostling heads, only to reveal nothing wrong, did little for one's confidence. And invariably, what little there was turned to ashes, as the inevitable question came from the mob, "Well, fitter what's the matter with it?"

This technically astute question was then followed immediately by a key sub-question, "How long will you be?"

This latter query had nothing to do with my height, but had everything to do with the fact that if I said it will take anything more than about ten minutes, all hell would break loose.

Still mentally praying, there were now two choices; bring out another spanner and try tightening the hydraulic pipes (of which there were many) in the hope that oil had leaked while in operation, causing the unit to lose pressure; or to state, as authoritatively as possible, that you had no idea what was wrong and that expert help would be needed from the workshops on the surface.

Whilst this latter ploy had the benefit of truth, it also had the disadvantage of being suicidal. Inevitably, the mob's mood would turn from that of a helpful group sharing a moment of advanced troubleshooting to one akin to peasants attending a packed programme at the guillotine. A number of succinct opinions would be offered ranging from, "Tha's bin to college and tha knows nowt," to the ultimate confidence booster, "See thee, thar't wust fitter we've ever had, thar's bloody useless."

Interestingly, on the extremely rare occasions that my prayers were answered, and it was a leaky joint, accolades were swift and unstinting, "See thee, thar's best fitter we've ever had, sit thee dern and have a chew old lad." And with that, tobacco tins would be opened and a fine length of chewing tobacco would be ripped off and offered. Refusing this honour was extremely difficult; however, when, in a foolish attempt to appear grateful, I did try a 'chew' once, it was the only time I threw up in a pit.

What I tended to do was politely decline the offer and ask for a pinch of snuff instead. At this, the traditional tin of Hedges snuff would be unrolled from someone's sock and I was offered a lovely 'line' on my wrist. Ah, the (transient) rewards of a job well done.

Hands up all those who don't know what I'm talking about—okay, a word of explanation.

Colliers had two main methods for combating the ingress of dust into the respiratory system. One was chewing tobacco and the other was the taking of snuff. The argument went that chewing kept the mouth moist and snuff cleared the sinuses of unwanted coal or rock dust. Of the two, I found that snuff taking to be slightly less revolting and relatively more socially acceptable than chewing (but only just.)

I think that chewing tobacco was more popular because, in those days, smoking was very prevalent but you couldn't smoke down a pit, so chewing became an adequate substitute. Remember, in the fifties most people smoked and cigarette adverts carried incredible claims for longevity and personal attraction. (,"For your throat's sake, smoke Craven A") Once the big film had started in your local cinema, you hoped it wouldn't contain too many night scenes, because you wouldn't be able to see what was on the screen through the thick smoke. Coughing was considered to be a normal attribute of a healthy life and definitely not related to smoking, in fact many aficionados swore that only by lighting up could they actually stop coughing. Another fine example of making the facts fit.

Chewing tobacco could be obtained in the canteen and came in what was known as a 'twist.' This was a dark brown substance about as thick as a knife handle and came tastefully wrapped in greaseproof paper. There were numerous makes and each consumer had their favourite—a bit like jam roly-poly versus rice pudding. The 'chew' was kept in one of two places; it was either rolled in the top of your sock, or tucked behind the inner headband of your safety helmet. It is true to say that being offered a chew from either location was not something high on the list of desirable experiences.

One interesting side effect of chewing tobacco was that it created a good deal of what might be called 'juice'. Now a key element in the art of chewing was that under no circumstances should you swallow this by-product. Instead, you had to spit it out and, the more you chewed, the more there was to jettison. This was OK when the chewer was busy shovelling coal or setting roof props. The trouble started when you were having one of our many informal meetings.

Don't get carried away with a vision of us all sat around a table exchanging views. Sitting, in our case, meant finding a spot on a heap of coal and wriggling down onto a smooth bit. Our day-to-day meetings were generally attended by Davvy our Overman, Eric, our Deputy, Kenny the electrician and me. Unfortunately for us, both Davvy and Eric were ardent chewers, whereas Kenny and I restricted such pleasurable pastimes to the taking of snuff.

The next part of this social history lesson is a bit disgusting, so anyone of a sensitive disposition may want to move swiftly on to another gripping chapter. However, for the stout-hearted, I'll explain, the meeting would proceed with the matters in hand, accompanied throughout by Davvy and Eric spitting lots of brown juice at their feet, or on a prop, or on the conveyor, or on your boots. They were never too particular with regard to aim and accuracy. If the meeting went on for some time, a puddle might form which soaked away very slowly, leaving behind a deep brown stain. One advantage of this residue was you could always tell where a meeting had taken place and, by studying the liquidity of the evidence—when. A bit like those Indian scouts in John Wayne films.

Snuff, contrary to chewing tobacco, was partaken in a far more ritualistic manner. People tended to occupy one of two camps—you were either a 'chewer' or a 'snuffer' but very seldom both and definitely not at the same time—assuming that is, you didn't want to overdose on nicotine. We engineers felt that taking snuff established our credentials as sophisticates far better than chewing could. The taking of snuff was a fine, delicate art, generally saved for a tranquil moment, when it was possible to relax and perform the proper ritual. Initiating such a session was prompted by someone asking the all important question, "Does want a snurch?"

Again, we are in the realms of lesser known dialect speak here. 'Snurch' was the word used to describe the taking of a pinch (or line) of snuff. I think it was possibly a derivation of the word 'sniff' but there again, I could be wrong. Anyway, on being invited to partake, the ritual went roughly as follows—we sat down (a snurch was never taken standing up) the benefactor would produce his silver tin of Hedges Snuff. Next, the lid would be tapped and gently removed to reveal the fresh contents, accompanied by an irresistible aroma of menthol and eucalyptus to an appreciative audience. (It was important always to have fresh snuff; when the lid was removed, the contents were supposed to look inviting, slightly moist and with a wonderful aroma. Stale snuff was appalling, it lacked 'body,' it was dry, it burnt the mucus membranes and had a tendency to blow away in a draught.)

The tin would now be offered to the lucky participants who each took a reasonable amount in turn and then added that all important individual way of partaking. This ranged from the 'pincher' who took a snurch between finger and thumb and then gently sniffed a portion up each nostril. Not many people utilised this method as it was prone to spillage and gave the impression that the snurcher had read too many Charles Dickens novels.

The favoured method was to take a portion and then very carefully place it into the little dip on the side of your wrist that appears when you stretch out your thumb. The technical term for this is the 'anatomical method'. Having gently smoothed out the 'line' you were then free to offer one end to the right nostril and then the other end to the left nostril. In this way, each nostril received a specific amount and there was no wastage due to spillage. I knew one chap who had an interesting variation on this anatomical method; he had a scar about an inch and a half long on the back of his hand and he would carefully fill the depression with snuff before imbibing in the approved manner. Incidentally, aficionados never, ever sneezed when taking snuff; sneezing was a sign of inexperience and was wasteful, even worse—it could mean that someone had offered you a snurch from a stale tin.

Although proper brown snuff was the product of choice, manufacturers were always on the lookout for new and exciting varieties. A bit like the Austin car which changed from being an A30 to an A35 by virtue of fitting a bigger back window. I think these days it's called 'added value.' Anyway, one snuff maker decided that white snuff might be a best-seller; the product, although it was a nasal snuff, had no tobacco in it. What I never found out was just what the basic powder was made of, but I do remember it came flavoured with aniseed or spearmint (they called this concoction 'medicated snuff' in a pathetic effort to convince participants of its credentials—it fooled no one.) I remember trying the new variety but it never really caught on and was generally considered to be a bit too Jane Austen for our liking.

One of the worst crimes, frowned on by all right thinking workers, was to have someone steal a snurch from your tin. My mate Les had this happen to him on a couple of occasions when we were on the afternoon shift. He used to leave his tin in his jacket pocket, which he left hanging on a hook in one of the sub-stations. Coincidentally, Les was, at the time, going through what he was wont to describe as his adventurous phase and favoured the taking of white snuff. Each time we returned to the sub-station for our break, he would open his tin and mutter a number of popular profanities on seeing the depleted remains. Obviously, Les had fallen victim to the worst of all criminals—a phantom snuff nicker. "I'll fix the bastard," he said and when I asked how he would catch the miserable git, answered, "Just thee leave it to me."

Sure enough, nothing more was said until one afternoon, we came upon a terrible commotion near to the sub-station. One of the haulage lads was bent double and retching terribly in between coughing and spluttering. Tears were streaming down his face and I thought he was going to die. However, just as I was about to summon help, Les let out a yell of, "Got you, you thieving toe-rag, I'll teach you to steal my snuff, you bastard!" I looked at Les and said, "Are you sure? The guy looks very ill to me."

Les, with a terrible smile, said, "Oh yes, I know it and he knows it."

"How can you be so certain?"

"I can be certain because I can see the powder on the front of his shirt."

"Then what the hell have you done to make the poor sod so ill?"

"I'll tell you and him what I did! I mixed a couple of spoonfuls of Steredent in with me snuff and he's just sniffed a whole pile of it up his nose. It serves the sod right."

(Note for younger readers—if you don't know what Steredent is, ask someone who is very old and wears false teeth; and if you want to faithfully recreate Les's revenge, try sniffing some up your nose.)

Anyway, enough sophistication for now. Although I must confess to a feeling of chagrin to think that forty years later some miserable drug addicts would hi-jack our innocent expression, 'having a line,' to mean something far more sinister. A bit like being unable to sing 'A Bachelor Gay am I' without being looked at in a funny way—oh well, time to move on.

As I mentioned earlier, our Deputy was known as 'Little Eric' probably because he was only about five foot tall and his name was Eric. He was extremely fastidious about everything and had a morbid dread of things going wrong. His other serious failing was that he had some sort of humour by-pass and couldn't see when his leg was being pulled. Unfortunately for Eric, we had, at the time, a terrible trio, merciless in the time-honoured pursuit of disturbing Eric's equilibrium. Our self appointed leader was Bill, a Shotfirer, ably supported by Ernie, a face worker and to a lesser extent, but learning quickly—me.

Eric was always in a hurry. He would scurry from one place to another, checking, counting, testing, worrying and generally mithering people. He would travel the complete district at least ten times more than any other Deputy. In fact, Bill and I, who were to be found in the main level whenever possible, used to have heated arguments as to which direction Eric was going, the last time we saw him.

One day, when we knew he was someway up the coal-face, Bill and Ernie borrowed a pair of boots from a nearby collier. Ernie then crawled into the waste area behind the roof supports to where a tremendous piece of rock had recently fallen. He carefully placed the boots just under the front edge of the boulder and completed the scene by placing his lamp at the side of the rock with the cable just disappearing underneath.

Bill then shouted up the face that Eric was wanted immediately and we all pretended to be hard at work, waiting for the inevitable, which wasn't long in coming. Eric arrived at a sort of half hunched gallop, whilst breathlessly shouting, "Bloody hell lads, what's wrong, what's up?"

At this point and with impeccable timing, Bill flashed his lamp on the boots and in a matter of fact voice said, 'By heck Eric, who's that?'

The next few seconds were very difficult to describe; but with a sort of strangled cry, Eric threw down his stick, dove into the waste, leapt onto the boulder and started to fling bits of rock in all directions, punctuating his actions with hoarse shouts of, "Oh my god, who is it?' 'Who the bloody hell is it?"

We, in the meantime, where in silent hysterics, when, at about the fifth incoherent shout, Eric made a tentative grab at one of the boots. We all leaned forward..............

The boot, not being attached to a foot, came away in Eric's hand quite freely, an event which had a terrible effect on Eric, who fell backwards with a despairing cry, thinking for an instant he had a dismembered limb in his hands.

At this point we could contain ourselves no longer, we heaved and shouted with delight and fell about like proper grown up lunatics.

Slowly the terrible truth began to dawn on Eric; he snatched the other boot and the lamp and hurled them at us, accompanied by a stream of profanities and reflections on our infantile behaviour before gathering up his stick and storming off on yet another of his rapid circumnavigations of the district.

Although we regularly played tricks on Eric, one thing could be guaranteed; he never, ever learned.

One morning he arrived at the main gate where Bill and I were lurking as usual and made another fatal error of judgement. He announced that we were about to have a lady visitor. Now visitors of any kind were a rare occurrence, but a lady visitor was unique. So Bill, in his role as senior interrogator, said, "Sounds interesting Eric, who is she?"

"Well lads, as far as I know she's pretty important. I'm told she's the wife of one of our Mines Inspectors and is on some sort of panel dealing with miners' welfare."

Bill said, "Then Eric, we must make her welcome. I'll pass the word around, no swearing and everyone is to help her over the rough ground."

I think even Eric was taken aback by Bill's offer to help and I couldn't help wondering whether he had gone soft; I needn't have worried—but Eric should have.

So, while Eric was busy checking there was no gas in the main level and that coats were hung correctly, Bill shot off up the face to acquaint the lads of the unique situation.

Having thoroughly checked everything for the fourth time, Eric made his way onto the face where once again he let out a strangled cry. Nipping smartly on behind him to see what was happening, I was met with what might be called 'not a pretty sight.'

Being rather hot on the face, most miners wore a pair of shorts; some wore singlets or an old shirt but mostly they hung their shirts on a prop and worked in shorts and boots. The notable difference today was the fact that the shorts had also been discarded. Poor Eric was confronted by a row of pure white, completely bare arses. What made it worse was that Ernie occupied pride of place at the first pack and, as he weighed about sixteen stone, his arse was proportionally large and, given he was otherwise covered in coal dust—proportionally white.

Eric, having recovered from the initial shock, which I must confess I shared, was now gabbling, "Oh bloody hell lads, oh no, now come on, what's going to happen if she see's you, oh no, oh bloody hell, I'll get the sack.'

The scene then became slightly nightmarish, as Eric grabbed Ernie's shorts and we were treated to the sight of a five foot demented man trying vainly to put a pair of tatty shorts on a sixteen stone idiot who was shovelling coal and pretending not to notice that he was being interfered with.

Isn't it interesting that one person's suffering can provide so much entertainment for others?

As the year wore on the coal face kept advancing by about twenty yards each week, which meant we had further and further to walk to get to the scene of operations. As it was uphill this became something of an effort and having arrived we needed to do something exciting to take our minds off the fact that we were now about three miles away from the pit bottom and freedom.

I say we, because there were generally three of us not permanently working on the coal face, Kenny, Bill and yours truly. Obviously Kenny and I were hoping that everything would work perfectly and they wouldn't need us (some hope,) whereas Bill was simply waiting to be called onto the face in order to commit explosive mayhem on the coal.

Being of sound mind, we devised a number of intellectual pursuits to keep us occupied. A great favourite was arm wrestling. Bill and I were about the same height and weight and, in those far off days I was reasonably fit, so I rose to the challenge immediately.

Each contestant leant on either side of an electrical transformer, which, by a happy coincidence, was just the right height. It was interesting to note that every time we organised a bout (best of three) it became a trial of strength between shotfirers and fitters; personalities were ignored—the status of the trade was now at stake. I don't know how many times we each won and lost, but we had a good deal of fun accompanied by lots of shouting, grunting, cursing and wide ranging personal insults.

We were happily engaged in a critical contest one day when Ernie appeared from the coal face. Apparently they were moving the cutter and he was in the way. Seeing Bill and I in mortal combat, he immediately wanted to join in.

Bill said, "No problem," but I had some misgivings. Ernie shovelled coal for a living, don't forget, and it was a bloody big shovel. He could move gargantuan amounts of coal in a shift. Oh, and in between times he would come out into the level and heave several five-foot steel roof bars onto his bare shoulders, drag the cutter cable onto the face, set hydraulic props and build a six-foot roof pack all on his own. Just to complete the picture, Ernie was built like a brick outhouse and as if this wasn't enough, he had been a rugby league player of some merit. This may have accounted for the fact that when Ernie faced the front, his nose occupied a position some fifteen degrees to the left.

So you can see that my enthusiasm at the prospect of Ernie joining the competition was tempered with a desire not to have my shoulder dislocated within ten seconds. Or, even worse, an offer by Ernie to put it back in again.

However, being British and extremely foolish, I tried to sound nonchalant and agreed. We made ready for the first contest, positions were taken, elbows were strategically placed, forearms were placed in the vertical position, Bill said "Right," tension was taken and my hand was immediately smashed onto the transformer. Trying to ignore the severe pain caused by what I was convinced were broken knuckles, I used excuse number one in the manual—"Ernie, I wasn't ready."

Ernie, who had the exact demeanour of someone who had just swatted a fly, said, "Right, let me know next time."

Next time? I looked at Bill, who simply nodded and said, "Aye - it's best of three as usual."

"Bloody hell," I thought, "If I have to do this twice more, I'll have hands like raw steak." I tried another ploy and suggested perhaps we should change arms this time, although I wasn't sure whether this was such a good move as I would probably then have two hands incapable of tying my boot laces. I needn't have worried. Ernie replied, "Nay, I'm comfortable where I am. Let's just stick to the right arm."

We readied ourselves (well at least I did) and the previous episode was repeated. I shouted ready and had just about got the word out when my hand met the steel top at about warp speed and the searing pain was renewed.

Bill, acting as unpaid referee, said, "That's two nil to Ernie."

With mixed feelings and eye watering pain, I said the wrong thing.

"Oh well, we might as well not bother with round three, I can't win now."

Bill, the interfering sod, said, "Aye, but you don't want a 'whitewash,' you could still win one."

I made one more fruitless try, "Okay but this time no holding onto the side of the transformer with our left hands." It was true that we had adopted an unspoken method of cheating and in order to gain additional purchase, would surreptitiously grip the lifting lug on the side and use the additional leverage to avoid being pulled over.

"This time," in desperation I said, "We both put our left hands behind our backs to make sure that only our right arms are being tested."

Honestly—what rubbish I came out with.

Anyway, the inevitable happened; Ernie stuck his left hand in his belt, gripped my right hand, I said "Ready," and my hand hit the steel.

Bill said, "That's three nil to Ernie."

I said, "Why don't you sod off back on the coalface Ernie?"

Because of the heavy nature of the work, colliers always worked in pairs and Ernie's mate was a guy called Joe. He was marginally smaller than Ernie in a similar way that the *USS Enterprise* is smaller than the *USS Nimitz*. He was also an inveterate prankster and it was nothing to see Ernie and Joe unceremoniously pick up an unwary colleague who had strayed onto their patch whilst trying to pinch one of their chocks and dump him some yards further up the coalface. Not a word would be spoken, but the message was always clearly received. My one dread was that Joe would be invited to take part in an extended wrist wrestling contest.

The four of us were standing one day in the main stable, waiting for the panzer conveyor to be pushed over, when Joe decided he needed a pee. He had just started a steady stream when the mood to join him took the rest of us. I find there is nothing like some pleasant company if you are to enjoy a good pee. Anyway, as we stood together, shoulder to shoulder, so to speak, I thought we looked just like that iconic scene in The Wild Bunch when William Holden and his gang arrive off the train to dispense summary justice. The main difference being that we weren't holding Colt 45s.

So there we were enjoying the moment and admiring the combined steams when Joe said, "You see all that foam we're making?" We agreed we did and he continued, "Well I got worried about that one day, I couldn't figure out where the bubbles were coming from, so I went to see the doctor."

Now I don't know why the mention of a doctor should have an adverse effect on one's natural functions, but one by one the streams died away and Bill, who had obviously been enjoying the moment said, "Bloody hell Joe, what's thee on about, I've always made foam when I pee, there's nothing wrong with that, surely?"

You could just feel, with that enquiry, nervousness had descended on the communal urinaters and we strained to hear the doctor's diagnosis.

Ernie summed up our feelings by grabbing Joe and yelling, "Well, what did he bloody well say, you daft bastard?"

This last act was something I shuddered to think about, as there's no doubt that had anyone else grabbed Joe, there would have been mayhem.

However, this was Ernie and so Joe, shaking himself free, gave us the results of the examination. Apparently the doctor said, "Joe, this is what I want you to do—if when you're peeing in the future, you notice an absence of bubbles—come straight to the surgery and tell me."

"Is that bloody it?" demanded Bill, "You're telling me that if there's no bubbles you're in trouble?"

"That's what he told me," said Joe, coming over somewhat defensive.

"Well I'll tell thee what Joe, yon bloody doctor's been pulling your plonker, that's what, you daft sod." We all nodded, agreeing that Bill had put his finger on it, so to speak. What a relief it was to find that peeing could resume as normal.

We must now turn to matters of a biological nature. The carrying out of experiments on mice has a long (and honourable) history. It could be said that we preceded the work of Cambridge Life Sciences by several decades in the pursuit of valid test results on the little swine. Why so, I hear you ask?

Well, there were lots of mice underground. They had arrived, it was rumoured, in the feed for pit ponies in the good old days before mechanisation. It's a salutary feeling to think that we engineers were largely responsible for the demise of the pony, many of whom had no option but to seek alternative employment on Blackpool sands.

Anyway, with the loss of their traditional dinner material they had to seek sustenance elsewhere and the main source turned out to be our 'snap' (a word of explanation, 'snap' or 'jackbit' was the colloquial term for what, in Liverpool, was properly referred to as 'butties.')

Mice, being non-discriminatory, looked upon it as a matter of honour to eat your snap before you did. This involved them in beating all the cunning methods you had devised to thwart the little buggers. We hung our snap bags and tins from hooks on the girders, we wrapped them in layers of discarded shirts and coats, we tucked them on shelves and we buried them in the stonedust barriers. All to no avail; you retrieved your carefully hidden snap, wriggled down in the coal and opened your package only to find that someone had been there before you. Remember, we hadn't yet been exposed to Tupperware or cling-film.

How could anyone be expected to enjoy a well earned after snap snurch after that?

So, tiring of the purely physical diversion of arm wrestling, we turned our attention to researching the physiological make-up of the mouse. This involved some careful thought and over time, we found there were two sources of stimuli that would achieve the desired outcome.

The first experiment involved picking the mouse up by the tail and whirling it round fairly quickly for about thirty revolutions. Care had to be taken not to exceed the optimum amount of centrifugal force as too enthusiastic an application could result in the experimenter being left with a tail whilst the intrepid volunteer was hurled off at a tangent and splattered into the wall.

Careful evaluation of mass, velocity, acceleration, centripetal force and mouse-tail tensile strength had all to be considered in our quest for the desired knowledge.

Having, with practise and numerous discarded tails, achieved the necessary revolutions at the optimum speed, the next step was to carefully place the mouse on a flat surface and watch what happened.

Amazingly, the outcome of this carefully controlled experiment was that the mouse had lost its sense of equilibrium and would fall over, lose control of its legs, spin around, try to get up and fall over again. Not unlike the popular image of a Glaswegian after imbibing well, but not too wisely, on an evening out. (In my defence, I have to say that this analogy was offered to me by a Scot who worked on our face.)

What we found interesting was that a couple of years later when men were going to the moon, part of their training was to be placed in a giant centrifuge and whirled around to establish the degree to which the human body can tolerate 'g' forces. We felt rather proud of the fact that we had invented (and tested) the prototype some years earlier. Unfortunately for NASA, we hadn't kept records.

The second experiment was rather more sophisticated and required the use of special equipment.

In order to conduct this important series of tests we needed a metal plate, a flat surface, a 'Megger' and at least one mouse.

In the extremely unlikely event that you don't know what a 'Megger' is, I'll explain. It's a piece of test equipment beloved of Electricians and one of its main functions is to test the insulation resistance of electrical equipment, switchgear and power cables.

What you do (or did when we were using one) is to connect two wires from the Megger to the kit to be tested and turn a handle at the side. This generated a DC voltage for several minutes and the device measured the current 'leaking' through the insulation. There now, aren't you glad you asked?

However, I bet you can now see a much more interesting application of the instrument vis-à-vis the mouse. Correct—the wires were fixed to the metal plate, the mouse was placed carefully in the centre, the handle was turned, voltage was generated (anything between, say, 600 to 2500 volts.) In our experiment, which was obviously to study the motor reactions of the mouse, the response could said to be immediate.

The best analogy I can give is to cast your mind back to those beloved Tom and Gerry cartoons. You'll recall that the unfortunate Tom was subjected to numerous massive and ingenious attacks by the diminutive Gerry, as a result of which, Tom would adopt the most amazing positions—generally involving splayed legs, fur standing on end, eyes popping, mouth agape, tail rigid, gargantuan leaps into the air and a general sense of dismay.

Well, you might say that we were able, in some small way, to redress the balance and provide similar stimulus to our 'Gerry.' Obviously this was undertaken in a thirst for knowledge (or revenge depending whether you're snap had been raided that day.)

There were some people who advocated the use of water on the plate and to combine experiment number one with number two, but we couldn't condone this as we thought it to be bordering on wanton cruelty.

Back to work.

Davvy, our Overman was one of the 'old school' miners and as far as we knew had worked in the pit all his days. He regarded us technicians with suspicion, which was, in his mind, exacerbated by a tacit acknowledgement that sadly, 'he couldn't do without us'. His major dilemma was that if the plant was operating efficiently, he was happy; this situation, however, meant there was nothing for us to do—which made him tense.

In this case, we could be found sitting in the main level chatting about earth-shattering issues of the day such as whether W. H. Auden's poetry better reflected philosophical aspects of the human race than T. S. Eliot's.

Well. Not exactly, to be honest—what we were interested in was whether Pillow Talk by Doris Day would outsell Rocks and Gravel by Frankie Laine. I recall hoping she would, as we were all in love with Doris Day.

This uneasy relationship between middle management and engineering prevailed until such time as a breakdown occurred. At this point Davvy would assert his authority and issue totally unnecessary instructions for us to get moving. He would then follow us to the scene and join the throng in chanting the colliers' mantra—"How long will you be, what's up with it, can you fix it?"

Obviously, another vitally important aspect of this pantomime was to be able, as soon as possible, to apportion blame.

I would start off by stating confidently that, "It's no wonder the bloody thing has stopped/broken/stalled/off its tracks, you've just dropped two tons of coal on it."

They, in turn would counter with, "Aye, and if you'd 'ave done your job properly and tightened/slackened/modified/renewed the unit, as we wanted, this would never have happened." Logic was never allowed to get in the way when such contradictory challenges were being issued—and just as firmly rebutted.

The next phase depended on whether I could in fact 'fix it' or whether a new part would have to be brought from the surface workshops. In the latter case, an unseemly race would commence, as both Davvy and I had to get to the phone first. This was located in the main level and winning this race was of the utmost importance, since I needed to convince my boss that the problem was due to colliers' malpractice, rather than poor maintenance.

Davvy, on the other hand, was equally determined to call the Under Manager in order to convince him that the costly stoppage was due to the fact that the fitter was incompetent and should be removed forthwith.

The phone we are talking about here shouldn't be confused with the nice plastic efforts to be found in all up-market homes today. Ours was a big, intrinsically safe, unit, mounted on a bracket fixed to the switchgear. Remember I mentioned that one of the jobs carried out by the boffins in Buxton, was to certify equipment for use underground? Well that's what 'intrinsically safe' means. In essence, having tested the equipment, they certify that the cast steel body is capable of sustaining a gas explosion within its assembly and that no flame can escape to the outside. Knowing this little gem, you might realise that these phones like this weren't built with aesthetics in mind.

It was similar in size and weight to a wall safe, had a fixed mouthpiece at the front of the unit and an ear piece, connected by a flexible armoured cable, which hung on a hook on the left hand side. This hook also doubled as the means by which contact was established or ended.

Assuming you had beaten off the opposition, the sequence of operation for making a call went roughly as follows; you took the ear-piece off the hook, which automatically rose off its rest in readiness to make contact. You then wound a power handle mounted on the right hand side in order to make the unit 'live.' This also sent a signal to the surface operator that you wished to speak to someone.

So, picture the scene; bursting out of the coal face like two Sumo wrestlers, we would both dive for the phone. At this point the fact that he was my immediate boss was completely ignored, as we scrabbled for the handle, tried to drag the ear piece off one another and all the time shouting idiot phrases like "Gimme the phone, let go you bastard, wait your turn, I was here first, gerrof."

No quarter was given or taken during this crucial contest; the honour of each department was at stake and besides, an amicable settlement wasn't uppermost in our minds. Still, there had to be a 'winner' and whoever did win would ignore the curses of the loser and proceed to tell as many convincing lies as possible, notwithstanding the fact that the loser would be attempting to shout his version of events into the mouthpiece at the same time.

Davvy had an interesting telephone style; whenever he beat me to it he would grab the handle and proceed to wind it at a phenomenal rate, while at the same time shouting "Hello, hello, answer the effing phone!" down the mouthpiece.

I remember Kenny saying to him one day that there was no need to wind it more than a couple of times, as contact with the operator was made almost immediately.

This gentle approach clearly didn't suit Davvy, as he fixed Kenny with a pitying glance and continued to wind away as if his life depended on it.

There was another situation designed to send Davvy into orbit. This concerned an extension to the phone. About a mile away from the face, the coal was transferred from our conveyor onto another, larger unit. This important junction was looked after by a semi-retired miner on what was laughingly called 'light duties' and his main job was to stop the conveyor, if the big unit stopped or a blockage occurred in the chute. His official title was the 'transfer man.'

Obviously, our retiree needed a phone to let us know when there was a problem.

Unfortunately (for him) winding our phone handle automatically sent a signal to his phone as well as to the surface operator. This meant that just as Davvy was bursting to convince management that this morning's catastrophe was all my fault, the phone would be answered by our transfer man. Who, it has to be said, was not overly confident with all this new fangled means of communication; and generally answered with a tentative ""Hello?"

For some reason, this unwarranted interruption caused Davvy to forget his carefully rehearsed pack of lies and he would launch into a tirade of incoherent foul language.

"Get of this effing phone," he would yell. "I'll come down there and wring your effing neck you bastard, get off the phone—NOW."

This last word was at such a decibel level that the poor devil on the other end could probably hear him without the phone. Interestingly (for us,) the fact that the transfer man was totally innocent of any wrongdoing had no bearing on Davvy's approach to the art of communication and man management.

I remember talking to Eric about Davvy's novel way of dealing with innocent interruptions and he said that quite often he had to go down to the recipient of Davvy's bile and convince him it was all an innocent mistake.

He said that on more than one occasion the victim had threatened to quit his job, as no one had explained that answering the phone carried with it the distinct possibility of being severely castigated by a ranting lunatic. Eric said he managed to convince the chap that it was all a mistake and not to worry as he would have a word with Davvy.

I said, "That was brave of you."

Eric replied, "Yes, I had a word, and told him that he was upsetting an innocent guy who was just trying to do his job and, if he heard the phone ring, he was duty bound to answer it."

"So what did Davvy say?"

Eric replied "He said, 'Don't talk bloody rubbish; I've never shouted at anyone in my life, he must be mistaken.'"

"What did you do then?"

Eric shrugged, "I gave up."

I knew what he meant; it's just a fact of life that there are some people whose management style is based loosely on the teachings of Attila the Hun, but who are convinced they have modelled themselves on St Francis of Assisi.

Davvy was older than us; I guess he would be in his forties when we worked together and on occasions, he would stop for a chat, despite his misgivings regarding our need to be there doing nothing. His favourite ploy was to steer the conversation towards the fact that, in his opinion, we may have had 'qualificashuns,' but we were novices regarding worldly wisdom, and conversely, that he had been everywhere and seen everything.

This made having a normal chat somewhat difficult, because no matter what we were discussing, he would emphasise his mastery of the subject. For instance we would often discuss the relative merits of Wigan and St Helens rugby teams and sure enough, Davvy would inform us that if it weren't for an unfortunate injury (unspecified,) he would have been Captain of the British Lions.

Now, although we were suspicious, we had no way, or inclination, of proving or disproving his assertions. Until one day, we were discussing the war and Davvy announced that he had been on the 'Murmansk Run.' Now, this came as something of a surprise but due to the fact that our reading was predominantly based on The Wooden Horse, The Colditz Story and The White Rabbit, we were agog for more details.

Davvy was happy to oblige, painting a graphic picture of extreme cold, danger and bravery under fire, interspersed with cocoa, Aldis lamps and U-boats.

For those who don't know, the Murmansk Run was the name given to the Arctic convoys that sailed through a deadly gauntlet of ice and German vessels to bring fuel and supplies to the Russian people during the war. In fact it was so dangerous and losses were so high that Winston Churchill called it the 'suicide run.'

As ever with true heroism and sacrifice—almost three thousand men perished in one convoy—it took until 2006 for the MoD to officially recognise the bravery of the servicemen and their fallen comrades.

The creation of an 'Arctic Emblem' (they decided that spending money on an actual medal would be going too far), was the result of a lengthy campaign for recognition by those few survivors there were left.

I suppose, if I am a tad cynical, you can't grumble; it only took sixty-one years to achieve. But maybe I am being unfair to the MoD.

Anyway, as this was still many years into the future, we were eager for more, and Davvy regaled us with tales of heroism and self-sacrifice. I have to say, I felt we had misjudged our worthy Overman and regarded him in a new light; such modesty and reticence was the stuff of Boys' Own adventures.

A couple of weeks later, as I was chatting to Pat, another Shotfirer, who became a good friend, I happened to mention our conversation with Davvy and the fact that he was such an unassuming hero.

Pat stared at me with amazement and said, "Are we talking about the same guy, Davvy—your Overman?"

"Yes," I said.

"Bloody hell," exclaimed Pat, "The nearest the lying sod has ever been to water is the kids boating lake in New Brighton, and the only reason he went there was because his wife took him. He's having you lot on! I'll bet if you ask him he can't even spell Murmansk, never mind been there."

Telling myself we should have known better turned out to be no comfort at all—conned again, something I guess we all have to get used to!

There's a phrase designed to strike terror into the heart of your average underground fitter, and it goes something like this—"Now then Briun, I've got a special job for thee." It was especially alarming when Neddy said it, as he was renowned for not having fully understood the task himself—I think nowadays they call it delegation.

On the face of it, this particular job seemed innocent enough as, by way of explanation, Neddy stabbed his finger at the front of a glossy brochure and said, "See thee, that's it, that's what I want thee to do, just build it in your district." As this was about as technical as Neddy got, I wisely, as it turned out, asked if there was a Manual. With some obvious reluctance, he opened his desk drawer and passed me the document.

Apparently, a company making underground mining equipment had invented a labour saving device called a 'Pneumatic Shovel.' I guess this inspirational title could have been because it worked on compressed air and had a shovel at the front. According to the manual it looked like a medium sized JCB running on tracks similar to an army tank. The shovel, mounted at the front of the vehicle, was designed to pick up a load of dirt, carry it over the top of the vehicle and deliver it into a tub located on rails at the rear.

It was actually a good idea and would save the road repair lads a great deal of backbreaking shovelling. My job, should I accept the challenge, was to assemble the beast with the help of the three road menders. These lads worked a permanent afternoon shift, which wasn't too bad, as long as you didn't mind missing Sir Mortimer Wheeler extolling the virtues of an Etruscan Vase.

The unit was dismantled on the surface, loaded onto about twelve low rail carts and finally delivered to the site. One nightmare scenario was a fear that the haulage lads would get the carts out of order; in other words, the part you needed first would lie back on cart number seven. Due to the confined space, we couldn't alter the running order, so a mix-up would mean that all the carts would have to be taken out of the district, shunted around into the correct order and brought all the way back in again. Whenever this happened (and it often did) there were fierce recriminations, accusations of incompetence, threats to the person, denials, gloom, schedule delays and an overwhelming need to apportion blame elsewhere.

Anyway, the four of us worked on the job for about three shifts until finally, we had a more or less complete vehicle. In growing excitement we coupled up the compressed air hoses to the operating unit and our appointed driver took his seat. What fun we had for the next hour, the shovel did all that was expected of it, we levelled off the roadway, re-laid the rails, moved forward and filled a tub in about ten minutes. The lads were ecstatic, I was their saviour, snurches were produced, tobacco was offered, a pint of Greenalls best would be waiting for me at the club bar, what more could you ask?

Returning to the surface and still basking in the glow of unstinting gratitude, I reported back to Neddy. Ever one to say the right thing, he said, "It's taken thee long enough, we had it dismantled in the workshop in one shift," ignoring the fact that he had four fitters working on it, with headroom, an overhead crane and a level floor.

I said, "Neddy you're an ungrateful bastard, we've just about killed ourselves getting the thing to work and all you can do is rabbit on about a couple of lost days."

"Aye right, as long as it works okay, I guess it's a good job done. What we want to do is come down and see the machine working and if it looks good, we'll order some more."

I don't know what it was, but Neddy's predilection for throwaway statements always brought on a feeling of dread, so I tried to figure out to what extent I would involved. "What do you mean, 'We'll' be coming to see it?"

"Why, me and one of the Area Engineers of course, who did you think I meant?"

"Oh good," I replied. So a date and time was arranged, which had to be after the day shift had finished so the road lads could be seen using the machine for real. So, after briefing them on the importance of the visit, I waited at the manrider terminus for Neddy while the lads went inbye to prepare for the demonstration.

I should have been forewarned that something was wrong as, shortly afterwards, we walked into the cloud of dust on our way to the demonstration, but due to the fact that I had been concentrating on keeping our visiting engineer from tripping over at regular intervals, I hadn't been paying proper attention.

However, as we got nearer, the dust got thicker, my visitors started to choke and soon we couldn't see a bloody thing. Finally we arrived on site, to find my lads with their heads inside their overalls and no sign of the machine. Then, peering through the gloom, I spotted Pat, and putting two and two together, realised he had just fired off about forty pounds of Nobel's less peaceful products.

In a pathetic attempt to gain control, I grabbed hold of Pat and said, "What the hell have you been doing and where's my machine?"

Pat, somewhat miffed by my accusations, said, "Well I've just blown six tons of rock out of the tunnel. Is that what you're looking for under there?"

Ever helpful and completely ignoring the fact that I was about to be sacked, he pointed to a huge mound of broken rock. And sure enough, I could just see the end of a very flat compressed air hose sticking out from under the rubble.

At about this point, the dust had started to clear, the visitors had stopped coughing, my lads had reappeared from inside their overalls and Pat had given me a sort of uncertain smile.

In an effort to retrieve the irretrievable, I said to Neddy, "Sorry about this, but as you can see we've had a bit of a setback. I don't think we can give you a demonstration today." (I think nowadays this is known as 'stating the bleeding obvious.')

Neddy stared at me with something approaching hatred and said, "Does tha' mean we've had a wasted journey then?"

There's no doubt that Neddy's grasp of the 'bleeding obvious' was keenly honed.

"Sorry, but as you can see, its going to take the lads some time to retrieve the machine and then we'll have to check everything to see what's been damaged."

Then, for the first time, the Engineer spoke. "Do you mean we'll have to walk all the way out again, before we can catch the manrider?"

"I'm afraid so, but its not too bad going out, as it's down hill for some of the way."

I thought for a moment he was going to cry. Anyway, realising there was no option, off they trudged.

Pat, who had been listening to the exchange, said, "Why didn't you tell them there's no manrider at this time in the afternoon? They'll have to walk out another mile to the pit bottom."

I replied, "There are some things in life you have to find out about for yourself."

Then, as there didn't seem to be anything more to add, the five of us sat down on the heap of rock and passed around a tin of nice fresh snuff. Just to clear the dust out of the sinuses, you understand.

Chapter Thirteen
Further Educashun

As time went on I was encouraged to attend the local Technical College for one day a week in order to obtain qualifications in mining related subjects. For some unaccountable reason, this went well and by some mysterious trick of the light I managed to be awarded a 'First Prize for Proficiency,' in the examinations. I never really understood what 'proficiency' meant in this context, until someone told me I had achieved the highest set of marks for that particular year.

So much so, that Geoff, the Deputy Head, who was a good guy, approached me and said I was entitled to a prize amounting to £2, and could I let him know what I wanted?

What excitement. I nipped out to the local bookshop, spied a book within the price range (thirty-five shillings) and reported back.

Geoff inquired, "What have you chosen?"

I replied, "The Second World War by Winston Churchill."

He looked at me and said, "Really - are you sure?"

Having misunderstood his concern I answered, "Yes, it's the abridged one-volume version."

He grunted, "Oh well, if it's what you want."

I asked Jack, another lecturer, why Geoff seemed a bit cool at my choice and he told me, "Well it's probably because Churchill's a Conservative and Geoff is a dyed in the wool Labour supporter."

Another sensitivity trodden on and what made it worse was that when I was formally presented with my prize, I was conscious of the fact that Geoff was somewhat terse in extolling the virtues of my choice.

Anyway, having attained this honour, I could then seek promotion to the lofty status of 'Mechanic of the Mine'. This was a position bounded by legislation and as such, I had to be sworn in—in a more formal sense than hitherto, as it were. This involved me having a rare meeting with the Chief Engineer and being lectured to on my new-found responsibilities.

Even to this day, I can recite from memory the role as laid down in the

Mines and Quarries Act, and I intend to quote it to you now.

After all, what's the point in me remembering all this stuff if you can't share it with your friends?

'It is the duty of the mechanic of the mine to:

Supervise or effect the installation of all such apparatus at the mine;

The examination, testing of all apparatus before it is put into use after installation, re-installation or repair;

The maintenance in safe working condition and in accordance with all requirements;

The systematic examination and testing of all such apparatus at the mine in accordance with the scheme for the time being in operation.'

How's that, impressive or what?

An invite to the chief's office followed, where I was indoctrinated, lectured, warned, congratulated and made to sign a number of official looking documents. This meant I was now accountable (in law) for the activities mentioned above and as such was required to sign a book known as M & Q Form 276 'Reports of Defective Mechanical Apparatus.'

And there's you thinking I was just a nobody.

This form (it was actually a book) had to be filled in and signed at the end of each shift, whereupon it was counter-signed by the Under-Manager before being placed on the Manager's desk (open at the current page.) He would then peruse the document, together with numerous others dealing with various activities, such as underground safety, locomotive transport, winding ropes and ventilation. He wasn't called the Manager for nothing.

It just so happened that after the first flush of excitement had worn off with regard to filling in the book day after day, I had a brainwave—or so I thought.

You see the M & Q Book posed a number of very important safety related questions to which, as an appointed person, you had to frame an accurate but succinct reply.

Then having completed a number of specific technical sections, you were required to add a comment at the end, the objective of which was to summarise the overall state of the mechanical equipment for which you were responsible.

In striving to be succinct, we used to pen such works of genius as, 'All in good working order,' or, 'All in sound working order,' or, 'All working in order,' or 'All examinations complete,' (a novel variation.) You can see the pattern emerging; a certain lack of imagination should be becoming apparent. It was then that I had my brainwave, and in the appropriate section I wrote –

'All Quiet on the Western Front.'

Brilliant!

This I felt, captured the true spirit of mining, it was relevant (we were on the west side,) it borrowed from a classic of the cinema and injected just the right amount of levity without being flippant—at least that's what I thought.

Surprisingly, as it turned out, I was wrong.

My first intimation that all was not well was when I discovered that my cap lamp and battery were missing from their assigned location. On querying this sudden disappearance with the lamp room technician, I was informed that the Manager had withdrawn my lamp and I was to report to his office at seven am prompt. Blissfully ignorant of what was to come, I knocked on his door at the appointed time and went in.

Both to my surprise and a growing sense of unease, I found myself face to face with the Manager, the Under Manager, Bert the Chief Engineer and Neddy my immediate boss. I suppose I should have guessed something was up when I wasn't asked to sit down.

Then, without so much as a 'Good morning' the Manager flung the M&Q Book across the desk and stabbing a finger on the offending section demanded, "What the bloody hell's this?"

And without waiting for a reply, continued, "Who told you to be a funny man with one of Her Majesty's legal documents?"

Rapidly followed up with, "I don't pay you to make ridiculous comments in statutory instruments you miserable bastard."

It dawned on me that up to now, although he had asked a number of questions, they all appeared to be rhetorical and he didn't actually expect me to answer. This was just as well; as I was terrified and anyway, I couldn't think of anything to say.

He then delivered his coup de grace. "Don't you realise that all these documents have to be counter-signed by me, acknowledging I have read and agree with the contents? Then they are all left open so that they can be examined and ratified by one of Her Majesty's Inspectors of Mines."

There he was, name dropping Her Majesty again—as if I wasn't sufficiently impressed. I now began to think that what I had done might be treasonable.

Meanwhile as he paused for a moment in this tirade, I noticed that his acolytes were all nodding vigorously in agreement, while at the same time trying to give the impression that I wasn't actually known to them—so much for loyalty.

Anyway, the upshot was I was forced to put a line through the offending section and we both counter-signed the changes.

I then spoiled what I thought was his return to sanity by asking if I could have my lamp back.

I won't go into the details of what followed—I've identified enough embarrassing confessions for one day—but suffice it to say I should have known better. At last, however, the renewed tirade finished and I realised I still had a job. As I walked, somewhat unsteadily, across the yard with Bert, he said, "I guess you realise you nearly got the sack just then, but for some bloody reason 't Manager's let thee off with a right good bollocking."

Continuing in what I now considered to be extreme caution, I said something pithy like, "Yes." When he continued, "Aye, but you did make the Manager smile—until, that is, he realised your masterpiece would be seen by the Inspectorate."

"Fine," I said, "He could have fooled me."

"Aye lad he could, that's why he's the Manager and you're not."

And with those words of wisdom, Bert went back to his office and I went down the pit, faced with a miserable three-mile walk, as the man-rider had finished its scheduled runs for the morning.

I have to say I was somewhat exercised knowing that my comments would be closely scrutinised from now on. Oh well, I thought, play it safe, back to variations on the theme of 'All in working order.'

(Note for younger readers—All Quiet on the Western Front was an Oscar winning film made in 1939 based on a book by Erich Maria Remarque. It is an epic saga of German schoolboys called up during the First World War. I guess the author was being somewhat ironic in his choice of title.)

Word of my brush with Her Majesty's representatives on earth soon spread and I was surprised to learn that Harold, a fitter working on the East side confessed that he had also been summoned to the presence. Apparently, he hadn't been as lyrical as me, but in a fit of misplaced indignation regarding perjury, he got into the habit of writing 'All OK where seen'.

This, he felt struck a correct balance between what machinery he had witnessed during the shift and what machinery he was aware of, but hadn't actually seen. I asked him what had happened.

"I was hauled in front of management, just like thee."

"'Yes, but what did the Manager say?"

"He said, 'Don't play bloody games with me you miserable sod, just tell me—did you bloody see the plant or didn't you? And, if you bloody didn't, what the bloody hell am I paying you for?'"

"Wow," I said, "I think I got off lightly."

"Aye, that's probably because you were cunning enough to quote from the First World War." I thought a hint of jealousy was creeping in, so I offered Harold a snurch and we changed the subject.

Later on, in a moment of weakness, I thought I might be able to learn even more than I knew already and signed on at Wigan and District Mining and Technical College. Notice the emphasis on mining in the title. This was an advanced course, still on day release, but was a lot further to travel into deepest Lancashire.

Now day release was okay but for one small snag. At the time I was working on a rota of alternate weekly day and night shifts, so attending college was all right when you were on days, but was considerably less attractive when you were on nights. You had to decide whether to come straight off night shift and attend the college, thus giving you the following night off. Or, you could take the night before off, attend college the next day and then go straight onto night shift that evening. Some choice.

In the end I found the latter system to be the lesser of two evils. Better to go on nights completely knackered and hope for a quiet time, rather than come off nights and go straight into an enthralling two hours of something mysterious called Thermodynamics.

Talking about Thermodynamics, we students found, to our horror, that this subject was largely based on a thing called applied mathematics—an apparently necessary skill that we had so far managed to get through life without ever needing.

Our lecturer was used to dealing with students who already had degree level maths and was nonplussed to find we weren't completely au fait with differential calculus, as applied to the enthalpy/entropy diagram for steam in the superheat region. Pathetic really.

Although we were reasonably good at 'sums,' all this applied stuff was new to us. Sadly, our undoubted ability to use algebra for wage calculations, turned out to be woefully inadequate—especially, as you know, when faced with the need to determine the stoichiometric air/fuel ratio for a given fuel.

So, partly in order for us to become clever and partly to avoid our Thermodynamics Lecturer having to seek counselling, they decided to give us extra maths lessons, an early example of 'care in the community.'

These extra curricular lessons were scheduled to take place at the end of the day, during which we had grappled manfully with such riveting subjects as Newton's three laws of motion, Euler's formula for slender columns and finally, 'The Law relating to safety and Health – Mines of Coal.'

So, fully stimulated and completely mind blown, we eagerly awaited our new maths lecturer. Sadly for us, he could only get to the college by seven pm, which meant we had to contain our excitement for another two hours. We drank tea, ate buns, read the latest issue of Reveille (very daring; it used to have great pictures of a girl called Sabrina, notable for her womanly measurements of 44", 17", 42"—there are some things you never forget). Or mostly, we simply nodded off.

Came seven pm and we were jolted into wakefulness by a man who seemed to know an awful lot more about differential thingy than we did. While all this extra learning was taking place, we looked forward to eight pm, so that we could get home, grab our snap and be on the pit bank by ten pm. Who was it said that an empty hour was a wasted hour? The prat.

Still, it must have worked because we did remember a good deal of thermowotsit and managed to bluff the examination board to such an extent that we passed our exams. Sadly, having committed all sorts of complex formulae to memory, I can't ever remember using my new-found genius. I recently came across one of my notebooks from the great learning era and if I hadn't recognised the writing, I would never have believed I had written the damned stuff. And as for understanding...

However, my new found Educashun provided me with yet another chance encounter with Bert our Chief Engineer.

Bert was renowned for two things—one, he had the biggest feet of anyone at the colliery and two, he would invariably offer the same highly technical advice whenever he came into the workshops. This compulsion to join in used to drive two of our best fitters mad with frustration.

Billy was a fitter of the old school and had for many years worked at Vulcan in Newton-le-Willows making locomotive engines for the whole world. He was fairly tall, well built with wavy black hair and looked a bit like a slightly worn version of Victor Mature. His abiding interest lay in Norton motorcycles, which he had raced until he had a serious accident on the Isle of Man. He had entered the TT races on several occasions, where he had twice lost gloriously to his hero, Geoff Duke. Leaving aside motor bikes for a moment, he once confided that sadly, as his wife had become disinterested in matters of a sexual nature, he had been forced to find solace elsewhere. In this case, with a lady who lived just 'down the road.' Although I was curious to know more about his marital problems (purely in the interests of research,) I never liked to ask and Billy never volunteered to elaborate.

His idol, Geoff Duke, had won the TT six times and the world championship six times as well. As far as Billy was concerned Duke was to be spoken of with reverence, and who can blame him? It would be difficult today to find an equivalent British champion, especially one who wore ex-army boots while so doing.

Jimmy, on the other hand, was unlike Billy in both build and outgoing demeanour; where Billy was stocky; Jimmy had a sort of haunted look (a bit like Anthony Perkins) and spoke only when asked a question. He generally deferred to Billy, except where in-depth knowledge of hydraulics was concerned, but together they made a formidable team.

Their main occupation during the day was as specialist designers and builders of new transfer chutes for various conveyors throughout the pit. They would go to the site, measure up, make sketches in Jimmy's notebook, bend brazing rods into complex shapes and return to the workshops.

Billy would set out the plan of action, Jimmy would nod in agreement and work would begin. Steel plate would be laid on the floor, marked out, flame cut, bent, welded, drilled and assembled on a dummy conveyor head mounted on trestles. They were highly skilled and unbeatable at fabricating what were at times, very complex assemblies, particularly as the angles and curves were based on the accuracy with which they had bent the brazing rods.

On arriving at the fabrication site, Bert would stop by the two lads and invariably open the conversation in the following manner—"Now then Billy where's tha makin this chute for?"

Billy would stare at Bert and say something like, "It's for the main gate transfer point at Rushy Park."

Then Bert would come out with his stock piece of advice.

"Great job lads, but I think you ought to just put a couple of 6" x 8" girders along the bottom, just to be sure."

And then, without waiting for a reply, he would put his feet into gear and saunter off.

His gem of wisdom would leave both Billy and Jimmy speechless with rage, and generally it was left to Billy, who worked on a shorter fuse, to give vent to their frustration.

"Bloody six by eight Bert, I'll swing for the bastard, if he keeps coming round here telling us to do the same thing time after time, why doesn't he sod off and mind his own business. I sure as hell don't need a pen pusher like him handing out daft advice."

And then Billy would finish his tirade with what he considered to be the clincher. "Anyone with feet that size needn't worry about girders for stability."

I never really understood the relevance of this last utterance, but it didn't seem to be the right time to ask him to explain.

Anyway, Bert sent for me one day just as I was starting the afternoon shift. This was an in-between shift where they didn't send coal, so it was an opportunity to advance roadways, lay tracks, clean up and maintain things.

"Now lad, I hear tha's got thee sen a new qualification?"

"Yes Bert," I said, wondering what was coming next.

"Well lad, it means I can promote thee while you're on afternoons."

"Gosh," I thought, "Promotion, this means more money, an office with a desk, a Davy lamp of my own"—and numerous other stupid flights of fancy. I then realised I was completely on the wrong track, as Bert continued, "I need to appoint someone to be the Mechanic in Charge in the Absence of the Engineer and, as you have the necessary certificate, you'll do just fine."

This was another statutory appointment designed to ensure there was always a qualified person on duty at all times. Obviously Bert had to go home at the end of the day and I was to be his official appointee while he was away grooming his ferrets, or whatever.

Believing that a little healthy crawling was in order, I said, "Thanks Bert, I'll do my best to see things are OK while you're away."

Bert then said, "Reet lad, now, as you might suspect, there's a standard payment for each shift you're in charge; and at present it amounts to three shillings."

At this revelation, all thoughts of buying a detached house faded away. Three bloody shillings? I could only stare at the sod, which he took to be delight and gratitude at the prospect.

Bert then delivered his coup de grace.

"Reet lad, just sign here. Oh and by the way, as I never leave before five o'clock, which is part way into your shift, I'll be paying you two and threepence instead of the full amount."

Once again my silent stare was taken for delight, but all I could think was, "Bert you're a miserable bastard."

Still blissfully unaware of my less than obvious delight, he added, "Now remember, if owt goes wrong with either the main fan or the winders, you're to call me immediately, no trying to fix things yourself."

I thought, "That'll be right, me tampering with the most critical bits of kit in the mine and all for two and threepence." I bet Billy would have known what to say and it would probably have contained a number of succinct references to Bert's feet.

When I was back on day shift, I mentioned Bert's magnanimity to Bill, our Shotfirer. He gave me one of those pitying looks and said, "Well, if you want to get your own back I can let you have half a stick of gelignite and a detonator. You could stick it in his allotment shed—that should sort the miserable git's seed trays out."

The trouble was, although the offer was very attractive, I probably would have blown myself up as well, so I never did find out whether Bill was joking or not.

While we were on the subject of using explosives to resolve minor problems, he told me a tale about a favour he did for a relative of his wife. Apparently, this guy had just moved into a new house and he was anxious to landscape his front garden. The only snag was that, when building the estate, the builders had chopped down a big elm tree but had left a gigantic root smack in the middle of what was now the front garden.

Knowing about Bill's job, he asked if he could loosen the roots so that it could be sawn up and removed. Bill, on being persuaded by his wife to help, said he would sort something out and arrived one Saturday morning, armed with sticks of gelignite, some detonators and a firing mechanism.

Working quietly, Bill and his brother-in-law dug under the stump and packed the purloined explosive in the holes, stretched the wires out, relayed them together and attached the ends to the turn-key ready for firing.

According to Bill, he said, "'Right, I'll run the cable up the side of the house, we'll take cover and I'll fire the shots. There'll be a whump and the stump should just shake itself free of the ground so you can cut it up.

"What happened then?" I asked, incredulous.

"Well," said Bill, "I fired off, there was a bit of a bang and a lot of dust, but unfortunately I'd slightly misjudged the force of the explosive. When the dust cleared, we found the bloody tree stump in the middle of the road and most of his garden was spread neatly over next-door's roses, their front path, garage doors, windows, washing, bird bath, a mongrel dog, two children and a parked milk float."

I then asked one of those stupid questions so beloved of radio interviewers.

"What did your brother-in-law say?"

"Oh, something along the lines of 'Sod it Bill, you're a mad bastard.' But that was nothing compared to what my bloody wife and her sister said when they came back from the shops and saw what had happened."

As I could see that even now the memory was still painful, I really didn't like to ask what they said—but obviously I did.

Apparently, having stared in disbelief at the carnage, his wife grabbed Bill by the shirt with one hand and commenced stabbing him with the other, in time to a tirade of his known and hitherto unknown faults. As she warmed to the subject, her voice became louder and soon there were a growing number of interested bystanders fascinated by the sight of a five-foot woman publicly dissecting the attributes of a six-foot four-inch man.

"Yes," I persisted, "But what did she say?"

"Well, she pointed out that I was a worthless, useless, great lump of crap, why she had ever married me was a mystery to her, her mother had warned her about me and she should have listened, I was responsible for her being totally embarrassed in front of her sister's new neighbours and how on earth could she show her face here ever again."

"Wow," I said, "What did you say to that?"

"Bugger all," replied Bill, "But I did offer to help move the tree root."

Chapter Fourteen
Food Fit for a King

The Government, in its infinite wisdom, during the Second World War, came to the conclusion that mining was of a somewhat manual nature. Therefore, being mindful of the need to keep our lads shovelling, they increased their cheese ration from two ounces a week to four and then eight ounces. Bear in mind, we are talking about ounces per week, not kilogrammes, so put aside all thoughts of gigantic cheese butties, as seen in pubs offering 'ploughman's lunches' which feature a lump of Cheddar the size of a small car.

In fact it wasn't until 1954 that cheese became unrationed. That meant you could buy as much as you liked—except that you couldn't, due to the fact that we'd eaten all the cows.

You need to also remember that sophisticated sandwich fillings such as cranberry and chicken, roast beef and horseradish, diced bacon and walnuts hadn't yet been invented. There were no 'Prêt a Manger' shops littering the high street and even Marks and Spencer hadn't realised that sandwiches could out-sell liberty bodices (whatever they are.)

So, sandwich fillings of choice might consist of condensed milk (messy, especially with added sugar,) Spam, boiled ham (very thin, no flavour,) or tomatoes (messy again.) However, the all time favourite filling was jam (consisting largely of swede, carrot and little wooden seeds to provide authenticity.) Fortunately, jam had two distinct advantages; it was easy to spread and it soaked into the bread.

A word here about bread. What I'm talking about was euphemistically called 'white bread,' and should not be confused with the multitude of types, shapes, contents and dubious flavours of the eighties and nineties.

Our bread was really a sort of off-white confection with a rubbery texture (this applied to the taste as well, for that matter.) Its main advantage was that it came wrapped in greaseproof paper, which turned out to be excellent for wrapping up your butties and stopping fillings such as condensed milk or jam from leaking out.

Due to the ungodly hour you had to be up, butties were generally made the night before, which allowed the jam to become more or less an integral part of the bread by morning.

On arrival at the pit, a fleet of buses would disgorge the huddled masses and we would all make our way to the canteen. Once there, we would order a bacon roll and a mug of tea. This, of course, was your breakfast and very welcome it was too. The tea was dark brown, very strong and served in a half pint mug with extremely thick sides and a sensible handle. Obviously some were chipped here and there and the skill was to circumvent the worst breaks in order to prevent second degree lacerations to the lips.

The canteen ladies were divided into two categories, the fearsome and the young; but at that hour of the morning even the young ones looked fairly fearsome, or maybe it was just a trick of the light.

Their uniforms were of the come-hither variety consisting of a floral wrap-around pinny, a turban of some indiscriminate material (sometimes allowing the odd wire curler to peep through) and, to complete the ensemble, a tea-towel gripped firmly under one arm.

Light-hearted banter was permissible, but innuendo of a sexual nature was severely restricted to a small number of guys who were in the 'prior knowledge' category.

I once saw a young haulage lad say something to one of the slightly younger ladies about "It being her lucky day and he could do her a power of good with a roll outside." I think he had learned his chat-up technique from a seed catalogue.

I should, however, have been prepared for the recipient's reaction, because on hearing his 'it never fails' spiel, the chaps to his immediate right and left moved swiftly to one side. They were wise to do so—the tea pot, which, until that moment, had been gripped firmly in her left hand, crashed down onto the metal counter, then, as though fired from a gun, her right arm shot out and grabbed our Lothario by the shirt collar. With one swift move she dragged him half across the counter and said, "Listen, you miserable weasel, when I want a proper man I'll send for one, tharl need to eat a lot more pies before thee can do me any good."

And with that parting shot, she pushed him away, retrieved the tea pot, looked up and without pausing for breath said, "Reet who's next?"

That being said, the ladies were able to deal quickly with numerous busloads of half-asleep pitmen, all impatient to be served. Watching one of the fair sex fill twenty mugs with tea from a giant pot, without pause or spilling any, was something to behold.

One thing I never really sussed was that although we were there in the early hours, the ladies were there before us, with bacon cooked, tea made and chewing tobacco ready for sale at the side of the till—another of life's puzzles.

At quarter past ten it was snap time, which lasted for all of twenty five minutes, so there was no time to waste. As soon as the conveyors stopped, tins, bags and pockets were emptied, people flopped down onto the floor and the surprise packets were opened for investigation. The odd curse generally meant that either a mouse had beaten the unfortunate diner to it or, it was jam yet again.

All this took about eight minutes, including a good swig of water to wash it down. The next vital move was to get to sleep for the remaining time. Erudite conversation was not high on the list of priorities for the average miner during this precious break time.

Then, inevitably, the conveyors would start up again; people would grumble and get back to work.

Water was carried in either a metal or a plastic bottle and as with snuff, was carefully husbanded. One of the least popular things was to have someone 'cadge' a drink, especially from a coal-face worker. The cadger had better have a good reason for so doing, or he would be met with a tirade of abuse, summarised as 'sod off and get your own water.'

Later on, we got into the daring habit of bringing a flask of tea down with us and very welcome it was too. The trick was to make it last as long as possible, as we generally stayed on until about five o'clock each day. On Saturdays we went down the pit at six am instead of seven (this late start was reserved for Sundays), so the hot tea was especially welcome, since there were no canteen facilities at weekends.

Neddy, our surface foreman, used to come down with us at the weekend, ostensibly to see how work was progressing. Unfortunately he was a 'cadger,' generally of water, but one morning, in a moment of weakness, one of the lads offered him a lid of tea from his flask. Neddy could hardly conceal his amazement.

"By 'eck lads,' he said, "This is grand, where does get thee flasks from?"

One of the lads told him, "You can get them off a stall on Wigan market, they're dead cheap."

I think this latter bit of information was a hint for him to get one of his own, but as Neddy wasn't exactly known for his sensitivity, we didn't hold out much hope.

Anyway, imagine our amazement on the Sunday morning when we

arrived at the pit bank and Neddy, with a flourish worthy of the little Daniels man, produced a flask from inside the front of his overalls.

"Now lads, what does think about this then? I went to the market, but decided no chep uns for me, this is a genuine Thermos and it cost a bob or two I'll tell thee."

At this point, the Banksman signalled us to get into the cage and tragically, as Neddy ducked under the raised gate, the newly procured flask fell out and crashed onto the steel floor. There was a stunned silence, as Neddy stared at the flask now nestling neatly between the rails. Then with a sort of strangled sob, he slowly he bent down, picked up his flask and gave it a tentative shake. Unfortunately, this caused it to give out a sound not unlike that of Edmundo Ross brandishing his maracas and going into rumba mode—his worst fears were realised—it was in bits.

The awful silence was finally broken by Frank who said, "Well tha's found out one thing Neddy, the dear un's brek same as the chep un's."

(For younger readers Edmundo Ross was a band-leader who introduced us to the rumba and samba. This was quite daring, as us male dancers were required to shake our hips—not something we were used to doing in Liverpool; on the other hand, our female partners were required to shake just about everything else—lovely).

Where was I?

Back to food. Pies formed an important element of the miners' diet and with superb timing, trays were delivered to the canteen just in time for the afternoon shift coming on and the day shift coming off. This meant that in one fell swoop, hundreds of chaps, half of whom were miserable and half of whom were ecstatic—were able to satisfy a craving for all things pie.

There were two types, a rectangular steak pie with a shiny crust, and a round meat and potato pie with a soft crust. The former was a deep brown colour while the latter was rather more pale and interesting. Both were excellent; and the ultimate in culinary heaven was to have at least one of each. Not only would this enable you to warm both hands at once, but it rendered pointless the endless discussions regarding the relative virtues of the steak over the potato.

However, any doubts you may have had regarding the intrinsic value of a canteen pie was resolved when a pie was all that stood between you and starvation.

As I may have mentioned, we engineering lads used to work a longer shift than the colliers. In general we finished at quarter past five and the extra three hours were laughingly referred to as 'overtime,' but as was often the case if things went wrong, we were stuck underground until the problem was resolved. One thing was of paramount importance; we had to have things ready to run for the night shift, who came on at a quarter past ten.

As these longer sessions were unplanned, it was invariably the case that any remaining butties had long ago been consumed (probably by about three in the afternoon.) So as time went by and, as the work was what social psychologists refer to as 'of a physical nature,' we became some-what hungry. There could, however, be one saving grace; if we needed a part bringing down from the surface workshops, we could beg the deliv-erer to nip into the canteen and buy some pies on our behalf. Most guys were happy to oblige, as they had all been in the same situation at some time or another.

I remember being stuck halfway up our coal face one evening, while we wrestled with a replacement cutter motor. All was going swimmingly until Les noticed that a critical bit of kit had broken and, of course, we had no replacement to hand. It's funny that on discovering what was now going to keep us underground for at least another two hours, we also dis-covered that we were starving. Still, we weren't known as rough, tough fitters for nothing—well, for about seven shillings and six pence an hour, actually. Les crawled off the face, telephoned an unfortunate surface fit-ter and ordered a new part. There was now nothing for it but to stretch out and try to stop our stomachs rumbling. This latter endeavour was made doubly difficult due to Les's predilection for describing the gargan-tuan feast of egg and chips he would have when he arrived home.

After what seemed like an age, we saw a light coming towards us and our volunteer fitter said, "Right lads, I've brought the new hydraulic con-nection."

And with that, he sagged back onto a pile of loose coal - job done.

Oblivious to the fact that we were now staring at him with something approaching hatred, our feelings were summed up by Les who said, "Never thee mind about lying back on the bloody coal—where's our sod-ding pies?"

Realising that all was not well, he raised an arm and said, "Oh, sorry lads, they're here." And with that he delved into the front of his overalls and brought out a number of white paper bags. The only thing was that at first glance, they looked ominously flat and there didn't seem to be anything inside.

However, on closer inspection we realised that the bags did indeed contain our supper. "What's this you bastard?" said Les acting as our spokesman. "The bloody pies are all flattened."

"Aye, sorry about that, but what with carrying the new part, I had no hands free so I stuffed them in me shirt to keep them safe."

"But why the hell are they flat?"

"They're bloody flat because I fell over a loose rail and if it hadn't been for the pies, I might have broken me ribs—now are you going to eat the sodding things or are you just going to moan about their shape?"

Realising we were in no position to moan about presentation, we gently peeled aside the paper bag (well most of it anyway) and not so gently manhandled the smashed bits of pie into our mouths. As usual, when you are in what might be called, culinary extremis, they tasted wonderful—although we didn't admit it to our careless pie carrier. And to think, that some years later, there would be an almighty fuss about the quality of hospital food; at least the patients didn't have it brought to them stuffed down a nurse's uniform—although I don't know, retrieval might have had beneficial side-effects.

Smells, both good and bad, carried an awfully long way in a pit and we discovered there were two items of food which could travel literally for miles in the intake air. The first was an orange and in the hands of a careless peeler could assault the senses for hundreds of yards. Les and I once worked on the afternoon shift with a lad called Hughie and when it was snap time we would repair to a nearby sub-station to enjoy our butties. Hughie was about six feet tall and had the same emaciated look as Jack Elam. His hair was of the lank variety and grease for grease, matched his overalls. And for some unaccountable reason, he insisted on wearing a helmet with a crack running across his left ear.

Having settled down and opened our tins, we noticed that Hughie, much to our surprise, had pulled an orange out of his overalls and proceeded to peel it. This was okay, but what was to follow caused us to stop eating and watch with a mixture of amazement and growing nausea.

It was the noise that first attracted our attention; there was the most alarming sucking and spluttering sound, followed by sharp intakes of breath followed by more sucking and muttering. It was a bit like the sound you might hear if you were unfortunate enough to be in close contact with a crocodile that has just enjoyed a meal of careless tourist.

On closer inspection, and with morbid fascination, it became obvious that Hughie wasn't so much eating the orange as trying to climb inside it. There were bits of masticated orange everywhere; the juice was trickling down his chin, onto his hands, down to his boots and ending up with

quite a bit of the floor. It became something of a puzzle to try and esti-
mate what percentage of orange had been eaten, versus the percentage
spread around Hughie and the sub-station. What was even more interesting, if that's the word, was that he was completely oblivious to our spellbound gaze; on he went—devouring, spluttering and occasionally wiping
his chin with an overall sleeve.

By now the smell was everywhere; it was incredible the distance travelled by the aroma; word came back to us later that tunnellers working
over a mile away wanted to know where the hell the appalling orange
smell was coming from.

At last and with the spectacular show over, we returned to our half
eaten butties and had a well deserved snurch to recover our equilibrium.
Later, as we returned to work, Les turned to me and said, "If Hughie
brings another blasted orange tomorrow, there's no way I'm staying in
the sub-station to go through that again. It wasn't just the appalling sight,
it was the bloody noise. Why he couldn't just bring a round of bread and
jam like the rest of us, is beyond me."

Interestingly, this emotional outburst came from a man who, some
weeks later, was responsible for releasing a smell of devastating proportions.

This time we were on nights and as we stepped off the manrider, Les
said, "Let's nip into the main sub-station, I've got a bit of a treat for us."

As treats in a pit were few and far between, I was somewhat puzzled,
but as the prospect of a treat, even from Les, was better than crawling up
a coal face, I was happy to oblige. We sat down and Les, pulling a package wrapped in newspaper out of his overalls said, "Here get stuck into
this lot."

The paper was warm and almost immediately the flavour began to per-
colate through the wrapping. As I unfolded it, there it was confirmed in
all its glory—a double portion of fish and chips.

We duly got stuck in, as they say. A fish supper, unheard of in a mine
thousands of feet underground, still warm, covered in salt and vinegar,
newspaper still readable: a dream come true.

"How the hell did you manage this," I asked between mouthfuls.

"Well," said Les, "It was on the spur of the moment. I was cycling past
that new Chippy on the Bold road and I thought—wow, I could just eat
a fish supper. So I got them to put extra paper around them and they've
stayed warm."

What we hadn't realised was, that as we unwrapped our parcels, the
distinct aroma of fish and chips had been caught on the breeze and was

being wafted gently through the tunnels, up five coalfaces, along the return airways and into all corners of the pit.

This time there were ructions; phones began to ring, Overmen and Deputies were dispatched to try and find the source of the smell, colliers, who had just started work, began to feel hungry and when they finally discovered that Les and I were the culprits, people went mad. Wherever we went, we were threatened, cursed, bollocked, cursed, warned, cursed, admonished, cursed and variously intimidated and not necessarily in that order.

Looking back, I think there was a measure of jealousy on the part of our attackers but even so, we never had the courage to try it again. Shame really—fish and chips beat jam butties every time.

One of our surface charge-hands used to come down with us at weekends; his name was Jimmy (Jemmy) Chatt. This name was unfortunate in some ways, as that was the last thing he would do. Trying to have any form of conversation with Jemmy was like pulling out your own teeth—painful, futile and great when you finally gave up.

He was the original professional misery as far as idle conversation was concerned, and as we generally had to walk all the way in and out of the pit at weekends, being accompanied by Jemmy was akin to taking a vow of silence.

He was about the same size as Dustin Hoffman but with a narrow face and a chin you could chop wood with. He wore clean and nicely pressed overalls and because of his uncanny ability to get others to do most of the work, they mostly remained that way.

He was renowned for two things; an unerring ability to thwart his partner when re-assembling a conveyor and a predisposition to eat in secret.

It went like this, the particular conveyor we had to repair each weekend was called an 'Armadillo,' and for good reason. It was a monster of a thing, made up of a series of flexible steel mats running on rollers and looked just like a giant escalator only lying horizontally. Each 'mat' was about eight feet long and four feet wide. As the armadillo carried a heavy load, it was prone to damage by great lumps of coal and rock landing on it from various chutes. This meant that at regular intervals we had to remove the damaged sections and then replace them with new mats. They were extremely heavy, very flexible, a swine to handle and were the ultimate 'finger trappers.'

Obviously, once we had removed a damaged section and wrestled the new part into place, it had to be joined to the existing mats. This was accomplished by fitting large steel 'pins' into connecting lugs at each end.

Fitting the first end was easy, but when you came to the other end, the mats had to be pulled together with giant ratchet grabs. There were two grabs, one on each side which were operated by a collier on each side, pulling on a long handle to align the lugs.

This was a distinctly ticklish part of the repair; the sweating colliers were straining at the handles, and the fitters, precariously balanced on each side of the conveyor, were shouting idiot things like, "Just a bit more, hold it there, back a bit," and other sophisticated engineering terms.

Each fitter would have his new pin at the ready and as soon as he could see any sign of alignment would jam his pin in the hole and smash it in place with a seven pound hammer.

Unfortunately, it was impossible to get the two pins in at the same time, so the guy who managed to get his pin in place first would sag back and tell the collier hanging onto on his grab to slacken off.

And this was where Jemmy unfailingly triumphed—somehow he always got his pin in first. This meant that the unfortunate fitter on the other side now had all the tension transmitted across to him, making it doubly difficult and hairy to get his pin in place.

No matter how hard we tried, we could never beat Jemmy to the punch and it frequently lead to accusations, recriminations, damaged fingers and frustration.

What was worse, it was about the only time the sod spoke to us and even then, it was limited to a phrase that we all came to dread—"Reet lads, my side's in."

I mentioned there were two things that Jemmy was infamous for; well although the second was on a somewhat different scale, it was no less maddening for all that.

Jemmy was prone to un-wrapping a toffee in his overall pocket and with some uncanny sleight of hand, slipping it into his mouth. He could do this when walking along (in bloody silence) or when we were working, especially after the magic words 'reet lads.' Either way, we never ever spotted the transference.

In fact the only indication that this had happened at all was when you smelled the toffee or mintoe. Examining Jemmy's jaw revealed nothing, as his other ability was to be able to eat a sweetie without either moving a muscle or causing his cheek to bulge.

Now you may be of the opinion that big hairy miners shouldn't get upset about a mere toffee. That's not the point. As with the chips, it was the smell, coupled with the knowledge that you weren't about to share in the goodies, that hurt. Again, you might wonder why we didn't bring our own toffees down with us and let Jemmy get on with his clandestine sweet eating activities? The truth is, Jemmy being a miserable bastard gave us something to moan about, involving a high moral principle—the willingness to share sweeties—and you don't get an opportunity like that every day.

Chapter Fifteen

That's Entertainmunt?

Obviously, hard working chaps like us needed to be entertained when we arrived back in the land of the living. This could take a number of forms, but the two most popular were undoubtedly watching Rugby League and variety acts at the Miners club.

In my case I'd been properly brought up to worship a proper sport, as played by the great Billy Liddell for Liverpool; and cricket with Brian Statham (including Freddy Truman, even though he played for York-shire).

So, faced with this wealth of sporting excellence, the world of rugby had passed me by. All through my formative working years, erudite conversation had centred on such weighty matters as the unerring ability of Albert Stubbins to take free-kicks and whether Bert Trautman would ever go back to Germany.

(Anyone under 70 reading this bit and not recognising the names should hang your head in shame and consult Wikiwhatsisname).

I remember mentioning rugby, the sport played with a strange shaped ball, to a fellow scouser one day and he was somewhat scathing in his reply.

He said, "Listen if God had meant you to pick a ball up, he'd 'ave purr a 'andle on it.'" While possibly not expressed in purely standard grammatical terms, I took his point.

Anyway, imagine my surprise, when joining my new-found friends for important underground discussions, to find that rugby league dominated their world. There was no mention of football, cricket, speedway racing, bowls, shove ha'penny, snooker, cribbage, or darts. Instead, the previous Saturday's clash of the titans was dissected, analysed, criticised, rationalised and lionised. What I had failed to realise was that only about forty miles from the Anfield, the Mecca of the beautiful game, there existed two implacable enemies, namely—St Helens and Wigan.

Both had achieved incredible success and considering that both towns were relatively small, they fielded a plethora of star players. A meeting between the two would result in one town or the other becoming deserted for the afternoon. I was foolish enough to mention that this would provide a golden opportunity for burglars, until Bill pointed out that this would be impossible, since no burglar worth his salt would miss such a game. The extent of the fans' support was brought home to me when I learned that the average gate for such contests was over 30,000 and when the teams met in the cup final at Wembley in 1960, there were 94,672 fans in attendance. Having dutifully absorbed the statistics, I now began to see just how important this game, with the funny ball, was, to my mates.

I was listening in to a post-match discussion one day and I must have been nodding at the right times, as I was invited to attend a match. Apparently, Wigan and 'Saints' traditionally played one another on Easter Monday and this year the game would be played at the 'Saints' ground. My hosts for this auspicious occasion were two Electricians, Brian, who was a Saint's supporter and his best friend Colin, who was a Wigan supporter. Continuing to maintain what I thought of as the right degree of scepticism, I nevertheless agreed and we met at 2pm outside the ground. Brian said we needed to be early as there were Greenhalgh's pies and Uncle Joe's mint balls to buy for half time and the ground would be full.

He was right, there were thousands of men, women and children, all wearing the appropriate scarf and/or woolly hat. There was banter, singing, back-slapping, derision, rattle waving—but funnily enough, no fighting. Meanwhile, as Colin tried to explain the basic rules of the game, Brian told me who I should pay particular attention to when the game commenced.

It turned out to be a glorious afternoon, during which I learned a host of new words such as scrums, pack, line-out, try, blind side, prop forward, hooker, loose play, and points. And, if this wasn't enough stress, the lads expected me to make praiseworthy comments about each of their favourite players.

I was introduced to a host of super-stars including Tom Van Vollenhoven, Ellery Hanley, Alex Murphy (who was renowned for being so fast, his quiff was never out of place), Brian McTigue and Vince Karalious (known affectionately as the Wild Bull of the Pampas, but I never liked to ask why.) Wigan's favourite son was a giant of a man called Billy Boston, who was the first black player ever to be taken on a British Lions tour of Australia and scored more tries than any man living before or since for the club.

You can see I was in for a treat and would have to pay attention, not ask daft questions, pretend to understand a good deal more than I actually did and be very careful about bias.

I must say, on reflection, you'd have to be dead not to be caught up in the noise, excitement, running, passing, incredible talent and devastating tackling. These were hard men and gave no quarter, the crowd loved it and when, on this occasion, Wigan won, nobody in St Helens had to have counselling, in fact the general consensus from the Saints supporters was, "Tha's played a better game today."

Can you imagine the average football fan saying that to an opposing supporter?

If you want to see an example of the sheer brute force of the tackling, take a look at This Sporting Life, made in 1963. Ignore the love interest and concentrate on the realism of Richard Harris's performance as a miner turned professional rugby player.

The other interesting thing for me was to observe the different reactions when a rugby player scored a try and a footballer scored a goal. Embarrassingly, there was a growing tendency in the latter case for members of the team to declare some kind of 'love-in' on the scorer. This manifested itself when they leapt on his head, threw him on the ground and then all piled on top of him in a most disgusting manner. We felt this growing tendency was due to some players having been exposed to Italian football, but this was never proved.

I couldn't help but notice a marked difference in rugby. Generally the try scorer, having dug himself out of the turf would stagger to his feet, shake his head, wipe the blood out of his eyes and run back to his position. At best, his team mates would nod in his direction or, at least help to pull him out of the ground, where the opposing team had half buried him in an effort to thwart his progress.

I mentioned my observations to Pat one day and he shuddered, saying, "Bloody hell, can you just visualise what would happen to anyone daft enough to throw their arms around Billy Boston, they'd probably end up in the third row of the stands! It doesn't bear thinking about."

Brian, the 'Saints' supporter, was of medium build with thinning sandy hair who had, rather incongruously, grown a military style moustache. It was carefully groomed and he had trained the thing to curl up at the ends. We all thought it made him look a bit like one of those retired Colonels who write to the Daily Telegraph. This hirsute affectation engendered some amusement and not a little derision among the mining fraternity, although he bore all the comments with fortitude (I was going to say, with a stiff upper lip, but we couldn't see it amongst the foliage). I asked him why he persisted in trying to look like the poor man's General Kitchener and he confided that it was all part of a carefully thought-out strategy for the future.

Apparently he felt he was bound for better things than working in a pit and as part of his grand plan, had secretly embarked on a correspondence course in Salesmanship.

I must have looked bemused, because he went on to explain that he and his wife were bent on becoming 'pillars of local society.' His wife was a hairdresser with her own small salon over a greengrocers and it was she who had sown the seeds of discontent in Brian.

Apparently she felt it to be socially unacceptable that the husband of a well regarded hairdresser (by appointment to the wives of executives), should come home dirty, having mixed with people of a lower social order. As a consequence, she believed an appropriate career for path Brian lay in having a job which would provide the necessary status in the community. This meant he would need a suit, a car, nice ties, a brief-case, cuff-links, polished shoes, a white handkerchief, a trilby, a rolled umbrella, a three-quarter length trench coat and a turned-up moustache to complete the ensemble.

The job—sorry career—in question was that of a 'Sales Representative.' This had, until shortly before, been known by a far less glamorous name of 'Commercial Traveller,' with all the attendant images of seedy mackintoshes, knocking on doors, a suitcase full of brushes and no car. However, the growth of consumerism in the early sixties and the need to keep shops filled with the latest useless goodies, had led to a new breed of traveller.

Working from a wholesale outlet in a secret location, our moustachioed representative had a wide area to cover, shopkeepers to charm, commission to earn, social intercourse to maintain, a company car to drive, bribes to distribute, 'salesperson of the year' dances to attend and later on, ulcers to deal with. This then, was Brian's ambition and, as he said, it explained the need for a moustache.

Coincidentally, in 1975 there was a wonderful sit-com on TV called *I Didn't Know You Cared*, written by Peter Tinniswood. It featured an awful, extended northern family called The Brandons. The son, Carter, was reluctantly engaged to a girl who aspired to an improved lifestyle. This manifested itself in each episode by her trying to persuade Carter that he was an up and coming 'executive' and as such, would need a briefcase. The similarities between Carter's and Brian's situation were astounding. I often wondered whether the author had ever bumped into Brian and his wife at some mayoral function and seen the potential for comedy; privately—we certainly did.

Miners' clubs or, in some areas, Labour clubs, also provided a significant amount of entertainmunt. Most of the clubs favoured a tried and tested programme; each evening there would be an item of unparalleled boredom called 'Bingo,' then on Wednesdays and Saturdays the excitement was brought to a fever pitch with was what was euphemistically known as 'live' entertainment.

On one of the west side coal faces, I worked with a fitter whose name was Clarrie Pye. I think his real name was Clarence but I never had the courage to ask. He was a pale looking chap with hollow cheeks and a sort of haunted expression. Witness my amazement one day when he proudly announced that he had just been appointed to the post of 'Entertainmunt Officer' for his local miners' club. (Now you see where the title of this section comes from —I was endlessly fascinated by Clarrie's emphasis on the last syllable—besides, one has to be faithful to the dialect).

Having accepted this key post meant he couldn't work overtime that day because, as he said, "I've to get around to a number of other clubs in the area to weigh up the talent and book new acts for the coming weeks."

Obviously I had underestimated the importance of the role and the sacrifice it entailed (giving up overtime was not something we took lightly.) I asked Clarrie what kind of acts he was looking for and he said, "Our members like a nice mixture. We need comedians, novelty acts and singers, so that the older people in the audience can sing along, while the younger ones like a bit of glamour."

I said, "What do you mean by novelty acts?"

"Well," said Clarrie, warming to the theme, "Last month we had a woman called Dolores and her Performing Doves and she came on in spangly tights with a dove on each arm and one on her head."

Trying hard not to visualise the awful scene, I asked, "What did she do then?"

"She played a record of In a Monastery Garden and did this sinuous dance."

"What did the doves do?"

"They just sort of sat there while she moved about; but then one night there was a bit of a problem."

Consumed with a sort of morbid fascination, I asked what had happened.

"Well," said Clarrie, "She was about half way through, you know where the record does that blackbird impression, and a guy in the audience shouted out 'They're not doves, they're bloody pigeons.' It seems he kept them and could tell the difference."

"Bloody hell," I said, "Did it put her off?"

"Yes, you could say that. She got a bit flustered, lost her place with the music and made a couple of quick steps to get back into time. This sudden move caused one of the pigeons to panic and it flew into the audience, where it landed on the beer pump handle and crapped on the bar."

Realising that Sunday Night at the Palladium had nothing to fear, I said, "Don't go into any more details Clarrie, it all sounds too exciting for words."

You have to remember that the early 60's was an incredible era for the live entertainment business. We were becoming familiar with names such as Tommy Steele, Adam Faith, Cliff Richard, Shane Fenton, Helen Shapiro, Mike and Bernie Winters, Freddie and the Dreamers, Billy Fury and Marty Wilde. They were regularly appearing in theatres, on the Telly, in what were laughingly known as 'Night Clubs' and in 'soon to be forgotten' films.

Although all of them had one thing in common—none were booked by Clarrie.

Being a good sort and thinking, mistakenly, that I was keen to sample this awesome talent, Clarrie invited me along to his club. So, not wishing to offend and being determined that I wasn't going to face this alone, I roped in Joe, another mate, and we turned up at seven o'clock one Saturday night. The club was a single storey building consisting of a large open area with a bar at one end and a stage at the other. There was a snooker room off to the left and some sort of committee meeting room opposite. Tables and chairs were set out in the body of the hall and other than the reflected glare from a multitude of fluorescent lights on the Formica tops, the atmosphere was pretty good.

The place started to fill up steadily, and we were enjoying a pint of Burtonwood bitter when we became dimly aware of an old guy approaching the table, staring at us, going away, coming back, staring and going away again. Noticing this strange behaviour, Joe said, "I think we're being eyed up because we're strangers, next time he comes across, tell him we're guests of Clarrie."

Sure enough the old chap limped across once more but this time he had another chap in tow.

"Now lads," said the newcomer, "What's tha doing sitting theer?"

We looked at one another, "What do you mean, we just sat at this table, it was empty when we came in, we're guests of Clarrie."

"Aye lads, that's fine, the trouble is dust see, thar't setting in owd Jack's seat."

We looked around at the multitude of empty seats.

"Aye I know lads, but owd Jack has sat here since t'club opened and he doesn't think its reet that strangers should be in his favourite seat."

Realising we were becoming something of an embarrassment; we picked up our beer and said to the chap, "Perhaps it would be better if you told us where we can sit." (All the time making a mental note to kill Clarrie.)

"Aye just follow me, I'm sorry about that, but Jack gets unsettled if things aren't just reet."

Having been suitably repositioned we couldn't wait for the programme to start, an anticipation which turned out to be wrong.

As a warm up, we were treated to several games of bingo, organised by a 'caller' who pulled numbered balls out of an empty pickle jar. As I had never played bingo I found it to be a mixture of embarrassment, banality, concentration, silence, disappointment, euphoria and shouting. Obviously neither Joe nor I won anything, which perhaps was a blessing in disguise, as our success might have had yet another adverse effect on Owd Jack.

I can't recall much about the main 'entertainmunt' which followed; there were singers (I use the term loosely) whose main talent seemed to embody that awful wobble in the voice beloved of uncles at funerals. The comedian was reasonably pathetic but he wasn't helped by the Master of Ceremonies interrupting him to take over the mike and issue the immortal words –"Reet everyone, just to let thee know, pies are ready when the young lad's finished."

At the pie eating interval we were approached by Clarrie who was obviously flushed with success and asked us how we were enjoying ourselves.

Knowing full well he was expecting us to be full of praise for the high standard of the acts, we found ourselves in the age-old position of lying to avoid hurting someone's feelings. In the event, it was Joe who managed to be confidently vague saying, "Aye Clarrie, we were just saying it's been a unique experience, we've never seen owt like it before."

This 'compliment' seemed to please Clarrie and he said, "Aye I thought you'd be impressed lads, great stuff."

Funnily enough, we never went back.

As well as entertainmunt, miners indulged in a number of hobbies or pastimes. Among the favourites were rearing turkeys, pigeon racing, breeding whippets, ferreting, gardening, drinking and ragging (this latter word rhymes with another well known expression which loosely translates as 'sexual intercourse,' but not necessarily with one's wife.)

Ragging was a popular pre-curser to marriage and was the subject of much boasting. During overtime there were many graphic descriptions of some guy's prowess in the trouser department, generally culminating with the modest comment "And she said I were reet good."

Pat Rimmer once told me that this boasting was mainly for the benefit of the rapt listeners and, as with many issues in the life of the average male, bore little resemblance to reality and was brilliantly captured in the TV series The Likely Lads. Pat summed it up by saying, "It's a well known fact with miners that all their 'ragging' was done in the pit and all the 'coal' was sent in the pub."

I asked him what he meant and he said, "If you listen to the so-called Don Juans, you find that their sexual conquests are brought to life and vividly described, in the pit. Then, I was in our local pub one night and heard some idiot telling his mates about a massive pillar of coal he had single-handedly removed.'

Pat continued, "As I'm listening to this rubbish, the daft bugger does no more than dive under the table to illustrate to his mates the height of the coal seam and how he managed to break some sort of record. I reckon he was working harder in the pub than he ever did down the pit."

"Mind you," said Pat, "There was one notable exception to the boasting rule; it concerned a collier by the name of Sailor Bill who practised ragging in its most extreme form."

I leaned forward in anticipation.

"His prowess in providing a service to various ladies in the area was legendary. Size, shape or age was of no relevance; all Bill needed was a willingness to participate and he was away like a jack-rabbit," said Pat, warming to the theme. I did think a hint of jealousy was creeping in, but Pat assured me that there was no way in which he could contemplate the risk, let alone have the necessary stamina.

"Did his wife know what he was up to?" I asked.

"Well there's no doubt she had her suspicions since, apparently, he was in the habit of telling her he was just popping down the road to help Mary or Joan or Alice or whoever with an urgent repair to a fuse or stuck window, as the particular lady's husband was on nights."

Over time, his missus became more and more suspicious, which was confirmed when she met one of the women in question and, on asking about the stuck window, was met with a blank stare followed by an embarrassed excuse that 'she must dash.'

"Bloody hell, he liked to live dangerously," I said.

"You're right," said Pat. "But it all came to grief one night, when Bill and his wife were invited to a party at a neighbour's and part way through the evening, Bill went missing as usual. By now the rumours had spread that Bill was paying rather a lot of attention to a lass about three doors away from the party and his wife, being unable to find her husband, finally put two and two together (or, in this case, one and one.) She announced to the invited guests that she was off to find him and, if he was where she thought he was, she would kill the randy bastard.

"Somehow," said Pat, "This enfolding drama seemed a lot more interesting than dancing to Frankie Laine recordings and with one body, the guests followed Bill's wife down the road.

"Sure enough her worst fears were realised as, on entering the back door and nipping smartly into the lounge, she saw her errant partner in what might be called a compromising position. In fact," said Pat, "Bill in flagrante delicto with the young lady. Although actually, all we could see was Bill's rear moving rapidly up and down between a pair of legs which we assumed belonged to the lucky lass."

I said, "Are you really telling me that even though the room was now full of curious people, Bill kept his mind on the job, so to speak?"

"Oh yes, and it was just about to get even more surreal, as Bill's wife, with a sort of strangled cry, leaped forward, grabbed Bill by the neck and proceeded to try to pull him off the object of his affections. At this point, the lady in question, noticing that Bill's measured stride was being interfered with, realised they were no longer alone and became aware that her lounge seemed to be full of curious neighbours, all clutching glasses of sherry or cans of beer and taking a considerable interest in the proceedings.

The awful knowledge that they were no longer alone in their love nest, then caused her to wriggle violently in a futile attempt to dislodge her paramour from his chosen position. And Bill, now realising (a) that the lady's increasingly frantic heaves weren't due to impending orgasmic delight and (b) that his wife was trying to strangle him—became aware that the game was up.

"Nevertheless," added Pat, with deep admiration, "Even as Bill's wife pulled and shrieked and his lady love twisted and turned, he managed to shout out, 'Bloody hell woman, stop pulling and let me finish!'"

"And to think," he mused, "The Italians believe they're the world's greatest lovers."

Funnily enough, I remember being somewhat taken aback some time later, when I proudly announced I was engaged to be married. This provoked an unexpected response from Ernie, who said, "Ha! Tha's bin a naughty bugger, tha's bigged her."

Having loosely translated this to mean that the object of my affections was pregnant, I said, "No I haven't, I'm just going to marry her, that's all."

Ernie looked puzzled and said, "Well if tha's not bigged her, what's tha getting married for?"

As I had no answer to this view of life as seen by Ernie waxing philosophical, we decided to have another wrist wrestling contest, which of course I lost—some things just don't change.

Chapter Sixteen
Getting About

The favourite (only) way of getting to and from the pit was by bus, and not just any bus. These were special buses laid on by the Coal Board who had contracted the job to the Ribble Bus Company. There was a fleet of five, and each morning they set out from Liverpool on a round trip to drop people off at all the pits in the St Helens area. In a similar manner, a fleet of buses would also make the trip from Wigan (wherever that is.)

My pick-up point was about a fifteen minute walk away, but you had to be on time as they didn't hang about waiting. The fleet would appear at six a.m. and in the beginning it was somewhat disconcerting to find that the first one roared past without stopping. Then, just as panic was setting in, one would stop, pick you up and miss out the next stop; it was a sort of leap-frog with buses and the drivers' unofficial way of making good time.

As we approached the first colliery, the bus would pause just long enough for you to fall off, then off it went to the next stop. Fortunately, our pit was the terminus where the mad ride ended and the drivers nipped into the canteen for sustenance before reversing the whole process with the night shift.

As time went on, and if you could stay awake, you began to see your mates climb aboard, get a ticket from the conductor, speak to no-one and try to fall asleep. However, if we did manage to stay awake, it was good to watch the antics of an old Overman called Andy.

Andy was picked up each morning outside Lea Green Colliery. He possessed a grim determination always to be on the first bus. This was not something the passengers on his bus looked forward to, as having surveyed the occupants, would haul a notebook, or as he referred to it his 'bible,' out from his shirt and start giving out jobs. As it was only about 6.15, the shift had not started and the men were still trying to sleep, Andy's man-management style went down like a lead balloon.

However, unbeknown to the watchers, revenge was on its way. It occurred one dark and very wintry morning as we were approaching Lea Green. On this particular occasion, I was on the second bus in the fleet. The first bus slowed momentarily to let one passenger off and was already accelerating away from the stop, when a wild, Mac flapping figure came pounding across the road. The apparition turned out to be Andy who had been hovering in the bus shelter on the opposite side and when he reached the rear end of the bus, he leapt for the door.

Unfortunately, for Andy, he was about to make forcible contact with a new design of bus, one where the door had been moved to the front of the vehicle. As a result of this daring innovation, we were treated to the remarkable sight of Andy sliding slowly down the side of the bus and landing in a crumpled heap in the gutter.

However, being of stern Overman material, he gathered himself up and with as much dignity as he could muster, re-fastened his mac and, having checked the whereabouts of the door first, clambered onto our bus. Funnily enough, this meeting of man and metal had left him strangely preoccupied and no jobs were given out that morning.

Andy's 'bible' was a large, stiff-backed black note book which never left his possession. Everything that happened, should have happened or didn't happen was noted down in its pages. One day in a moment of weakness and I guess, trying to impress us disorganised engineers, he brought out the current volume and, tapping the cover in a sort of confidential manner, told us he had kept such a diary since he began his career as a humble Shotfirer. And what was worse, he had every single one locked in a box at home. In case, he said darkly, "I need evidence."

This last cryptic statement led us to imagine Andy confronting the Prosecuting Counsel and much to the alarm of the judge, suddenly plunging his hand into his shirt, only to produce irrefutable written evidence of something or other.

I mentioned Andy's paranoia to Pat my Shotfirer mate, who said he wasn't surprised, as it was well known that if Andy were off ill or on holiday, he would lock himself in the coal house with a number of back editions and re-live past glories of transport difficulties overcome, fitters put in their place, gas detected, costs minimised and roofs well supported. Still, I suppose if retired Brigadiers can do it with toy soldiers, why not Andy with his books?

The current bible, safely tucked in the front of his shirt (which also carried an apple and several rounds of bread in greaseproof paper) was secured with a large elastic band with a Biro held firmly at the side. In this way the blasted book could be produced at a moment's notice, so that yet more secret notes could be made. MI5 would have been proud of Andy.

Those who didn't arrive by bus generally arrived on a bike. There were several covered racks close to the back door of the canteen, which enabled the owners to nip smartly in and get a bacon roll before the buses arrived.

One or two people had cars and Charlie, who invested his money wisely, owned an Austin 30. It was a sort of battleship grey—primarily because that was the only colour obtainable. This limitation had one advantage, however, as we painted all our refurbished machinery in a similar shade. This enabled Charlie to 'touch-up' scuffed parts without having to bother British Leyland.

He was a big, gangly lad whose footwear of choice, as we know, was the clog. He came from a village about eight miles away and his route took him past a bus stop where another of our fitters used to stand waiting.

This was the notorious Dickie Pye (no relation to the aforementioned Clarrie of impresario fame.) Dickie was small, wizened, toothless and possibly the grumpiest man I ever met. In fact, by comparison, Ebenezer Scrooge was the embodiment of stand-up comedy.

One person we used to feel sorry for was an apprentice who had been allocated to Dickie by an unfeeling Training Department. This poor lad was a bundle of nerves to start with and being confronted by someone who looked like a cross between Gandalf and a badly worn garden gnome did little to bolster his confidence.

It was Dickie's firm belief that an apprentice had been allocated to him for the express purpose of making his life easier. This meant the lad would be employed in a number of vital enterprises on Dickie's behalf, such as buying the Daily Mirror, fetching overalls from the laundry, nipping to the canteen for a pie, cadging fags from anyone in the vicinity, chopping up bits of scaffolding for firewood, sorting out old rags, cleaning assorted tools and scrubbing old bearings in a paraffin bath.

Having carried out these intellectually challenging tasks to Dickie's satisfaction (implied but never spoken,) the lad was then entrusted with the most sensitive job of all—making a brew. This was traditionally made in a white enamel can with a blue rim, sometimes known as a 'Billy Can,' but don't ask me why. It was about four inches in diameter and eight inches high and I guess held about a pint of liquid. The real beauty of the can was the lid, which fitted inside the top rim and doubled as a cup. The whole ensemble was completed with a wire carrying handle fixed to the sides.

Now we also need to be clear here on what we mean by 'a brew.' Obviously the main constituent consists of tea-leaves (loose - not in the form of tea-bags, which hadn't been invented at the time.) We are also not using words such as Oolong, Darjeeling, Assam, Lapsang Suchong, or Lapsang Formosa. Neither are we in the realms of herbal, nettle, olive leaf, mint, or raspberry leaf tea. In fact, anyone producing such a brew would be looked on with deep suspicion—something akin to being seen using hair conditioner.

What we are talking about is a neat mixture consisting of a cheap Co-op blend mixed with a dollop of condensed milk and placed carefully in the centre of a piece of greaseproof wrapping paper taken from a loaf. This was then folded carefully into a makeshift envelope and placed in the bottom of your snap tin.

For younger readers, condensed milk (or 'conny-onny' as it was more popularly known) was cows' milk from which water had been removed and sugar added, yielding a very thick, sweet mixture which came in a tin. You can also make fudge with it, although it's so sweet you could hear your teeth scream when eating a piece. Anyway, back to the plot.

Having assessed the lad's intellectual brewing potential, Dickie produced his precious envelope and taking down his can from the shelf, told the lad to 'mek a brew.'

The lad, cognisant of the fact that he had been accorded a singular honour and completely missing the point that Dickie was just too lazy to do it himself, trotted off to the hot water urn in the toilets. "Although," as Dickie later remarked, "It seemed to tek him a long time to put a can under the hot tap, open the brew and pour on the water."

He had no idea of the horror to come. Finally the lad reappeared and with something of a nervous flourish, placed the steaming can on the bench. Dickie, on turning towards the can, let out a strangled cry. "What's tha done to me can, you daft bastard, tha's ruined everything! Oh bloody hell, I should never have trusted thee, tha' wants sacking."

We craned forward to see what terrible thing the lad had done and there it was for all to see. The reason why he had taken so long became obvious—he had scrubbed the can inside and out to achieve a pristine whiteness, a colour never seen since the can was bought new about ten years before. All unknowingly, our lad had removed years of carefully preserved layers of deep brown tannin which, in Dickie's opinion, was the key to enhanced flavour.

Les, having tasted Dickie's brew, thought that any claim to flavour enhancement was probably due to the fact that he smoked Capstan Full

Strength and that the miserable sod used the cheapest tea available. Sadly, comments such as this had no bearing on Dickie's firm opinion the lad's misguided effort was tantamount to an act of criminal vandalism and therefore, physical violence was the only answer.

Fortunately, as the terrified lad backed away, he was saved by one of Dickie's even less endearing qualities, which was to suddenly interrupt what he was doing in order to attack his inner ear. This nightmare scenario would be accomplished with anything that came to hand. A finger was the implement of choice, but if that failed to achieve the desired effect, he would probe the orifice with a biro, a nail, a matchstick or a small screwdriver.

This revolting procedure would go roughly as follows—having pushed a rigid finger or some other implement into his ear, there would begin a series of manoeuvres of increasing intensity. Starting slowly, he would waggle his arm up and down in a most alarming fashion whilst at the same time forcing his finger ever deeper into the ear canal

By now a large part of the finger had disappeared from sight and was fast approaching the ear drum.

The increasing violence of this activity caused Dickie's mouth to open, a fearsome grimace to appear, then, as the up and down motion intensified, his eyes to water and his glasses to dislodge and work their way towards the end of his nose.

As if this wasn't enough, we also noticed two interesting side effects to this procedure. As his finger approached the cochlea, Dickie's sense of balance became somewhat compromised, which would make him lurch to one side and crash into the front of his locker. The second side effect was that about this point, Dickie became lost to us—all conversation had ceased and he answered no questions. This led us to believe that he had now penetrated his skull to a point where his finger was preventing nerve fibres from transmitting information to the brain.

Anyone seeing this attempt to reach the centre of his head for the first time, would stare in disbelief, shudder at the awful sight and walk away. Then, as quickly as he had started, Dickie would remove the implement, regain his balance, inspect it closely for God knows what; and carry on with the conversation, which had been interrupted by this exercise in self-mutilation. Fortunately, the lad, on seeing this awful ritual begin, nipped smartly into the toilets and was sick, either with revulsion at the sight of someone trying to bury a finger in his cranium; or relief at having just missed being killed.

Would it surprise you to know that on top of all his other endearing qualities, the daft old bugger was deaf?

In an unexpected and rather affectionate way, Dickie was inadvertently responsible for a phrase which has since become part of our family's lexicon. Any time anyone has an itch in their ear and there is an overwhelming need to poke at it for relief, we say we've 'got a Dickie Pye.'

So I suppose in a strange way, Dickie's memory lives on.

Inevitably, for one so 'nowty' as we used to say, there came a time when Dickie got his comeuppance and, once again, it all started off innocently enough, as they say.

It happened one morning, when Charlie spotted Dickie standing in the bus queue and, in a moment of undeniable weakness, stopped to give him a lift.

Then, as is the way of things, this became routine. Charlie would drive towards the queue; Dickie would wave, Charlie would stop; Dickie would climb aboard and together they would travel to the pit.

Until one day, that is, it all went horribly wrong.

I had called into the workshop for something and seeing Charlie making a brew at his locker, stopped for a quick word and a lidful. We had just started discussing the relative merits of Chubby Checker and Helen Shapiro, when the door was flung open and a small, toothless maniac raced across to Charlie and went berserk.

Most of it was incomprehensible, but the gist of it was that, in Dickie's opinion, Charlie was a miserable git; he had left him standing in a queue in the rain, when he, Dickie, was fully entitled to expect that Charlie would duly arrive and pick him up as usual.

As that patently hadn't happened he, Dickie, had come to the very reasonable conclusion that Charlie had met with some disaster or, at the very least, had contacted the bubonic plague. Then, having managed to catch the last bus he, Dickie, had been full of concern for Charlie's wellbeing, which lasted until the door opened and he saw Charlie as large as life, supping a lid of tea and obviously not suffering from some terminal illness.

It was all too much for Dickie. However, as he continued to list Charlie's shortcomings, I noticed that Charlie had begun to tap his clogs on the floor.

Interestingly, for students of human nature Charlie had, throughout this tirade, maintained an icy silence. This, together with the tapping of clogs, now ended abruptly.

"See thee tha' wizened bastard, I'm not you're bloody chauffeur, I'm the one doin' thee a favour and if I want to take t'other road round that's my bloody business. There's one thing thee can bet on owd lad—and that's from now on thar'd better mak thee own arrangements to get to pit, 'cos I'm done with thee."

And with a last flick of his clogs, Charlie swallowed his tea, shut his locker and moved off, leaving Dickie who, being in 'extremis', did the only thing possible—he shoved a finger in his ear and waggled.

Sadly, Charlie and I never did resolve the Checker—Shapiro dilemma.

Then one day Charlie himself arrived on the bus and when we enquired about the whereabouts of his beloved A30, he said the cylinder head was blowing and a new head gasket was needed.

You have to remember that in the early sixties car engines weren't quite up to the technical standards of today and things that would make you sue the manufacturer for millions now, were more or less the norm. Gaskets would blow, points would burn, spark plugs would get covered in soot, fan belts would snap, wiper blades would fly off, brake shoes would come adrift, windows would leak, doors would fail to close, the bodywork would turn to rust and engine oil would leak all over the path.

And this was just new cars – with second hand models it was even worse.

So Charlie's need for a new head gasket was nothing new. What was new, was that he'd instructed his wife to buy a new one from the local dealer, in readiness for a workover on his return from the pit. We were surprised, therefore, to see Charlie the following morning once again alight from the bus and, as he was a very competent fitter, we wondered what was wrong with his pride and joy (the car – not his wife.)

On being asked, Charlie went all tight lipped and replied, "I geet home last neet and said 'Nay owd love, hast geet me gasket?'

'Oh aye,' she said, 'I've got it here.'

And with that she opened her handbag and pulled out me gasket. The only trouble was it was folded in half. I couldn't sodding believe it.

'Nay lass, what the bloody hell have you folded it up for?'

'Well,' she said, 'I couldn't carry it on the bus with all the shopping, so to keep it safe I put it in my handbag, the only trouble was it were too big, so I folded it up—Why what's wrong with it?'

'What's bloody wrong? I'll tell thee what's bloody wrong; it's no bloody good that's what's wrong. Tha's put a bloody great crease in the copper lining which means it'll be about as much sodding use as the old one.' That's what's wrong."

"Blimey," said Les, who had been listening to Charlie's emotional outpouring and was trying to figure out what would happen if he spoke to his wife like that. "Then what happened?"

Charlie stared into space for a minute and said, "What bloody happened was, I didn't get any bloody tea and she said she would divorce me if I ever asked her to get anything for the car again. And that's why I'm still on the bloody bus."

There didn't seem to be anything to add, Charlie was evidently in the grip of both a strong emotion and his wife, so Les and I beetled off down the pit for another exciting day at the coalface. (I've always wanted to use that phrase in its true context.)

It's now the end of another long day and I want you to picture the scene—you're about three miles in from the pit bottom, it's eight o'clock at night, you've been down since six-thirty that morning, you've had nothing to eat for about five hours, you're as black as the ace of spades, your cap lamp is just about ready to die away, you've bodily manhandled a thirty hundredweight gearbox into place with no room to stand up and you're absolutely knackered.

You are now faced with a walk all the way to the shaft as the manrider train doesn't operate at this time of the day. And there alongside, as you stagger towards home, is a thirty-six inch wide conveyor belt travelling in your direction—what would you do?

Well so did we. However, hitching a ride on a conveyor was not something you just 'did.' Well, not if you wanted to live to tell the tale, that is.

First of all you need to understand a little bit about the conveyor and how it works. I know; boring, but just think you now have a unique opportunity to learn new words like modulus of elasticity, inertia, surge control, linear velocity, belt pre-tension, gravitational effects on inclines—but not from me, you'll be glad to hear.

Anyway, a coal conveyor is a series of flat metal trays with rollers mounted on the top and the underside, along which runs an endless belt. Each conveyor could be anything up to a mile long and carried a massive amount of coal each shift. There were three rollers in a line across the top; with the outer two angled upwards to form a dished effect. This roller layout was designed to keep the belt running true, enable more coal to be carried and to prevent it from falling off en route.

The bottom roller ran straight across, as it just had to carry the empty belt back to the starting point; with the added bonus that, being straight, it could be easily modified to make a car exhaust.

The drive end was a huge affair with a series of drums around which the belt was wound. The main drum was connected to a gear-box and driven by an electric motor. So at a given signal the wee man in charge of the beast would press the start button and away she went, except that she didn't—well not straight away.

Remember that lovely word 'inertia?' Sadly; it doesn't just apply to teenagers. Our motor, being sort of powerful, was now trying to pull a mile of belt fully loaded with coal, rock, broken spades, empty snuff boxes, butty crusts, the odd pit prop and sundry other bits of unmentionable detritus.

What happened was that the top belt stretched, increased in length, wound its way through the drums and became slack underneath.

It seems there's always something mechanical just itching to spoil your day.

However, being engineers and under threat of the sack, we overcame the problem by having an idler drum mounted on a frame with a bloody great counterweight hanging off the end. So when the belt started to throw slack, our weight pulled the idler drum along and kept the tension constant.

Simple, you say—what's clever about that? Well nothing really until, as sometimes happened, the belt snapped under the strain and made a terrible mess for the wee man to clean up.

Anyway, although the conveyor was mounted in a frame at each end, the long in-between part was hung from the roof of the tunnel by wire ropes fixed to the trays at six feet intervals. Being suspended, it enabled a semi-retired, knackered collier to start at one end and work his way along, cleaning up spillage from underneath and, accompanied by a hacking cough, throw it back onto the belt. You see in our pit, just like true socialism in the USSR, there were jobs for everyone.

Back to the plot. Remember you're on your last legs with several miles still to walk and there, swishing past, is this lovely means of alleviating all that pain. So putting to one side idiot thoughts such as, "What if I'm caught?" and "Is it safe?" you decide to hitch a ride.

Doing this for the first time was a bit like to watching open heart surgery and thinking, "Looks easy, I bet could do that." The other interesting thing was, having decided to hitch a ride, you were about to bring a period of untold joy to any seasoned belt riders who happened to be in the vicinity.

Your first foray into the noble art of belt riding went roughly as follows...

You clambered up, and then, standing on the side of the conveyor, you jumped on.

A millisecond later you found yourself back on the floor in a tangled heap. This was because, having held on to a rope support, you forgot to let go as you jumped onto the belt. You were now in the grip of a thing called centrifugal force, which, due to the forward motion of the belt, flung your feet horizontally into the air and tried to revolve you around the rope support. Realising you were no longer on the belt, you made another fatal error—you let go of the rope and, since you were now in mid-air, no longer holding on to anything, gravity took over from centrifugal force.

What has happened, if only you were in the mood to appreciate it, was your body has just proved the first law of thermodynamics which as you know, states that 'energy can neither be created nor destroyed.' Although, as you lay on the floor, most of your body felt it had been—destroyed that is.

Time for another go.

This time, you remembered to let go of the rope as soon as your feet hit the belt.

A mille-second later you found yourself flat on your back, lying on a heap of coal, being hurled along in pitch darkness at about 60 mph, or at least that's what it seemed like.

What has happened is that, once again, you have neglected to consider the effect of placing your feet rather tentatively on a conveyor which is travelling at speed away from you.

This brings into play another of our old physics favourites—velocity. The alarming effect of a stationary object (you) being placed on a fast moving object, was to have your feet whipped smartly from under you. The net affect of this was that you once again adopted a mid-air horizontal posture, before crashing back down onto the belt. It's that damn gravity thing again.

Setting aside the momentary terror, pain and disorientation, was the realisation that all this violence had dislodged your cap lamp. You are also dimly aware that if you stayed where you were, then pretty soon you would be deposited down a chute and into a bunker with about 200 tons of coal.

Obviously it was time to leap off, only to land once again in an increasingly painful heap.

Time for another go.

This time, setting aside the pain, you look back over your previous mistakes and rehearse in your mind what you have to do.

Check your lamp, climb up, step smartly onto the belt, let go of the rope, adopt a leaning forward position to counteract the velocity of the belt and quietly but confidently kneel on the coal with your hands on the belt in front to steady yourself. Then with stability achieved and cap lamp ablaze you can at last enjoy the ride.

So repeating this mantra, you're ready to go again.

This time, all the lessons have been remembered, you swing smoothly onto the belt, let go of the rope, adopt a forward position, kneel down, place your hands on the edges of the belt and a millisecond later experience an unbelievably searing pain in your fingers.

Sadly, in your euphoria at having landed safely, you had curled your fingers over the lip of the belt, trapping them between the underside and the guide rollers. Before you realise what's happened, you've travelled over another six rollers with fingers still locked in position, with the combined weight of coal and yourself trying to flatten them.

Finally, coming to your senses, you snatch your hands away from the source of the pain; unfortunately, this causes you to fall forward, landing with your face in an assorted heap of coal, dust, rock and bits of iron.

Stemming your tears of both pain and frustration, you realise it's now necessary to leap off again before you land head first in the bunker.

Remember, while all this has been going on, you have been providing no end of amusement to the lads, but perhaps the worst part is the laughter as an experienced sod rides past and shouts, "Nay Briun, what's tha doin dern theer, has't lost summat?"

Just as you have hit the ground for the third time.

Time for another go.

So, clutching the rope as best you can with flattened fingers, you adopt the downhill ski position, step smartly on, kneel down, keep your hands on top of the belt and—hey presto, we have lift off.

This is the life, no more long walks, as you swish silently along the roadway and then, just as you raise you're head to see how far there is to go, you are dealt an enormous blow on the head, you fall backwards once more and this time you have the added joy of being completely covered in stone-dust.

What you had failed to remember was that dust barriers are mounted at intervals just under the roof and, as the roof is prone to undulate due to weight of strata above, some of the barriers were lower than they should be.

Panic sets in, your eyes are full of dust, you're quietly choking, your lamp is wound around your neck and you have forgotten how far ahead the bunker is.

Time to get off.

Time for another go.

At last (disregarding the fact that had you just kept on walking, you would have been under a nice warm shower by now, you wouldn't be in pain, you wouldn't be embarrassed and your fingers would have been capable of gently holding your Willy,) all the lessons have been learned, balance is perfect and you can now join that select band of belt riding brothers. No more derision, eyes wide open, no more fear of the bunker—until that is, you have to get off.

This means you now have to stand upright on a belt travelling towards the bunker at Mach One speed, reach for a rope hanger, time everything to a millisecond and step smartly off—or not, as the case may be.

Funnily enough, in my case stepping off was not a problem due to a skill I had learned in childhood and which now stood me in good stead. Growing up in Liverpool meant that the transport of choice was a tram. These were known, for some unaccountable reason, as 'Green Goddesses;' well they were green—but goddesses?

Anyway, what you learned at an early age, was that anyone with macho pretensions (most of Liverpool really) never, ever waited for the tram to stop before getting off.

In fact, if the tram was full and you approached a popular stop (outside Woolworths for instance) there would be considerable jostling for position on the second step down. Then, swinging gracefully from the chrome bar and facing the direction of travel, you stepped off, ran smartly alongside, slowed to a walk and with a modest smile, went into the shop.

Again, this method of alighting could provide endless amusement for the people in the queue waiting to get on. Inevitably there were those who took the art of alighting to undreamed of heights and the favourite was some prat who decided—wrongly as it turned out—to be the first to leap off, while the tram was still doing about twenty mph. This resulted in our hero having to suddenly run parallel to the tram at about the same speed as Jesse Owens on a good medal day.

The only significant difference was that Jesse wasn't encumbered by a flapping gabardine mac, wellies, a hand rolled fag, an Everton scarf, a boiled sweet, a flat cap, a shiny Burtons suit, a roll of Fablon and a pair of wire rimmed glasses held together with Elastoplast. I think if only Hitler had had the foresight to make tram hopping a compulsory Olympic event in 1936, it may well have affected Jesse's speed on the bends.

Being now firmly in the grip of two more bits of physics, namely the slipstream of the tram and his own momentum, the idiot found that stopping was rather more difficult than starting. The end result was that he either shot past the now stationary tram, much to the amazement of the driver or; he crashed into the queue, just as they moved forward to get aboard. Sadly as most people were concentrating on getting a good window seat, they were unaware of the impending doom, until they found themselves skittled in all directions.

However, this latter event did have one advantage—it brought our hero to an abrupt stop, but with the distinct possibility of being duffed up by the irate crowd.

It's like everything else in life—perfection needs practise.

So, although getting on the belt was initially a painful experience, getting off simply required me to pretend it was a tram.

Years later, the 'powers that be' decided to legalise manriding on belts and so built proper platforms with emergency signals and handrails for getting on and off.

So, no more adrenalin rush, no unusual skills to be learned, no thrill of breaking the law, no having to lie flat to get under low roof girders and no collecting the odd bruise or two. How us macho men would have scorned such softy progress.

As I mentioned earlier, all this working late, so that the general population could keep warm, meant that I missed the going home bus far more times than I caught it. Then one bright summer's day, as I was once again making my weary way across Lancashire in a vain attempt to get home before it was time to go back, I had a brainwave and bought a Scooter. Freedom at last! I could work overtime for as long as I liked, I could have fifteen minutes more in bed in the mornings, I no longer had to run for the bus, stand in the rain, find the correct fare or sit on the top deck with visibility down to about two rows of seats, coupled with a distinct lack of breathable air.

The vehicle in question was a state of the art machine known as a Vespa. Actually at the time, there was a choice of two—the Vespa and the Lambretta, both of which were produced by Italian companies.

The Lambretta was made by Innocenti and the Vespa by Piaggio. I like to think I chose the Vespa because Piaggio also made two fearsome motor-bikes—the Moto-Guzzi and the Gilera. But it wouldn't be true, as I had no idea what else they made at the time.

All I did know was that both models were currently thrashing the pants off our Norton bikes at the Isle of Man TT races. The other sad truth was that although the Vespa was less powerful than the Lambretta—it was cheaper.

Interestingly, Innocenti got into financial difficulties and was bought by that icon of British automobile engineering, the British Motor Corporation, better known as BMC. Remember the Innocenti Mini—of course you do. Now BMC were not really geared up to be the saviours of anybody, especially themselves. With amazing foresight, they had bought into a fashion trend that was rapidly coming to an end and, as most of their year was taken up by strikes, motor scooter sales took a nose-dive and Innocenti closed.

Just another fine example of British industrial know-how and sense of timing I suppose.

Unbeknown to me, at about the same time as I was driving to the pit, in the deep south of the country, about twenty thousand idiots were also driving scooters, each one tastefully embellished with about a hundred wing mirrors mounted on the handlebars. They all wore an ex U.S. Army surplus outer garment known as a 'Parka' in order to protect their cutting edge mohair suits, pointed shoes and pressed shirts. The parka was a sort of light brown coat that came down to the knees at the front, with a longer 'fishtail' at the back. The ensemble was completed by a hood with a length of dead cat fur sewn around the edge. Collectively, this sartorially challenged group were known as 'Mods.'

On any given weekend they polished their wing mirrors and headed en masse to exotic places like Clacton, Margate and Brighton. On reaching their destination, they would await the arrival of another bunch of lunatics, this lot favouring an assortment of fast motorbikes. They were referred to as 'Rockers' and the difference was not just in the mode of transport, as they were, by comparison, a bunch of scruffy herberts whose dress code consisted mainly of oily leather jackets, jeans and an assortment of boots.

It was reckoned that the difference in transport was explained by the fact that 'Mods,' having spent all their money on clothes, hadn't much left for transport.

Having all arrived at the same resort they would parade up and down the promenade, make a good deal of noise, frighten old ladies and convince themselves that they hated one another. At which point, the scooters and bikes were jettisoned and a pitched battle would commence. This was known as the weekly battle for supremacy between the 'Mods' (don't crease me suit) and 'Rockers' (don't split me jeans.) Newspaper reports of our youth at play were united regarding one thing—nobody knew why and this applied not least of all, to the protagonists, as they emerged from the various Out-Patient departments.

Still, as we used to say on reading the latest bulletin, "What can you expect from people who, for some unaccountable reason, had decided to live south of Whitchurch?"

Enough of the social history—on with the plot.

I was now the proud owner of a 'set of wheels' as we independent spirits' called them. Mine was tasteful green with a chrome wing mirror and an engine capable of unleashing nearly six horsepower (downhill with a following wind of not less than ten knots).

Obviously, owning such a powerful machine (well relatively, compared to a bike,) required specialised protective clothing. Here I was fortunate; I already owned the main item—a duffel coat. All that remained was the need to purchase a safety helmet, goggles and some big gloves.

Now don't get confused here thinking, oh I know, it's the same type of helmet as worn by Valentino Rossi. No, my helmet bore a distinct resemblance to a pudding basin and was just about as useful as a means of preventing brain damage. It was a tastefully covered with a thin layer of black leather with protective flaps on each side. These covered the ears and were perforated so that you could hear the bus just before it hit you. The flaps ended with straps, which were fastened under the chin by press studs in order to stop the helmet flying off in a breeze.

The inside had crossed webbing under the crown, with a bit of string to allow for minute adjustment. The whole thing was lined with cork, the better to absorb shock as you hit the road head first. Wearing the thing increased my overall height by about eight inches giving me a look reminiscent of a very tall bollard.

Obviously goggles were a must. I may have mentioned I wore glasses to see with and wearing them on a dry day wasn't too bad, if you discount the fact that within a mile or two, they were covered in a various assortment of squashed bugs. No—clearly the answer was to wear goggles over my glasses.

Designed to emulate a World War II flying ace, they had a protective screen around the corners of the eyes and were made in a one piece moulding, sometimes of leather, or, in my case, a sort of leatherette material left over from a three-piece suite. Some misguided idiots favoured lenses with a yellow tint, but this had two disadvantages; in dim light you couldn't see anything, and seeing someone staring at you for the first time with bright yellow eyes was off-putting, to say the least.

I knew one guy who tried to make some kind of fashion statement with his and took to wearing them on top of his helmet; this was OK until he reached about twenty mph when they blew away. Not put off by this minor setback to the cause of looking swish, he modified his approach and—in the manner of Baron Von Richthofen alighting from his Fokker Dr1—left them slung casually around his neck. Forgetting for a moment that the Baron, when flying, wore them as designed; our idiot set off at great speed, at which point the goggles, becoming aerodynamic, shot up and hit him in the face. And to think, this guy was in charge of the Washery Plant.

The final must-have item to complete the 'dangerous biker' image was to buy a pair of gauntlets. Again, the idea was to affect the dispatch rider look and if they could be made to simulate real leather so much the better. The extended wrist guard had to be reasonably stiff, both to avoid it collapsing when buffeted by wind and to enable you to stuff the arms of your duffle coat firmly down the inside.

So—you had the 'wheels' and you had the biker gear; all that remained now was to ride the damn thing. There's no doubt that due to the novelty and new-found freedom, things worked well all through the first summer months. As I sped along the highway, passing cyclists with distain, scattering wildlife and pretending to be Barry Sheene, I realised there was one small niggle which tended to spoil this new 'king of the road' image. It was the flapping that was most noticeable. L plates were difficult to fasten on securely and as a result, the string kept coming loose and the things would rattle against the bodywork like demented pigeons. Not only was this annoying, it also meant that about every three weeks I had to buy another pair, tie them on and the whole cycle of destruction would start all over again. Something had to be done.

I applied for a driving test.

Forms were filled in, payment was made, the Highway Code was purchased, new L plates were fitted and a date was set for the examination.

Now in those days, for some unaccountable reason, the driving test for scooters was held right in the centre of Liverpool. So what? I hear you say. Well this is what – the City of Liverpool at any one time is full of buses, taxis, delivery vans, hills, traffic lights, pedestrian crossings, one-way streets, signs pointing everywhere, buskers, drunks falling off the pavement and on the day I took my test, 247,000 shoppers bent on suicide. You have to remember that Zebra crossings had only been invented about ten years before and were looked on by the average Scouser as a challenge to the motorist. The favourite game was to wait until the approaching vehicle was about three feet from the crossing and then step smartly onto the first stripe while at the same time staring fixedly at the driver in a manner roughly interpreted as—'Go on then pal, I dare you.'

Mothers would encourage their kids to believe that once on a crossing they were safe from harm. A sort of modified version of the childrens game—'barley on the wall can't touch me.' Sadly, no one had told the motorist about this infallibility claim and, as a result, kids were being skittled all over the roads, A&E facilities were filled to overflowing, the police were engulfed in paperwork, insurance claims for bodywork dents caused by children were being rejected; and parents were beginning to question the wisdom of the Government in naming a so called safety feature after a daft African animal.

It was something of a shock then, to find I was expected to take my test in the middle of all this mayhem. Not only that, but I began to realise that restricting my study of the highway code to the section on 'Courtesy when meeting horse-drawn vehicles,' wasn't going to be uppermost in the Examiner's list of likely questions. As if that wasn't enough, the damned test was to take place on a Saturday.

So we can now add the odd six or eight thousand Everton/Liverpool supporters intent on having pre-match drinks in various hostelries and using suicidal road crossing techniques in order to reach the next watering hole.

The scene was set, as they say.

I arrived at the test centre at the appointed time and after some minutes was introduced to my Examiner. He turned out to be a sad looking man in a trilby and the kind of long gabardine mac beloved of flashers. Having introduced himself, he said he would start by asking a number of road safety questions, prior to the actual test taking place. I have no idea whether, or if, I answered satisfactorily, for reasons which will become apparent in a minute. Anyway, after a short time, he said he had asked all the questions he wanted and could I now make my way outside, retrieve my scooter and he would provide instructions for the next phase.

We met as indicated and as I wheeled my scooter to the end of the road, he gave me a set of detailed instructions. Remember, this was a scooter, so he couldn't accompany me, but apparently, whilst I was negotiating the course, he would station himself at strategic positions in order to observe my progress, adherence to the Highway Code, general demeanour and whether I knocked anyone down.

His instructions were detailed with some rapidity and no notes were taken. In essence he told me the route he wanted me to take, with numerous references to take the first right, follow the signs for the University, take the second left, go straight on for 200 yards, bear left, cross over the bridge, take the second right into Renshaw Street, go left at the second set of traffic lights and pull up opposite the entrance to the test centre.

Throughout all this imparting of key information, I was putting on my helmet, donning my gloves, fastening my duffle coat and kick-starting the scooter. He finished by asking, "Is that clear?" And not wishing to seem more idiotic than usual, I replied in the affirmative.

Off I went and took the first right, so far so good, but it then dawned on me that I hadn't committed his route to memory and I was now sailing down one of the busiest parts of the city at thirty mph, with absolutely no idea where I was actually going, let alone where I was supposed to be going. In some panic and realising that if I were to make it back at all to the test centre, I had a stroke of brilliance—keep bearing left. And I have to say my plan seemed to be working until that is, I met a one-way street. Swerving rapidly out again I pressed on.

The next ten minutes were a blur. I tried to find my way back to the start by whatever roads became available, but ended up doing a grand tour of the city. By now all thoughts of ever seeing my Examiner again had long since faded and, realising that I had most probably failed, I drove home.

There was nothing else for it—I tied the L plates on with thicker string.

Sadly, however, as autumn merged into winter a number of new short-comings began to emerge.

Most notable was the onset of hypothermia. It became increasingly obvious that nylon trousers (even when tucked into your socks) were no proof against cold, damp November mornings and what was worse, my duffel coat toggles were being stretched to breaking point, causing the garment to billow out like a half inflated balloon. This in turn, sent a stream of freezing air down each sleeve, which on reaching the gauntlet, created a back pressure sufficient to force the cuffs back up your arms so that you were now in the happy position of driving along in a flapping coat with short sleeves.

And then, strangely enough, the roads became icy, bringing a whole new driving experience, which in my case, was based largely on what the prats in the Institute of Advanced Motoring call 'a failure to read the road.' Unfortunately, this 'failure' occurred at one particular spot, at one particular time each morning and in front of one particular (captive) audience.

Each morning I sailed up the hill out of Prescot and on reaching a level section of road took a sweeping left-hand bend leading to St Helens. Located on the apex of the bend were two bus stops, one on each side of the road. Invariably, at each stop, there was a queue of sad looking folk all waiting for their respective buses.

As the summer months went by, we became an almost familiar site, they watching a bloke on a scooter several sizes too small for comfort; me glancing at the queues and feeling quite superior as I zoomed past in a cloud of oily exhaust fumes.

And then came that fateful morning when I realised in a rush of adrenalin that all I had learned about coefficients of friction was true. This was borne out by the fact that as I turned nicely into the sweeping bend, the scooter decided to go straight on.

In the space of a millisecond I began to realise that all was not well. The wheel has been turned as usual, I had glanced at the queues as usual, I had retained the same speed as usual; but it now begins to dawn that nothing usual is happening.

What was happening was that I was racing, on a green scooter, towards the queue on the opposite side of the road, with the wheel and handlebars turned at about thirty degrees to the left. I was making futile, and as it turned out,incorrect, attempts to apply the brake, definitely not slowing down and the crowd were beginning to move smartly out of harms way.

At about two thirds of the way across the road, balance became an issue. The scooter, realising the front wheel was both stationary and pointing in a different direction to that of travel, decides to tip sideways. We then observed a classic case of divided momentum, the bike carried on its frictionless way as before, whilst I, having landed sideways on the road, began to slow down. This meant that although we were both still travelling towards the rapidly disappearing queue, the scooter arrived at the kerb some seconds before I did. Finally, having both stopped abruptly, I was reunited with my machine, which meant we were now both lying together in the gutter, jammed up against the kerb.

Realising I couldn't continue to lie there, I needed to leap to my feet, retrieve the bike, re-mount and drive off as though nothing untoward had happened. Unfortunately, this simple strategy contained a couple of significant unknowns—one of which was that I had to make the episode look like a minor setback and then I had to pretend I wasn't hurt.

All of this under the rapt attention of about thirty people on both sides of the road. Not, as it turned out, an easy thing to achieve.

In order to try and convince my audience that all was well, I contemplated waving as I set off. However, as my entire body was in severe pain, my handlebars were bent at a strange angle, my wing mirror was swinging in the breeze and my goggles were halfway around the back of my neck—I decided against it.

It also began to dawn on me that nylon trousers and a duffle coat were no match for tarmac.

The following day saw a change in tactics in that I approached the dreaded bend at about three mph with both feet trailing along the road for added stability. I also noticed that my audience on seeing me, leaned forward in anticipation of the fun to come. They were however, disappointed, whilst selfishly, I was extremely relieved.

All went well for the rest of the week until, despite my new cautious riding style—it happened again. The only consolation was the fact that it had also taken the audience by surprise and both the scooter and I crashed into the kerb before they were ready.

Something would have to be done, it wasn't just that I was scarred for life, or that I was now wearing shredded trousers. No—it was an increasing awareness that having finally arrived at the pit, I could no longer dismount.

Somehow or other I seemed to be unable to perform simple tasks with my hands, I shivered, muscles appeared to be in a state of lock-down, exposed skin (of which there was a lot) had taken on a sort of bluish tinge, my eyeballs were frozen, I had no inclination to perform the complex task of walking and I started to have hallucinations about the wonderful warmth to be found upstairs on a bus. So I did the only thing possible; I sold the bloody thing and bought a Mini-van.

Why, I hear you ask, did you buy a van? Well, it's obvious really; a van was cheaper, (in fact when I bought it, the optional extras were a choice between a heater and a passenger seat.) It also had room in the back in which to throw the three children we had produced by then.

The Coal Face—This is where the fun starts. Ours was 200 yards long, which is why the deputy looks so miserable, as he realised he still has 180 yards to crawl, while the Davy Lamp is burning his willy.

A Coal Shearer—The steel picks cut the coal as the drum rotates. The shearer is pulled along the face by the chain. The Cutter-man is coiling the electric cable as the machine moves along.

A Conveyor Belt—Coal is being sent out of the District to the main storage hopper. The Overman seems to be wondering why the electric cable is on the wrong side. You can see the hangers we used to grab in order to swing on and off the belt.

The Main Loading Point—Sixty tubs, each holding three tonnes, being filled from the hopper. The black hole underneath the tubs is where Joe and I used to meet Joe Gormley in the chapter Knowing Famous People

(Left) A New Installation— The switchgear is cunningly mounted above at just the right height to knock your helmet off. Notice the 'manhole' on the left of the tunnel. We managed to get seven of us in one of these when all Hell broke loose in the chapter entitled An Uphill Struggle.

A Driller At Work—Preparing the tunnel ready for blasting. The entrance to the coal face is on the lower left, but as you can see, there is not a lot of headroom

A Tunnel Collapse—What might be called 'a small setback,' as the pressure of the rock above becomes greater than the tunnel supports can bear. Our tunnel looked a bit like this after the escapade in the chapter entitled An Uphill Struggle.

A Mechanical Shovel— I had just built a machine similar to this when Pat rather carelessly, buried it under a pile of rock.

Twin Branch Tunnels—The one on the left is a victim of weight coming on both the roof and the floor. The one on the right is luckier, it is only being squashed from the sides. Neither option looks very exciting.

(Right) Another Bad Day at the Office—And just when you think you're winning!

After the Dust Cleared—More hours of endless fun on the coal face. You can see on the right, the Shotfirer has just finished playing with his dynamite.

Happy Smiling Miners—Despite the fact that the big guy in the front looks as though he has just won the shovel in a raffle.

Chapter Seventeen
Knowing Famous People

You may be wondering, "If he works so far underground, just where do the famous people come in?"—bear with me and prepare to be amazed—later.

I had my own early warning system of impending mechanical problems on our coal-face, in the doughty form of Joe, my willing partner on matters social. Joe was an 'Oiler' and his role was to work his way around the district checking bearings and gearboxes on the plant and machinery.

He carried a grease gun in the manner of a mafia hit-man and each morning would collect a jerry-can full of oil from the workshop, bring it down the pit and carry it in to our district. Joe would travel round, feed the machinery and let me know which bearings were 'getting hot,' or whether there was an oil leak in a gearbox.

It was early warning information you couldn't buy and on a number of occasions, saved me from having to deal with what might have been serious breakdowns. This, of course, meant that I was unable to show off my undoubted engineering skills, but hey—sacrifices had to be made.

Joe was about fifteen years older than me; he was tall with reddish hair and wore glasses. He hailed originally from the Durham area, which accounted for his funny way of speaking. He had entered the industry straight from school and worked in the local pit just prior to nationalisation.

We spent many a happy hour chatting, as we went on our way around the district, Joe operating his grease gun and me operating my spanners. We were clambering along a back road one day and had to crawl on hands and knees, as the roof was doing its best to meet the floor. Stopping for a breather, I said, "I hope the roof will stay where it was long enough for us to get clear."

Joe said, "I was once trapped underground for three days due to a roof fall."

"Bloody hell Joe," I said, "What was it like?"

Yet another fine example of my renowned 'in-depth' questioning technique.

"What do you think it was like? It was bloody awful. There were three of us on the face when weight came on and the roof on either side of us collapsed. Fortunately air was still coming across the top of the fall, but the gap was too narrow for us to climb through. Anyway it took the rescuers about three days to clear away the rock and fortunately, by the second day, they could hear us and were able to push some food and water over the top of the fall."

"Finally," continued Joe, "We were able to crawl over the debris and the rescue team took us to the Safety Room where we were examined by a local Doctor."

Thinking of something pertinent to say, I said, "I'll bet the Manager was pleased you were all okay."

"Oh aye," said Joe, "The old sod greeted us individually and I'll never forget his words. He said how relieved he was to see us, but obviously he couldn't pay us for the three days, as we hadn't been working."

I stared at him. "Nice one Joe, you certainly fooled me. As if anyone could be that mean."

"Nice one be blowed," said Joe, "That's exactly what the miserable bastard said; and we never did get paid."

I did wonder whether Joe had been offered counselling for his ordeal, but thought it wiser not to ask.

One of our most important joint enterprises concerned the main coal transfer point in the main tunnel. Here, the coal from all the districts was delivered into an enormous container, with a chute at one end. It was located on a girder frame high up in the air and held about two hundred tons of coal. It was so big that the locomotive could deliver sixty tubs at a time underneath.

Once in place, the tubs were then rammed forward and on arriving under the chute, the door would be opened and each tub would be filled in about twenty seconds. The door would close, another tub would be rammed underneath then, when all sixty were filled, the loco would couple up and take the whole load to the pit bottom.

Exciting—no; dusty and noisy—yes.

Our job, at the end of each shift, was to check the hydraulic rams to see that all was well and they were ready to operate throughout the night shift. Unfortunately (for us) the rams were mounted underneath the rails and the only access for inspection was via a narrow 'pit.' This wasn't too bad except for the fact that, as we had been loading coal for seven hours non-stop, there was a considerable amount of spillage. Obviously, the first thing to fill up was our inspection pit.

There then followed what became an extremely boring routine. Taking a shovel apiece we would start to fling coal out of the pit until slowly but surely, we would both disappear under the roadway. The only sign of life from then on would be airborne coal, cursing, flashing cap-lamps and lots of dust rising gently in the breeze.

At about the time when we were both completely out of sight, a light, accompanied by a disembodied voice, would shine on us and the 'voice' would say, "Nay lads, who's that and what tha't doin' dern theer?"

On the first occasion, it was Joe who answered, "It's OK Joe, it's only the fitter and me, were just looking at the rams."

The 'voice' would then say, "Aye but thee aren't colliers. It's not reet that tha' should be shovelling coal. I'm not having this lads, I'll be seeing the Manager when I get up top and I'll get it stopped."

And with that parting shot, the mystery 'voice' departed.

"Who the hell was that, Joe?" I asked.

"That's Joe Gormley. He's our NUM rep and he always goes up early to attend to union business."

Bloody hell—even I had heard of the great Joe Gormley; and to think he cared about us enough to make such big changes! I mentioned as much to Joe.

"Don't hold your breath. He's been stopping like this on and off for months and making the same comment. So far nothing's changed, I think it just makes the great man feel better."

Mind you, to have spoken to the man (well listened, anyway) who was to become the President of the NUM, do battle with Ted Heath (and win) fight Arthur Scargill (another win) and end up as Baron Gormley of Ashton-in-Makerfield, is not to be sniffed at.

Not only that, but if we are to consider fame by association then, as Joe Gormley came from the Wigan area, so did George Formby. Mind you, in my formative years I had the misfortune to see a couple of George Formby films and in my opinion, he was no Danny Kaye.

(For younger readers, Danny Kaye was a very talented clown and made a number of funny films, often with Virginia Mayo, with whom we were also in love. Take a look at his genius in The Secret Life of Walter Mitty.)

Then there was the time when Sir Alfred Robens, the NCB Chairman, was to pay a visit to our pit. Everything was made ready, the canteen was painted, paths were weeded, the flag was flying, overalls were washed, white lines were painted, oil lamps were polished, a new tea-service was purchased and broken machinery was hidden behind the workshops. All was in order. We were briefed about not speaking unless the great man spoke first, not to call him 'Alf,' we pretended to be busy—and he didn't turn up.

Little Eric our 'road runner' Deputy arrived one morning and proceeded to single-handedly spring clean the main gate. He tidied cables, re-arranged snap boxes, picked up stray lumps of coal, tested for gas, straightened props, checked the time and generally made a nuisance of himself.

Bill the Shotfirer and I were in our usual standby-alert mode, leaning on a nice warm transformer until, on Eric's third pass, Bill could stand it no longer.

"Bloody hell Eric, sit thee down, thar'll do thyself an injury. What's going on?"

"Oh lads, there's a famous Bishop just been appointed to the area and he wants to see what it's like to be a miner—as he says, they're all a part of his flock."

"Famous, what's he bloody famous for?" asked Bill, in a voice that seemed to be somewhat lacking in reverence.

"Now Bill," said Eric, "Don't thee be giving me any trouble. He's famous for having set up a special unit for unmarried mothers and apparently he was given some sort of award from Buckingham Palace."

Bill stared at Eric and said, "If I'm any judge of the sodding clergy, he probably put half of them in the club himself. They're all bloody hypocrites, the lot of them."

I began to suspect that Bill had a powerful tale to tell involving the clergy and illicit relationships and determined to wheedle it out of him later.

Eric, however, was now in an advanced state of panic and started to ask Bill subtle questions like, "Won't you have to be the far end of the face ready for firing anytime now?"

Bill, ever the diplomat, said, "Well I might, but then again I might just stay here and have a word with his lordship."

Eric, having consulted his watch for the tenth time, said, "Oh heck, he'll be here any minute, I'll just see that everything is okay on the face." And with that he shot off, little knowing that fate was about to conspire to the extent that worrying about Bill would pale into insignificance.

Sure enough, a short time later, lights appeared and his Reverence arrived, accompanied by Norman, our Training Officer.

"Aye up lads," said Norman, "This here's the Reverend and he's come to take a look at where the coal comes from."

Now Norman was a great guy and quite relaxed, he was wise enough to stop for a chat while his bishopness got his breath back and had a surreptitious lean on our transformer.

It was at about this point that things began to go seriously wrong for Eric.

Suddenly, a disembodied voice boomed out, "Cutter's bloody stopped again, we need the sodding electrician up here now."

Several things happened at once—Eric gave out a wail, the Bishop jumped and looked sort of heavenward for the source of the voice, Norman looked puzzled and Bill gave me a terrible smile.

Then with a fine sense of timing, the voice continued.

"Now we're bloody stuffed, the effing thing won't move. We'll just have to pull the effing, sodding cable out of the tray and re-lay the effing sod."

And then it went quiet. The Bishop by now probably thought his past sins had caught him up and Eric went ballistic.

What the Bishop was experiencing first hand was the result of a longed for stroke of genius on the part of the Electrical Department. Remember I said earlier that if you were wanted on the face, a message had to be shouted down from person to person until it reached the recipient? Well, some inventive chap reckoned that we could install 'jack-points' at intervals along the face so that a portable telephone could be plugged in and messages relayed to the main gate. Obviously, because of the noise, the phone was connected to a tannoy system set at 'burst ear drum' decibel levels. Similar to, but at a much lower pain threshold than is enjoyed at the average pop concert—or so I am told.

On receipt of the second succinct message from the cutter-man, Eric leapt at the tannoy pole and tried vainly to stuff his jacket into the source of the noise. Realising that: a) it was futile and b) he was now about to receive the next plea from the face in an ear which was about two inches from the tannoy, he leapt off and tried another gambit.

Grabbing the return telephone, he conveyed what turned out to be the wrong message.

"Nay Harry, don't thee be shouting like that and watch your language; we have a Bishop come to visit us in the main gate."

Probably because Eric's frantic appeal was somewhat unusual, the cutter-man replied in kind.

"Well Eric, if tha's got a Bishop with thee, thar'd best send him up here and see if he can work an effing miracle on this sodding cutter. But I'll tell thee; it's going to take more than effing holy water to make this bastard move."

By now, Eric was taking no further part in the proceedings. His head was in his hands, he was slumped over the nearest transformer and was chewing on the sleeve of his jacket—most of which was still stuffed inside the tannoy.

Fortunately, Norman, realising that things weren't going to improve said, "Right Reverend, I think me and thee had best be on our way. See thee lads." And with that Norman and the Bishop moved off.

Throughout all this, both Bill and I had not moved, but on the departure of our guests, Bill took the phone out of Eric's hand, called Harry and said, "Hold on Harry, I'll send for the experts and for God's sake stop shouting like a bloody lunatic."

I said to Bill, "Nice touch that, calling on the almighty to stop Harry yelling."

Bill, with the most sinister smile I had ever seen replied, "I don't know what you're talking about, but I will say it were the best fun I've had for a long time."

I said, "Did you know all about this visit before Eric?"

"Aye well, maybe," was all he would say.

It was later, when I was leaving the canteen that my conspiracy theory started to click into place, probably because I saw Bill and Harry getting on the Wigan bus, laughing like lunatics and slapping one another on the back.

A couple of days later, having let Bill beat me at wrist-wrestling once again, the time seemed right to ask my in-depth question, purely, you understand, in the interests of serious research.

"Bill, what's the problem with your lack of admiration for the clergy?"

I thought for a minute I'd overstepped the mark, as Bill stared at me and began playing with a stick of dynamite. Thankfully, after a couple of failed attempts to catch it in mid-air, he said, "Aye well, as far as I'm concerned they're all a bunch of bloody hypocrites, preaching one thing and doing another."

I needed to know more and, as he had stopped throwing explosives around for a moment, I pressed on in my quest for sociological wotsi-sname.

"What happened to make you think like that?" (Another penetrating question).

"Well, I'll tell thee, it started when the wife insisted we attend her cousin's wedding and while we were in the church, who should I find officiating, but a bloody vicar who, it was well known, was 'knocking off' his organist. As if that weren't bad enough, he gets up in the pulpit and starts rabbiting on about the sanctity of marriage. So I says to the wife, 'He's a sodding hypocrite. The bastard's married with three kids and it's not just the church organ that's being played with.'"

"Wow," I said, "What happened then?"

"Well it seems that I'd been speaking in a bit of a loud voice, which meant that half the congregation and the sodding organist heard what I said. The wife went mad and dragged me out, shouting as how I'd spoiled her cousin's wedding day, how she'd wasted her money on a fancy hat, a present, a bag of confetti and how we now couldn't possibly attend the function laid on for the evening."

"Then what?"

"I tried reasoning with her, saying it weren't my fault if her cousin decided to let a randy vicar marry them, but I could see it were hopeless, she was embarrassed and I'd ruined her day."

"Bloody hell Bill," I said, "So you just went home, did you?"

"Well we were just about to, when her cousin's father made a bee-line for us. I thought now I'm for it, he's going to want a punch-up for ruining his daughter's big day. Anyway, the wife's hissing at me to apologise, when the bride's father reaches me, grabs me by the hand and starts shaking it. And all the while he's shaking, he's saying, 'Bloody well done Bill, I told me daughter she should have gone to another church, as it's well known the dirty sod's been ragging the organist for months. Now, make sure you're both at the function early; I want to buy thee both the biggest drinks in the world.' And, with that, he shot off to find his wife, muttering about me being the best relative he's ever had."

"So it all turned out for the best," I said.

"Oh aye, we had a reet good knees up and I never bought a drink all night."

"Did your wife forgive you then?"

"Well, when she heard what her cousin's father said, she became quite proud and I heard her telling one of her aunties, 'It's a pity other people didn't have the courage to speak out like her Bill.'"

"What about the vicar, did he turn up?"

"Funnily enough, he made some excuse and never came to the reception; but the best thing was a couple of weeks later, the wife came back from the shops and told me the organist had gone off with a lad who worked in the local butchers."

Pat Rimmer and I were chatting one morning whilst waiting for him to blast the next round of shots and cover us in our daily dose of dust, when the talk turned to heroes. As Pat was a dyed-in-the-wool St Helens supporter, he waxed lyrical about the prowess of great past players. A number of these guys had been humble pit men before their talent for the great game propelled them to glory. Oh, how Pat envied these local giants and the adulation he felt was due to them.

I tried to put myself in Pat's position and had to agree that as lads we all wanted to be Stanley Matthews (he of the flapping shorts) or in summer, Godfrey Evans, the great Kent and England wicket keeper. We both sat back and tried to visualise just how wonderful it would be to achieve heroic status, when Pat removed his glasses and blew an accumulation of dust off the lenses.

Looking up and seeing things clearly for a minute, Pat gave out a sort of strangled cry.

"Just look at that sod over there, the bastard."

I looked, but none of what I saw made any sense and, as it wasn't like Pat to explode (no pun intended) like this, I asked what was wrong.

"Wrong, I'll tell you what's wrong! You see that sod over there cleaning up the coal, he's a miserable git that's what's wrong."

As I still hadn't grasped the significance of his outburst, I said, "Pat, what the hell are you on about? The guy's just shovelling away and minding his own business."

Pat stared at me as though I was a halfwit and said, "Look at his bloody shirt! The sod's wearing a British Lions shirt! If I'd won a shirt like that, it would be hung over our mantelpiece in pride of place, so everyone could see just what a brilliant career I'd had and how I'd played for my country—he just doesn't care! It's not right, the sod."

And with that he fell back exhausted.

Looking closer I could see the guy was indeed wearing the coveted shirt, you could just see the badge with the rose, shamrock, thistle and feathers.

"Are you sure it's his?"

"Of course it's bloody his! I know him, he played several times for the Lions and went to Australia to play the Wallabies. How anyone can treat such an icon like he does beats me, he doesn't deserve it," said Pat, still in the grip of some strong emotion.

"So he's not really a hero of yours then?" I asked.

Pat just picked up a lump of coal and threw it at the conveyor; I suppose that was the only answer I was to get, so we changed the subject.

Heroes—who needs them? Feet of clay if you ask me.

As I said, Pat wore spectacles, as did I. Although glasses and coal dust weren't the best combination for seeing clearly, it was definitely better than walking into walls, falling down holes, not recognising anybody and being unable to check your pay-slip.

In my case the deterioration became noticeable when I was about eighteen and I found it increasingly difficult to focus on anything further away than about six inches. Obviously, being a chap, I did nothing about it, as I was firmly convinced that wearing glasses would destroy forever any chance of ever getting a girl friend. Pathetic really, but then again—as I'm sure your all aware—you never saw John Wayne wearing specs (even when, as Rooster Cogburn, he had a patch over one eye.)

So I struggled on, memorising local landmarks, shop names, friends, next door neighbours, the furniture, road signs, traffic lights and Doris Day. In the last case I was faced with a terrible dilemma—how could I go through life being in love with someone who was becoming less and less distinct with every new film? Something had to be done. A secret visit to the local opticians revealed the worst—I couldn't see.

Glasses were produced, chosen, purchased and immediately hidden away in a drawer. The only concession I made to this sensible regime was to take them with me to the cinema and, as soon as the lights went down, I whipped out the specs and with one surreptitious movement stuck them on my nose. Oh what joy a combination of darkness and bits of glass can bring, for there on the screen was the lovely Doris in all her blonde, clearly focused, glory. Then, as the interval approached, a reverse of the process took place and the specs were swiftly returned to the top pocket. Clever or what?

This system for seeing the important things in life prevailed until I did in fact 'get a girl friend' and having indoctrinated her in the fine art of film-going, we began to see each other regularly (well, to be honest, she saw me clearly—mostly I saw her in a sort of blur.)

Sadly, my cunning ocular strategy fell apart one evening as we were waiting for a bus to take us into town and, as usual, I couldn't see the blasted numbers until the damned thing was about three feet away. This meant that it was far too late to stick out your hand to make the bus stop and pick you up.

Until then, I had adopted another clever piece of subterfuge. As the bus approached, I would casually say to my girl, "Oh look, here's the number

10." This was said with a faintly interrogative tone as though I already knew the answer, but was including her in my pronouncements out of courtesy, thus allowing her to gently but innocently correct me if I was wrong.

However, being a girl and infinitely cleverer than me, the ploy didn't fool her for an instant. This terrible truth was brought home one evening when she said, "You can't see the bus numbers, can you?"

"What," I said.

She repeated the accusation, "You can't see, and I know you need glasses, because I've noticed that when we're in the pictures you slip them on while you think I'm watching the screen. Have you got them with you now?"

I mumbled something evasive like "Yes."

"Then why on earth don't you take them out and put them on, then we can both see what number bus is coming."

Sometimes we mere males are totally helpless in the face of such unerring logic, even despite the fact that I could now get the right bus home.

However, she may have been right as we have been together for forty-seven years, she is no longer blurred and I can still see bus numbers.

This sorry tale of male obfuscation was being recounted to Pat and his wife one evening and Pat's wife began to nod in agreement. She then said that one of her many embarrassing moments regarding Pat's failure to wear his glasses in public, occurred one Saturday morning in St Helens.

Apparently, they were going shopping in the town when a chap stopped them and asked the way to Lennon's Supermarket. Before she could stop him, Pat said "No problem," and launched into a detailed description of how to get there. This involved a number of left and right-hand turns, with a firm instruction for the chap to be sure and make a final right turn at the giant Guinness sign on the corner.

With profuse thanks, the chap went on his way, Pat beamed and his wife went spare.

She said, "Pat for god's sake will you wear your glasses, you've just sent a man in a completely wrong direction, just what he'll think of us is beyond me."

"Listen woman," said Pat coming over all masculine. "I've lived here all my life and I know my way around this town blindfolded." This, as it happened, turned out to be an unfortunate simile.

"Oh you do, do you? Well let me tell you, the giant Guinness sign you cleverly referred to was taken down six months ago—now for the last time, will you just wear your glasses?"

Logic again—but there you have it—two idiots in a pit, unashamedly wearing glasses, and all due to our failure to fool the opposite sex.

Chapter Eighteen
Fringe Benefits

The Coal Board, being a nationalised industry, hit on a wonderful scheme which enabled them to seem magnanimous whilst at the same time avoid having to pay us in actual money.

This brainwave was dreamed up by some genius in headquarters and came under the heading of 'concessionary'. In effect, they gave you nothing of any value to them, but the goods were packaged in such a way that the recipient was left with a warm glow.

The simile is appropriate, as the major concession was coal. Each underground employee was entitled to twenty tons of coal each year for the princely sum of £1 a ton.

When I excitedly ordered my first load, I naively thought it would be delivered in bags and tipped into your coal bunker just like everyone else's. This turned out to be a false assumption and the first indication that things were different, was when my wife answered a knock on the door and a man covered in coal-dust asked her where she wanted the coal tipped.

Looking past the apparition, she noticed a giant NCB tipper wagon outside and realised there would be no nice sacks and that things were about to go horribly wrong.

Mistaking her failure to answer, for tacit approval to proceed, he signalled the driver who promptly backed the lorry part way up our new path, which I had tastefully laid in broken flags, known, on upmarket estates, as 'crazy paving.' (This, in the light of events, turned out to be lucky.) Then, with a terrible shudder, the vehicle deposited twenty tons of best household coal on the now even more randomly broken flags.

If you've never had the benefit of seeing twenty tons of coal on your path, roses, flower bed, boundary fence, front porch and back gate, it may be difficult to picture the scene. But imagine for a moment that you live in the shade of Mount Etna and one morning, just as you've finished polishing the step, there's a sort of dull rumble and a massive pile of red-hot lava arrives on your path, climbs halfway up your wall, ruins the flower bed and covers the newly polished step in dust. Well, change the lava for coal and you have an idea of the mixed emotions you are about to experience—on the one hand, you're going to be nice and warm in the winter, on the other hand, you have arrived home to find you can't get in, and your wife can't get out.

I think it's called having mixed emotions.

I don't want to be cynical, but when you think that our pit regularly produced 21,000 tons of coal every week, even when sending most of it to the nearby Power Station, they were left with an awful lot of coal. Selling some of the residue to the workers seemed to be an economically sound move on the part of management.

So, having shovelled a path through the mountain, filled the laughably small bunker, offered a few barrow loads to the lady next door and re-discovered the roses, we realised that comfort and plenty of hot water was not going to be a problem.

This was borne out by the fact that friends used to come from miles around just to bask in the heat and the only added cost to us was the need to replace the burned out grate every three months.

The next 'concessions' were at the opposite end of the spectrum so to speak, involving as they did—cleanliness.

Now I realise that soap, as a captivating subject, may not quite be on a par with an in depth discussion on whether Doris Day looked more ravishing in a black rather than a white sweater (I went for white every time.) However, probably due to the fact that you got dirty in a pit, we could buy soap at a vastly reduced price. I'll explain how and where later.

This was no ordinary soap; this was big, green, hard, lasted a long time, smelled soapy, lathered well and didn't turn to jelly overnight. It doubled as a shampoo, removed ninety percent of ingrained dust and acted as a moisturiser on your skin, although we didn't know that at the time.

What we hadn't realised was that we were trying to manage skin care with soap made largely of palm and olive oil (called Palmolive – see, clever marketing,) not knowing that just a few decades later we could have been taking advantage of Regenerist (with added peptides) or Pro-Retinol or Dermo-expertise wrinkle de-crease collagen filler or Boswelox (a breakthrough phyto-complex.)

Just think how smooth we could have been if only the pit baths could have stocked such goodies. Mind you, on reflection, the sight of big Ernie staring intently into his little metal mirror, whilst liberally applying these new miracle complexion aids, is not something I want to dwell on.

The second concession coming under the general heading of cleanliness was 'towels.' Now we're not just talking about your average, run-of-the-mill drying facility here, these towels were about the size of a small African country, were invariably green (to match the soap), were so thick you could use them as a fireside rug and they could soak up enough water to fill a beer barrel. These were, without a doubt, the Bayeux Tapestry of towels.

You could always tell when chaps were going on their annual hols, they could be seen carrying arms full of the things onto the bus, all in readiness for spreading on the sand, sheltering under from the rain and carrying out that most British of activities—holding the towel like a tent and attempting to remove a wet swimming costume, whilst standing alternately on one leg, then the other—just prior to falling over.

Just think how different it would have been if package holidays to the Costa Brava had been around in those days. The Germans wouldn't have stood a chance when measuring their puny towels against our giant blankets. I reckon that had we spread our towels over a pool recliner, we could have covered at least two at a time and hidden half the shallow end as well.

Another fringe benefit of the NCB's largesse was having free, if unofficial, run of the workshop after the finish of our shift, or at weekends. This meant we could avail ourselves of iron (flat, round and tubular), saws, drills, welding facilities, blacksmiths, oil, grease, lead based paint (a choice of NCB brown or grey,) bearings, files, wire rope, brazing rods and any amount of nuts, screws, washers and bolts. In other words—heaven. But best of all, during these clandestine operations, was the absence of Albert.

Picture if you will, a person of medium stature with thinning hair, a skinny neck, acne scars on both cheeks, a failed attempt to grow a moustache, teeth like Victorian gravestones, wire rimmed glasses with a delicate twist to the right, a racking cough and a personality that made the witches in Macbeth seem like the Three Stooges. This then, was Albert, our esteemed Storeman.

Our good fortune was the fact that Albert didn't work overtime or at weekends. This was definitely to our advantage, as his philosophy during the week, was to refuse all requests for materials, based on an erroneous belief that the NCB had entrusted him with the entire contents of the store and under no circumstances were they to be issued without a fight.

Albert's idea of heaven was to take delivery of new stock, at which he would close the hatch and lovingly sort, count, cross-check, tick-off, file the manifest and then, humming tunelessly, place the items in the appropriate bins.

Trying to obtain your requirements became a battle of wills, bluff, counter-bluff and threats. On any average day the ritual would go as follows;

"Albert, I need twelve one inch Whitworth bolts and washers."

"Twelve, what's tha' want twelve for, won't six do thee?"

"No, I asked for twelve and I bloody well need twelve."

"What's tha' want them for?"

"I'm renewing the holding bolts on the main transfer chute, not that it's any of your business."

"Well, can't tha' save some when tha' takes out the old ones?"

"Albert, no I can't, now for crying out loud give me twelve, so I can get on with the sodding job."

"Reet, here's your twelve bolts, but this is going to leave me short and anyway, are you sure you need twelve washers; tha' could save some of those."

"Albert, if you don't give me what I asked for, I'll come over the counter and ram this pinch bar down your throat."

"Okay, okay, there's no need to get nasty. Here's your bolts and washers, but I've no sack to put them in, thar'l just have to carry them loose."

And with a grotesque smile, he would clatter the gear down on the counter and start to roll a fag.

Over time, we did try the old double bluff, whereby, if you wanted six of anything you asked for eight or ten. Albert, however, was on to this like a rocket and generally you lost out when, all unwary, he would ask, "What's tha want eight (or ten) for?"

Then, without thinking, you would say, "Oh, they're for the Panzer motor."

Albert would then pounce.

"You're a lying sod; I know the motor only needs six bolts and that's all tha's getting."

There was one exception to Albert's one man attempt to save the NCB money and that was when Jemmy approached the counter. Pausing only to unwrap a toffee in his pocket and pop it into his mouth (unseen by anyone) he would ask for what he wanted.

At this, a frightening transformation would come over Albert and, with a rictus smile, he would say, "Certainly Jemmy, I'll get them straight away. Is there anything else you want while I'm about it, I've got washers, lock nuts, all sorts?"

Jemmy would say, between sucks, "Nay that's all Albert, just what I asked for."

"Well there's no need for you to be standing here Jemmy, I'll just get the stuff, put it into a sack and bring it over to thee."

Our only revenge was the sight of Albert's face when, on opening up on a Monday morning, he realised his precious stock had been pillaged during the weekend. Obviously there were no witnesses and everyone denied all knowledge of any purloined items. I remember Charlie saying to Albert on being questioned, "Tha's imagining it owd lad. Problem is, tha's probably miss-counted and got thee inventory wrong."

I thought Albert was going to burst into tears, instead, he muttered something about not trusting us shower of bastards, and went off to roll a fag.

So, here we were at the weekend, sans Albert, fresh brews on the go and the entire workshop a hive of activity, with an assortment of guys banging, bending, welding and painting

Ambitious projects were undertaken—garden furniture, swings, see-saws, roof ladders, plant stands and wrought-iron gates (flat packed, to be bolted together later.) We could also have made wonderful barbeques, but they hadn't yet been invented. Sadly, B & Q, or 'Dodge City,' as they were known at the time (an apt description considering the quality of its stock,) hadn't been exposed to the Australian delights of burning food outdoors.

Car exhausts were fabricated out of two-inch steel water pipe with the silencer made from a defunct thirty-inch steel conveyor roller and stuffed with a random mixture of wire wool and fibreglass. The only trouble with these exhausts was that they were massively stronger than any part of the average car and, as the rest of the vehicle rotted away, you were prone to losing the exhaust while driving along the road. This sudden loss could result in considerable embarrassment—if it hit the ground at a forward angle; the car did a sort of pole vault, generally culminating in the exhaust spearing up through the floor and joining you in the cab.

If, on the other hand, it hit the ground at a backward angle, there was the most unearthly screech of metal and a shower of sparks as it tried its best to dig a six-inch furrow in the tarmac before flinging itself in a shower of red-hot sparks onto the pavement—sadly, with most of the exhaust manifold still attached.

In either case, you would be faced with gathering up the bits, stuffing lumps of hot metal in the boot, pushing back as much tarmac as possible with your foot and driving casually off, accompanied by the most god-awful noise from the engine.

I once made a tow bracket out of four-inch angle iron which was bolted to the underside of the floor with stainless steel bolts. Unfortunately, as I came to find out, the assembly was distorted as a result of careless welding, the upshot of which was, being infinitely stronger than the car, it pulled the rear chassis out of alignment. This caused the car to adopt a sort of crabwise forward motion, coupled with an overwhelming tendency to scrub the tread off diagonally opposed front and rear tyres. It also did interesting things with the direction of the headlight beams.

Another fringe benefit was our ability to 'borrow' things on a sort of long-term loan. I remember lamenting one day about the need to barrow away the mountain of blasted coal which had just arrived when Charlie said he knew just where to find the answer.

Off we went to the far end of the pit yard where a small, but beautifully constructed sewage plant was operating. Somewhat mystified and trying to get used to the smell, I said, "What the hell are we doing here, Charlie?"

"Just keep thee mouth shut and follow me. I saw this while I was having a mooch around the other day."

Still trying to figure out why anyone would mooch around a sewage works, I dutifully followed.

Rounding the side of a small building, Charlie said, "Theer, it's just what tha needs."

And sure enough he was right, there lying on its side was a lovely metal wheelbarrow with a big pneumatic wheel, long handles and no evident signs of congealed sewage. Perfect.

Meanwhile Charlie had continued to mooch and came back with a superman-sized shovel and throwing it into the barrow, issued fresh, command mode instructions. "Reet I'll stay here, you go and get the mini-van and we'll load the gear in the back before anyone misses it." I was obviously in the hands of a master purloiner, so off I went for the getaway vehicle (or 'wheels' as we in the fraternity call it.) Taking every precaution, we threw the barrow and spade carefully into the back of the van, parked in a far corner of the car park and strolled back for a well earned brew of Charlie's finest. You can't buy friendship like that. Someone who, without a thought for himself, is willing to sacrifice time and expertise to help nick much needed bits of kit.

Interestingly, I really did intend to return the goods, but there didn't seem to be a time when they weren't in use. Later on I seriously considered it once again, but found to my everlasting shame that some forty years had passed, I now lived 450 miles away and the pit had disappeared.

No option really, but to keep the 'borrowed' goods.

So there we were, able to buy as much soap and as many towels as we liked, wash, whether we were dirty or not, dry the parts that other towels couldn't reach, be burned by a raging inferno in the grate, have full use of workshop facilities and shovel and barrow coal to our hearts content. Who says the NCB didn't care about us?

Chapter Nineteen

Cleanliness is next to Dirtliness

Look, I know the popular image is one where the miner returns home to be met by his wife in a pinny holding aloft a cast iron kettle full of hot water, ready to pour over our hero as he discards his dirty clothes and sinks gratefully into a tin bath in front of the fire, the kids, the dog, grandma, a budgie and three cats. This, you have to realise, is romantic rubbish.

That was in the dark ages; we on the other hand, were of the modern, thrusting, upmarket, 20th century, man-about-town age. We were clean and shiny when we arrived home. We were ready for the pictures, the pub, the pigeons, the whippets, the ferrets, the lass down the road, the fishing pond, the woman next door and the allotment. And not necessarily in that order—a lot depended on your luck at the time.

We had Pit Head Baths, a big, hot, white tiled building full of lockers. Believe it or not, but before the advent of the NCB, miners had clubbed together to build their own baths. Putting aside something like two shillings a week, they saved enough to achieve their aim of sinking the now defunct tin bath in the backyard, filling it with tap water and forking out for three or four half-dead goldfish.

Obviously, the mine owners couldn't help to buy the baths; their money was needed to build mansions, landscape the gardens, create fountains, dig lakes, collect artwork, take continental holidays, pay their staff (a pittance,) hold shooting parties, support their tame MPs, build great useless structures and hunt tigers. No wonder miners voted Labour—I'm becoming bitter and twisted.

Our pit head bath worked on a very simple principle. On arrival and full of bacon butties, you would go into the 'clean end,' remove your everyday clothes and hang them in your first locker. You would take out your soap, flannel and towel, which incidentally would be dried as stiff as a board, due to the heat.

Then, naked and unashamed, you walked past the showers and into the 'dirty end.' Opening another locker, you would climb into your pit clothes (in our case—overalls,) grab your helmet, put on your boots, deposit soap, flannel and towel and slope off to the lamp room.

On your return, surprise, surprise, you went into reverse mode. You threw off your increasingly dirty clothes, stuffed them in your locker, grabbed your soap, flannel and towel and went into the showers.

Now the showers weren't designed for the preservation of either dignity or modesty. Ours consisted of long rows of white tiled walls about six feet tall, with individual shower heads mounted at intervals along their length. On arrival, you found an empty shower, threw your towel over the top of the wall, put your soap in the dish and turned the lever.

An amazing amount of hot water then crashed down on your head and away you went with your ablutions. As you might be accompanied during this time by about five hundred other guys all doing the same thing, the room quickly filled with an impenetrable blanket of steam.

The gulleys located along the middle of the floor were soon running with a nice mixture of coal dust, sweat, hair, foam and, if you were careless, bars of soap. Then slowly but surely, white bodies began to emerge from the steam, towels were pulled off the wall and the process of drying began.

The first time you were exposed to this new regime several points emerged. One is the fact that never in all your sheltered upbringing have you ever seen so many naked male bodies in one place or at one time. The second is that you can forget all the stories you have read about the behaviour of chaps in public schools, with tales of playfulness, sexual innuendo, towel flicking and general high spirits.

Our miners had only one thing on their minds when they were in the showers—to get washed and get out as fast as possible, in order to enjoy that first mug of tea and/or a fag. So forget all your preconceived notions about male bonding—there was none.

I do however, confess to becoming very nervous one day, as I was quietly sloshing soap all over myself, to find a miner in very close proximity. Moving ever so slightly away, I stared at him when, without a word, he thrust his soap into my hand and turned his back to me. Oh no, I thought, I've read about this in the News of the World, when, realising nothing was happening, my new friend turned round and said, "Come on owd lad, scrub me bloody back, what's the matter with you?"

Another lesson learned. I realised it wasn't uncommon for colliers to seek help, as they often worked stripped to the waist and it was impossible for them to wash their own backs. So off I went, somewhat tentatively at first, and then realising we would be there all day, with increasing vigour.

As time went by, you became blasé about the whole thing, with one possible exception—you tried to steer clear of big Ernie, who was massive, muscular and covered in hair—it was a bit too much like washing a gorilla.

Miners came in all sorts of shapes and sizes. They were tall, short, fat, skinny, tapered, hairy, bald, dangly, straight legged, bent legged, pigeon toed, ten-to-two footed, pot-bellied, toothless, bulbous nosed, bat-eared, freckled, pock-marked and pallid.

No wonder the average miner's wife had a secret yearning for Clark Gable (especially in his role as Rhett Butler in Gone with the Wind.) Although, come to think of it, I reckon his ears were too big, but that could be just jealousy on my part.

There was another bit of the body you couldn't wash with soap and water and that was the eyes. For some strange reason, coal dust settled around the eyes and was impervious to the attention of the flannel whilst in the shower. The upshot was that having dressed in all your smart going home togs, the illusion was spoilt because you looked something like a cross between Elizabeth Taylor made up as Cleopatra and a sad looking Panda. Later on, the look was popularised by Dusty Springfield and although it looked okay on her, on us, it lacked the same emotional appeal.

There were two ways by which you could remove the residue. One was to spit on the corner of your towel and delicately rub your eyelashes until the dust came away. The other method was rather more dubious; rumour had it that some guy's wife swore by the use of Vaseline to remove her eye shadow. So, based on this idiotic premise, tins were produced; liberal quantities were rubbed into the eye lashes, the eye balls, the eyebrows and then rubbed off with your towel. The end result was that your eye lids were firmly glued together, your towel became impervious to water and your vision was blurred for the next two days.

Soap and towels could be purchased from a small man who lived behind a hatch in the clean side of the pit baths. For some unaccountable reason, he had decided to wear a short off-white coat about four sizes too large, which gave him the appearance of a slightly demented barber. His day was spent counting bars of soap, folding new (green) towels, taking bets, swearing a good deal—although I never found out at what and cutting up old stock towels to make flannels, which could also be purchased for an indeterminate sum, for an indeterminate destination. Still, despite the unfortunate resemblance to Sweeny Todd, he provided a much needed service.

There was one other facility in the baths, namely the toilets. I don't intend to dwell on the bodily functions of your average miner, but there was one product with which I did come into close contact and which I hadn't seen since leaving my infants' school. I refer to that most remarkable invention—IZAL toilet paper.

So what? I hear younger readers reply—well first of all, you have to know something about its unique construction. It bore no resemblance to your modern, softy, scented, multi-ply, embossed, colour coded, Sudoku imprinted, quilted, inspirational jumbo, essential luxury, toilet roll, as played with on the television by a blasted pup.

Izal toilet paper came in a flat pack, with a window on the top, through which you pulled out a leaf. Having done so, the system was designed so that withdrawing one sheet revealed the tongue of the next. So far so good.

No—it wasn't the packaging that was at fault—it was the composition of the material itself. This paper wasn't built for those of a delicate disposition for a start, primarily because, for some unaccountable reason, it was shiny on one side. When I was in the infants during the war, it was used mainly as tracing paper (shiny side down.)

It was virtually untearable (a bonus in some ways) and wiping your posterior on the shiny side was akin to using a plastic gro-bag for the same purpose. In fact I really don't want to dwell on the matter any more, so I'll just mention that prolonged use of this reinforced paper probably accounted for a significant increase in the use of Zam Buk ointment, sold conveniently by the little man in the large white coat.

Incidentally, for any cynical reader needing further confirmation, I'm told you can still get Zam Buk from any African grocery shop. A long journey, but maybe worth it, in the interests of scientific research.

While we're still on the subject of all things ablution, we also discovered a new miracle cleaner quite by accident. We were milling around in the workshop one morning while trying to decide what work to avoid, when Neddy entered stage left clutching a gallon can. Not being one to let modesty stand in the way (remember the thermos flask incident) he put it down on the workbench with what he thought of as a flourish and said, "Nar then lads, see what I've geet."

With that cryptic remark, he undid the cap to reveal a colourless liquid inside. Curiosity being a fine thing, we gathered around.

"Fetch me an old bearing off the shelf, will you?"

One was duly 'fetched' and without further ado, but with considerable drama, Neddy poured some of the liquid into a steel tray and dropped the oily, greasy bearing into the fluid.

We moved in closer, but with some trepidation—would it blow up, what the hell was Neddy on about, and what was that strange smell?

Stirring the liquid with his fingers we began to see what the 'miracle' was all about. Within a couple of minutes the congealed oil and grease began to melt away and a short time later the bearing was removed to reveal a shiny, grease free, brand new looking article, together with a very clean finger.

Gasps all round, and Neddy beaming at his captivated audience (not a pretty sight.)

"Now lads, what does think about that?"

We were astonished. No more nasty paraffin baths, no more scrubbing, scraping or leaving things to soak overnight, no more bullying the nearest apprentice into paraffin tank duties. Wow, what was this stuff called, and could we get an endless supply of it?

Neddy the oracle was happy to oblige. "It's called 'trike' and it cost £20 for this gallon can, so we need to keep it under lock and key and only use it for special jobs."

Billy said, "What the hell's 'trike' when its about?"

"Well," said Neddy, who was obviously dying to tell us, "Its proper name is Trichloroethylene and it has amazing de-greasing properties."

Now this last statement was significant for two reasons; one was, we didn't know Neddy could say long words and the second was, he said it without swearing.

"Too bloody right it's got properties," said Billy, "And you're telling me a gallon costs more than my week's wages."

"Aye, I know it's expensive (another big word) but we've ordered a twenty gallon drum of the stuff so we can try it out on gear-boxes when we strip them down."

From that moment on we cleaned everything in sight and it soon became a habit to wash our hands in the stuff before making a brew. After all, there were hygiene standards to maintain and it sure beat lathering up with Swarfega, scrubbing with an old brush-head and splashing about in a big sink for ten minutes, whilst trying gamely to remove an ingrained mixture of oil, grease and fine coal dust.

Our new miracle cleaner laughed in the face of such stains. All it needed was a brief dip into the tin, a light washing motion, a rinse off, rapid evaporation and, 'hey presto' hands like a surgeon. Brilliant!

It wasn't long before we discovered that what it could do for the hands—

it could also do for grotty overalls. And it wasn't unusual to see a length of steel bar lying across the top of the drum with several pairs of overalls dangling in the fluid. Another bonus was the discovery that on removing the garments, all you needed to do was waft them around in the air for a minute or two—and they were perfectly dry. Magic!

The only slight drawback to this new cleanliness regime was the strange fumes. Leaning over the fluid and breathing in at the same time had a slightly disconcerting effect on one's equilibrium. There was a tendency to sway and in some cases the effect was mesmerizing, to the extent that you weren't quite sure where you were or, why you were wherever it was—if you see what I mean.

Some idiots reckoned it was far better than Vick for clearing the nose and others made dubious claims that since being exposed to the fumes (so to speak) they hadn't had so much as a sniffle.

However in time, many of the claims died away and we simply used the stuff for de-greasing, overall cleaning and hand washing.

Interestingly (if that's the word we're looking for) – in the 1970's some spoilsport discovered that Trichloroethylene had carcinogenic properties. Dire warnings were issued regarding such exciting side effects as impaired heart function, nerve, kidney and liver damage, unconsciousness and death. A bit like the warnings they give today on children's cough mixtures.

So there we were, blissfully ignorant of the consequences, bathing in the stuff and using the fumes to clear the sinuses. Mind you, looking back, it would be difficult to establish whether, with some people, the fluid was to blame for their erratic behaviour, or whether they had always been toe-rags from choice.

Chapter Twenty

Did the Earth Move for You?

If you dig a great big hole in the ground, go down about three thousand feet, drive a tunnel at right angles for a mile or so and start taking coal out of the rock for about another three miles, I guess it might occur to you that there was a hell of a lot of weight pressing down on the spaces.

Correct—I think it's something to do with a thing called geology. Now our coal was known as 'deep mined coal,' probably because it was deep and we had to mine it. The clue, I often find, is in the title. Anyway, if we were to avoid being squashed flat, it paid to understand a little bit about geology, but rest assured I won't be going into great detail about carboniferous rocks, the Devonian period, sedimentary deposits, synclines, anticlines, up-thrusts, fault lines, the Silesian subsystem or a fluvio-deltaic environment. The main reason being, that I can't for the life of me remember why I had to learn about them at the time and looking back, I don't recall having interesting conversations, where we debated the relative merits of metamorphic rocks.

What you might be forgiven for thinking is that with all that rock above, it wouldn't be bothered with us having removed a little bit such a long way down. You would be wrong.

It seemed that as soon as we removed any coal or rock, the rest of the stuff above took umbrage and decided to remove the gap as soon as possible. You really wonder at this perverse behaviour, after all, taking out six feet in three thousand is only about 0.2% at the most—you really wouldn't bother.

Not so, the main aim of geology was to flatten the gap as soon as we had made it. This meant that we had to support the roof. So, in the main roadways, we set rings of girders at six feet intervals and on the coal-face we used hydraulic props. While all this was going on, there was another perversity of so-called nature, which used to drive us mad with jealousy. This was the fact that there were lots of caves lying around the country consisting of great gaps in the rock, and for some reason, geology had decided this was okay for caves and there was no need to try and crush the space.

We, on the other hand, had only to remove just a small amount and geology went mad. Cracks appeared, lumps fell down, the roof collapsed, the floor heaved up and, as if that wasn't enough, there were the most frightful, cracking, crunching, thumping sounds you ever heard. When I was first exposed to this tendency of nature to make disconcerting noises, a collier, noticing that my reaction to the noise was to flinch and duck like a punch-drunk boxer, said, "Tha' doesn't need to worry about the cracking, its when it goes quiet tha' needs to worry."

Now as an attempt to reassure, these words of wisdom fell somewhat short of useful in my estimation, as I now had an overwhelming urge to sit listening rather than getting on with any work. Besides, what was I supposed to do if it did go quiet?

The other interesting thing was the fact that every crack was accompanied by a shower of dust and bits of rock which landed with unerring accuracy down your neck.

In the meantime, great chunks of rock would suddenly dislodge and crash down in the waste area behind you.

Foolishly, I asked my collier friend why the rock suddenly broke up like that and again, his reply lacked the necessary degree of reassurance. He said, "Aye well our rock is what's called friable. It just means it crumbles easily, that's why you can't trust the bloody stuff."

All this exposure to 'geology having a bad hair day' meant we had a constant battle to stop being crushed. The funny thing is, it reminded me of a serial we used to watch at the Saturday matinee about a secret agent called Sexton Blake. Despite supposedly having a superior intellect, he kept falling into the hands of a dastardly oriental fiend whose torture of choice was to put our Sexton into a locked room and, just before the episode finished, would pull a switch and the roof and floor of the locked room would start to move towards one another.

We stared in horror as the credits rolled and a sombre voice told us urchins to be sure and watch episode two hundred and forty-nine next week. Obviously we did, but funnily enough, in the next instalment, Sexton was out of the room and a voice-over told us that—'with one bound he was free.' Conned again.

Anyway our battle was on a grander scale and it was amazing to witness the never-ending attempts of nature to do the oriental fiend thing and squash us all flat. Very soon after we removed the coal, the 'waste,' which is what we called the gap, either settled lower or great lumps fell out of the roof. If you shone your cap lamp towards the back it was not uncommon to see that the roof and floor were now joined together. Very impressive.

The story was much the same in the main tunnels. Despite being supported by an arch of girders every six feet, nature took no notice and almost immediately began a two-pronged attack. Weight would come on the girders and do its best to twist them out of shape, whilst all the time squeezing them down towards the floor.

As if this wasn't enough, the floor would start to heave upwards, causing no end of problems with rail tracks, conveyor drives, electrical switchgear, headroom and the ability to walk without breaking your ankle.

This is where the afternoon shift came into their own. Teams of road repair gangs would take up rail-tracks, dig out the floor, smooth everything off and re-lay the rails. While somewhere else, teams would drag out the twisted roof supports, drill and blast the descending rock and re-set new rings.

In old workings, nature would be allowed to have its own way and it was not uncommon to see what was once a tunnel twenty feet wide by fifteen feet high crushed to such an extent that the only way through was to crawl. The worst example of this delightful experience was when, having finished yet another exciting job, we found that due to a tunnelling operation, our only way out was to navigate an old return airway. This was crushed to such an extent that we had to lie flat on our stomachs, tie our toolbag to a foot and drag our way through in the manner of a particularly sadistic commando course.

Now, just to really test our resolve (stupidity) you have to remember what happens to air when the same amount flowing through a big tunnel has to pass through a much smaller gap in the same time. It's that physics thing again—it goes faster.

So you're on your stomach, trying to keep your head down, a bag full of spanners is tied to your left leg, a water bottle and an empty snap tin is tied to your belt, your lamp battery is catching on the roof and you've no idea if, or when, you'll be able to stand upright again.

While all this is going on, the air is now whistling past you like a demented jet engine, carrying lots of dust, small stones and bits of wood because, in scraping the roof and floor, you've loosened all sorts of hobgoblins.

You now have a number of enviable decisions to make—shall I close my eyes to avoid them filling up with dust, in which case I can't see where I'm going; or shall I try to crawl quicker and get out of this idiot situation, in which case all the accoutrements will snag more often and disturb considerable amounts of high speed rubble.

The only thing to cheer you up throughout this minor discomfort is that you are on overtime and this slight delay is probably worth another ten shillings (before tax and other sundry stoppages dreamed up by a caring government.)

Chapter Twenty-One

How Much?

Talking about money, which we have to do sooner or later, there were two distinct sides to the coin (pun intended.)

The colliers (or face workers) were on piece-work and their wages depended on the amount of coal they dug out in a week. And, in our opinion, they were grossly overpaid.

We, on the other hand, were paid a flat rate for the standard shift, with overtime for hours worked outwith the norm. And colliers thought we were grossly overpaid.

You now begin to understand the potential for mutual hatred and name calling when there was a problem with the machinery since, until we fixed it, the colliers made no money. The funny thing was that at weekends a truce was called as we often needed some colliers to help out with heaving, dragging, lifting and swearing, while installing some new machinery. In this case, we were a band of brothers at time-and-a-half for Saturday and double-time on a Sunday. Hooray.

There was just one golden rule which management didn't like, but were powerless to prevent. It was that whatever progress was made on a Saturday, everyone finished in time to get home, have a bite to eat and be on the terraces for a three o'clock kick-off.

Obviously this meant that if we hadn't managed to do at least half the work the day before, we had to finish the job on Sunday no matter how long it took.

Obviously being paid double-time had nothing at all to do with it.

When a new coal face opened, a price had to be negotiated between the colliers and management. This brought into play all sorts of interesting issues, such as the ease with which the cutter could slice into the seam, the amount of rock inclusion in the coal, the length of the coalface, the number of colliers, the angle of the incline, the likelihood of breakdowns and the number of convincing lies that could be told.

Each week the Overman and the charge-hand would take a long tape-measure and working from the previous week's closely guarded chalk mark would agree the distance travelled. They would then measure the coalface from top to bottom and agree the results. Then, knowing the height of the seam, they could work out the cubic yardage of coal cut that week. All you did then was multiply the result by the negotiated price per cubic yard, divide by the number of colliers and, hey presto—you had wages.

The really interesting element of this strategy was to be found at the negotiation stage. This meant that, after having cut the coal for some weeks when everyone on the face felt confident that the rate was readily achievable, a crucial meeting would take place in the Manager's office.

At this point, the scene was set for a classic industrial relations trial of strength. Management were appalled at the colliers' totally unreasonable demands, whilst the colliers were convinced that Management were determined to impose starvation conditions on hard working families. In other words, each side was convinced they were dealing with a bunch of unfeeling, unrealistic charlatans.

Management would plead that their offer was magnanimous in the extreme and adding another penny to the price would close the pit, whilst the colliers' representatives would plead extreme poverty, how it wasn't worth coming to work for, how children would have to go barefoot and how amazed they were that management (in this enlightened age—always a good appeal) had no feelings of loyalty towards their hard working employees.

And this was day one.

I remember Pat telling me about some protracted discussions he was involved in before he became a Shotfirer. They had met in the conference room, all oak and polished tables, with tea laid on and grim looking oil paintings of past Managers staring down at them from around the walls.

Apparently, negotiations had reached another stalemate, the management team were adamant that acceptance of their more than generous terms would guarantee a fortune for the workers and that to pay any more would bankrupt the NCB. The collier's team were equally convinced that management were hell-bent on destroying morale, reverting to Victorian principles, denying human dignity, forcing penury on innocent families and how, if they went back to the team with such a figure, they would be lynched.

Pat said he was always amazed by the lyrical turns of phrase that so-called uneducated colliers could call on when 'in extremis.'

Anyway, in order to get a breathing space, the charge-hand asked for "Time out Mester, to talk things over with the lads in private."

No doubt sensing victory, the Manager said, "Nay problem lads, you just go and use my office, take as long as thee like."

Now an offer of the Manager's office was not something the lads were used to, but in they filed and after some time and considerable in-fighting, they realised a compromise had to be reached. Convinced they weren't going to get all they asked for, an acceptable sum was reluctantly agreed, one which management could not fail to find fair and equable and which they could take back to the lads without being accused of a 'sell-out'—or so the theory went.

Time to re-convene, and with a knock on the conference room door, in they filed.

"Well lads, have you had time to think?" beamed the Manager. But before the lads could table their elegant and hard-fought compromise, the Manager continued, "We've been doing a bit of thinking ourselves while you were out and we think we've got the answer."

Then without waiting for a reply, he delved into a drawer at his side and brought out a big adding machine. As he tapped rapidly on the keys and pulled down on a lever at the side, paper started to emerge from the top which appeared to be full of calculations. Then, with a sort of theatrical flourish, he ripped the paper off and, laying it on the table in front of the lads, said, "There thee are, final figures, machine can't lie, just as we've bin saying, it's a good price. Now what's tha got to say to that?"

Pausing only to throw down his tatty bit of paper covered in pencil scribbles, the charge hand turned to his team and said, "Now we're well and truly f.........Manager's used a sodding machine to screw us—games up lads, we might as well quit and go home."

Some time later, when Joe Gormley had become a full-time union representative, we were chatting again about the age-old battle of union versus management. A collier, who was obviously 'earwigging' on our conversation, chipped in with one of those fatuous statements, based on jealousy and a complete lack of understanding. "In my opinion," he said, "I don't see why Joe Gormley should have been given a three litre Rover to drive around in. After all," he pronounced, "it's the likes of us that has to pay for the bloody thing out of our union subscriptions."

Pat stared at him, "You're a bloody half-wit, how the hell do you expect him to negotiate from a position of strength, when management turn up in their cars and Joe arrives soaking wet on his bike?"

"They all hang their Gannex driving coats on the hat stand and Joe shoves his cycle clips in his pocket. That should send a right message regarding equality and no mistake." I could see that Pat was in the grip of some strong emotion, so I tried to change the subject.

"I guess it pays to have a strong union when doing battle with the NCB."

"It's nothing to do with strength," said Pat, "It's about unity. All other industries have to deal with dozens of small unions, most of whom have no interest in presenting a united front; consequently there are constant stoppages, arguments and recriminations. The other advantage we have is that Joe gets on well with Alf (Lord) Robens."

"Oh aye," said our Daily Worker reader, "I call it sleeping with the enemy."

"The trouble is," said Pat, "You're a tin-pot bloody communist but without the brains to spell Karl Marx."

"Never heard of him and anyway what's he got to do with the workers?"

Pat stared at him, "Sod this, I'm off to fire some shots."

And I realised I still had a lot to learn about industrial relations, including Karl Marx.

Little did we know then, that in 1984 the celebrated and envied miners' unity would be broken forever.

However, this book isn't about bitterness and recrimination, others have dealt with the subject far better than I can—besides, by then, I was an onlooker, thank goodness.

Many years later when I had left the pit and was lecturing on Mining Engineering. I got into an idle conversation with Peter, who was an ex-Mine Manager and, like me, had changed jobs. I was recounting the story about the adding machine and Peter said they used to have many protracted arguments before a settlement was reached.

He then said that one day after another long, fruitless session, he quietly asked the collier's spokesman out for a pint.

Peter said, "After our third pint of Greenalls best bitter, we both realised that if we didn't change our approach we would never reach a settlement. It dawned on us that neither side could afford to 'win' over the other and that both parties had to come out of the discussions feeling able to defend their decisions."

"So what happened," I asked.

"Well the next day, we tried hard to meet in the middle and after some more to-ing and fro-ing we reached an agreement; and I learned a valuable lesson."

"Which was?"

"Never, ever, back somebody into a corner from where they can't move; you must always leave enough room for them to get out with dignity."

Much later on, when faced with some tricky offshore contractual negotiations, I remembered Peter's words of wisdom. In fact, numerous books have been written about the art of negotiation, often known as the 'win-win' situation. But I reckon that Peter, many years before, was one of the first Managers to recognise the power of reasonable compromise. You can see that mining wasn't just about whippets.

Pat also introduced me to another interesting character named Steve, who worked at the bottom of the downcast shaft. Now remember, this was the shaft where the air entered the mine and obviously, in the winter, the air coming down was freezing cold and at times, dripped icy water down the sides, the cage, and the occupants and, as our friend worked close by, largely on him.

He was recognisable by the fact that he wore an old waterproof jacket and a sack, cut down one side and worn over his safety helmet in the manner of a lunatic. It was, he said, to stop the water dripping down his neck. I have to confess, he had a bloody awful job.

Pat took great delight in chatting to Steve and the conversation went something like this..........

"Hi Steve, how's it going?"

"How's it bloody going? I'll tell thee how it's going, I'm chucking this job, they can stuff it. As soon as I get up pit I'm seeing the Manager, they don't pay me enough to work like this and I'm going to tell the sod, that's what and he'll just have to find someone else—that's what, I don't care if the pit stops I'm not putting up with this any longer, I'll tell him, 'Nay Mester how'd thee like to work in these conditions, you don't pay me enough to do this job, it's not fit for a dog is this.'—That'll shake the bastard.'

And with that Steve sagged back exhausted against the side of the tunnel.

As I had never heard anything so vitriolic and sustained, I looked at Pat in some alarm, but he seemed oblivious and said, "I don't blame you Steve; it's terrible what you have to put up with. What do you think the Manager will say?"

"Say? There's only one thing the sod can say—"Nay Steve, don't thee be talking like that. Tha knows how valuable the job is, we can't have this wild talk about chucking it. I'll tell thee what, let's see if we can't give thee a bit more cash, shall we, and let's hear no more talk of leaving. Now what do you say?'"

"That's it Steve,' said Pat, 'that's just what he'll say."

And bidding him goodbye, Pat led me to the manrider.

"Bloody hell Pat," I said, "You're a right stirrer, the bloke will get the sack if he talks to the Manager like that."

Pat said, "That's just the point. I've been saying things like that to Steve for about four years and I just love the reaction. He's no more intention of seeing the Manager than I have of water skiing. Offloading like that makes him feel better and I provide a valuable service in relieving his tension."

I thought this last bit to be a load of rubbish, but on reflection it seemed harmless enough and it's not often you get to hear such a command of the language from a wee man wearing a wet sack on his head.

Coming back to the thorny subject of wages, obviously the face workers earned more money than we did, so the only thing left that could redress the balance was a thing called 'overtime.' Notice also we didn't talk about 'salary,' what we got in a 'safeseal-easy-check' envelope were wages. And these generally comprised of a couple of fivers, some pound notes, the odd half a crown, a shilling or two and a pile of pennies.

The envelope was cunningly designed with a triangle cut out of the top corner so that you could count the notes without opening the packet. Very useful for those sad characters that had to hand over their wages unopened to a loving (and trusting) spouse.

And just to complete the cunning design, the bottom third of the envelope was perforated. This allowed you, with much careful shaking, to count the coins.

There's one thing for sure—you couldn't mistake that little lot for a salary.

In order to receive this largesse, you had to wait until Friday when the NCB van arrived from headquarters bearing the stuffed envelopes. Then on the dot of two-thirty, a window opened in the wages office and a man passed you the precious package when you shouted out your number. Sophisticated or what?

Try to imagine the scene today—there, trundling along numerous country lanes, is a shiny dark blue van with big white letters saying NCB on each side (to make identification easier,) being driven by two miners wearing flat caps who can't work underground any longer due to ill-health.

Reaching at times the dizzy speed of thirty-five mph, it stops off at each pit to deliver boxes full of untraceable money. At about every third pit our exhausted drivers leave the van (locked obviously) and repair to the canteen for a sustaining mug of tea and a pie, before moving on.

I did raise the thought that our wages could be somewhat vulnerable, should some toe-rags take it into their heads to execute a daring robbery before retiring to Spain. I was informed that obviously, this had already been thought of and, in order to thwart the baddies, the driver was instructed to vary his route each week.

I was going to ask how effective they considered this to be, as there were only two roads leading to our pit, but I didn't want to sound panicky.

A missed opportunity for 'the great train robbers' if you ask me.

I mentioned my (academic) concern to Bill one day and he said not to worry, a mate at area offices told him that the driver was armed with a pick-axe handle which he kept under his seat.

I said, "Do you think he'd use it to prevent a robbery?"

Bill said, "Don't be daft, by the time he bent down and found the handle, he'd be wheezing and coughing so badly he wouldn't have the strength to wind up the window."

In order to supplement their income, some guys had little enterprises going. One of our fitters had a nice sideline making kitchen wall cupboards in his garage. Remember, in the early sixties so-called 'fitted kitchens' were the thing to have, words like worktops, Formica, extractor fans, wall tiles, double ovens, chopping boards, stainless steel sinks and cushion-floor, were becoming the topic of conversation among socially ambitious wives, who were no longer content with kitchen cabinets, oil-cloth, single wooden draining boards or Fablon covered window ledges.

As word spread, via satisfied customers, he was kept very busy making and fitting units to order. He once mentioned that every now and again a wife would offer an alternative method of payment, but he tried to resist, as he was often working in close proximity to the unsuspecting husband.

Whether we believed him or not was often debated, one thing we all agreed on was that he was a lucky sod and that fitting kitchens obviously had extra-curricular potential.

One of our shotfirers had set himself up as a TV repair man and, as these were the early days of the BBC showing black and white pictures, the job sounded simple enough. The problem was that the TV sets were generally crap.

They were huge affairs about the size of a small shed and in a misguided attempt to make them appear sophisticated, were disguised as a cocktail cabinet in artificial oak or walnut with double doors to hide the screen. This of course was the ultimate in inverted snobbery; on the one hand you were at the cutting edge of entertainment technology, but on the other hand you didn't want anyone to know. Another minor drawback with this attempt to fool burglars was the fact that the average owner thought a cocktail was something to do with keeping hens.

Sadly, from a visual point of view, the screen was completely out of proportion to the size of the unit as, on opening the double doors, you were confronted by a curved glass screen about ten inches square.

Switching on had to be done some time prior to the start of the programme, as the set took about an hour to warm up. Finally, the screen began to glow, but if it was in competition with daylight, you couldn't see anything except the reflection of a family all peering in the same direction.

This meant that the curtains had to be drawn which, unfortunately, gave your neighbours the impression that someone had just died.

Later on, in an effort to avoid eye-strain, some clever manufacturer came up with a magnifying glass which could be placed in front of the screen. This worked reasonably well if you were viewing from a forward position, however, if you were viewing from an armchair at the side, all the figures took on a distorted outlook similar to those mirrors you used to see in fairgrounds. So peering sideways at a magnified version of Cliff Michelmore gave the distinct impression that he was suffering from a terminal case of Elephantiasis.

I digress. Our first TV set was a second hand affair given to us by my mother-in-law. At the time, she lived in Bristol and we lived in Rainhill, a suburb of Liverpool and famous for its mental hospital. This proved to be very handy when chastising naughty children as for years, mothers in Liverpool would threaten their recalcitrant offspring with the immortal words, "If you don't sodding behave, I'll put you in Rainhill."

Anyway it was a kindly gesture on her part and so one weekend (overtime sacrificed) we drove down and loaded the set into the back of our Mini-van. Now the journey was not as it is today; the M6 was still known as the Preston By-pass and as Preston was north of us, not much use. Our route therefore is still embedded in my mind (you don't forget pain like that in a hurry.) We travelled back through strange sounding places like Gloucester, Worcester, Tewksbury, Kidderminster, Whitchurch, before regaining familiar ground on emerging from the Mersey tunnel.

This took about seven hours on a good day (remember it was all of 160 miles to Bristol) and on what were laughingly known as 'A' roads. Meanwhile, despite driving with due care and attention, the TV, accompanied by three children, is lurching about in the back and absorbing humps, bumps, roadwork's, severe bends, sudden stops, acceleration (not a problem), traffic lights, hills and tram lines.

Having arrived home safely, avoiding a hernia lifting the thing out, rearranging the furniture to accommodate the set, erecting an aerial and plugging it in - we waited for it to warm up, ready to enjoy the show.

Unfortunately, despite our best efforts, the journey must have been too much for the valves and all we got was a glow, accompanied by a hissing sound. No amount of adjusting, fiddling, checking or having the children carry the aerial around the house made any difference, except perhaps to change the hissing tone.

One other minor problem was the fact that my mother-in-law couldn't find the manual. However, if I'm honest I don't think it would have made a ha'porth of difference. I have generally failed to understand the contents of any instruction manuals which arrive with domestic appliances. That's why I'm an engineer.

Time to call in the expert.

The expert, in this case, was a small weasely looking chap named Tommy; again, since he was a Shotfirer by profession, I have no idea where or how he became familiar with the inner workings of a television set. However, as you do, we got talking one day and I mentioned the fact that we had this well travelled TV which resolutely refused to show pictures. Tommy then uttered those fatal words – "I can fix tellies."

I invited him home one afternoon (overtime sacrificed again) and without further ado he took the back off and started poking around with a screwdriver. He pronounced that all the valves were in order, but a number of (unspecified) adjustments would be necessary. In some trepidation we switched the set on and he began twiddling in the back while getting me to rotate the aerial. I then entered into unchartered seas consisting of words like co-axial, gain, auto-lock, 405 lines, signal strength and horizontal hold.

The upshot was, as if by magic, a picture appeared followed by sound—and lo and behold we had television. Even if it was black and white, with an unnerving tendency for the picture to roll to the top of the screen at irregular intervals and for no apparent reason.

Be that as it may, it was on this was the very set that in 1969, we got the children out of bed to watch Neil Armstrong set foot on the moon. Even though some of their leaps seemed to be increasingly dramatic, as every now and then they rolled to the top of the screen.

Pat and I were talking about Christmas, as you do in July, and I had expressed the up and coming gourmet's opinion that frozen turkeys were pretty tasteless.

Pat said, "Why don't you get a freshly reared turkey from Alec?"

"Who's Alec?" I asked.

"Alec's the Shotfirer on 4 West face. You know him, he's a short stout guy with a big Adam's apple."

"Why should I get a turkey from him?" I asked.

"Because," said Pat with enforced patience, "Alec has a smallholding and every year he takes orders and breeds a hundred or so turkeys for sale. You want to tap him up in the canteen and get your name down for one— they're very tasty."

So, not wishing to miss out on the prospect of having a turkey with added taste, I found Alec and placed my order. This of course had to be done surreptitiously, as entrepreneurship of this magnitude was sort of frowned on by management. He was, however, as good as his word and just before Christmas, he sought me out in the canteen saying, "Thee turkey's ready. I'll be in the car park tomorrow at three o'clock, be there and thee can tak it away with thee."

As all this was said out of the corner of his mouth while drinking a mug of tea, I felt it prudent to say I'd be there—out of the corner of my mouth—obviously. It dawned on me later that this little scene must have been repeated a hundred times.

The following day I was in the car park waiting to complete the transaction when I noticed a shooting brake (now known as a 'sports utility vehicle') make its way into the car park. The interesting thing was it moved very slowly, the back end was almost touching the road and you couldn't see through either the rear or side windows. As the vehicle ground to a halt I noticed that Alec was crammed in a sort of crabwise position in the drivers seat, as the passenger side and half of the drivers side was occupied by a solid mass of plucked turkeys. Opening his door, he fell out onto the tarmac and said, "I've brought thee turkey, I'll just open the back."

On so doing, another interesting thing happened, it became increasingly obvious that the back wasn't entirely filled with turkeys, because there was a heaving sound, a number of birds were pushed to the side and a young girl appeared from under the carcases.

I must have looked startled because Alec said, "It's alright, it's me daughter Claire. She helps me to pluck the bloody things."

Throughout all these fine examples of entrepreneurship, there was one important competition which dominated our lives. This was to be the first fitter to earn £20 in one week—after stoppages. This meant, as a minimum, staying down each day until at least five or six o'clock and working weekends (ignoring the siren call of rugby matches or shopping with the wife.) The problem was, the longer we worked, the more proportionally the taxman would take as his share. In mathematical terms we had to work longer and longer to make a smaller and smaller net gain. I think it's called the law of diminishing returns, but that's not we called it. As far as we were concerned we were the victims of a government conspiracy.

Week after week, we would compare pay packets, convinced each time that we had reached our goal, but no—there were cries of "Bloody hell, I've got £18-7-6;" "I've got £19-3-5; sod it I was certain I'd made it this time;" "It's £19-12-6."

Now for younger readers, I realise the figures must seem incomprehensible, but long before you were born we had a different way of counting money. It was called Pounds, Shillings and Pence. This then, is to what the figures refer, but as I want to keep the boredom level to a minimum, I'll go no further, other than to mention that we didn't use PSP as the initials, instead we used LSD (I often had the feeling that we would have been a whole lot happier had we been able to get hold of some LSD – the happy variety anyway.)

Enough, if your I-Pod battery is flat and you want to know more about ancient British currency—try Wikipedia.

The good news is that one Friday there was a shout of "Yyesss!" and we all crowded around Gordon who was waving his pay packet around like a Morris Dancer without his bells. He had broken the wage barrier. What we realised later was that in order to do so, Gordon had worked all weekend and right through the night on Sunday.

Still, we all felt a small glow, as we had at last beaten the Inland Revenue, or at least, Gordon had.

One last comment before I become bitter and twisted again; at the time our basic pay was the princely sum of seven pounds, twelve shillings and sixpence (about £7-62p) per week for working underground. So you can see a good deal of overtime was needed in the good old days, to get to the magic figure of £20.

There is a postscript to my obvious bitterness regarding pay, which I would like to share with you.

In July 2000 I received a letter from the Mineworkers Pension Scheme that said,

"I am writing about your pension entitlement and am pleased to inform you that you are entitled to receive your pension from March 1992 or from your 60th birthday, whichever is the sooner. To claim your pension, please complete the attached form. When I receive the form I will contact you again with details of your entitlement."

I thought, WOW—another pension, and working on the premise that you can't have too many, I filled the form in and posted it off. How much will it be? Should I order a new car? What about a cruise? After all it's going to be back-dated to 1992 - I could hardly wait. It may also be worth mentioning that I had never heard of the Mineworkers Pension Scheme, but it sounded like a wonderful organisation.

Anyway, in October 2000 I received another missive setting out my pension entitlement, which said:

"I am pleased to tell you that you are entitled to a weekly pension of £0-40 payable from the 30th October 1995".

As I am sure you are doing now, I thought it was a misprint and the figure really should have been £4-00 or even £40-00 per week. However it all became clear when I read further. It said....

"This has since been increased to:

£0-63 per week from 25/09/2000, this includes bonus.

The first payment will be made with arrears on 17th November 2000 and every 52 weeks following this date."

So, hardly containing my excitement and already choosing the colour of the new model, I quickly calculated that I was due to the princely sum of £32-76 per annum (as they say in accountancy circles).

There was another paragraph.

"Your pension may be taxed..............if you have any questions about tax deductions you need to contact the Inland Revenue."

I didn't.

And then in August 2003 I received another letter, that said;

"As the total value of your benefits (what?) is less than £5 per week, you can take a final lump sum payment of £359-17. If you agree, you will no linger be a member of the Scheme."

So I commuted (as they say in accountancy circles).

What really cheered me up was to see that my pension included 'bonuses'. I did try to work out what I could buy for sixty-three pence, but it became too depressing.

As I don't want to end this section on a sour note, let's just say something fatuous like   'money isn't everything'—well, working for the coal industry certainly proved that!

Chapter Twenty-Two
An Outside Interest

What about life after the excitement of shovelling coal? I realise that fun filled days of dust, gas, mice, breakdowns, explosions, arguments, pies, overtime and roof falls should be enough to satisfy the most jaded palette. Not so, coal miners enjoyed a wide variety of hobbies, pastimes and illicit liaisons once the dust was washed off.

There is an image, put about by those unfortunate enough to be living in the south of the country, that everyone in the north of England is distinguished by flat caps, whippets, pigeons, ferrets, betting, eating rabbits and growing leeks. Well I'm here to tell you that when I worked in the pit, it was all true and nothing to be ashamed of.

It's also true to say that people in the south were not always held in high esteem by us in the north. This was probably due to the fact that they didn't play rugby league, they all wore bowler hats and the government didn't know where we were.

The other thing pit people had was an incredible pride in their county, for instance being 'Lancashire folk' was looked on with pride (I called it the Gracie Fields syndrome, but not out loud.) Even coming from Yorkshire was infinitely better than coming from Middlesex. This is why I was looked on with considerable suspicion by the miners, as one pointedly remarked, "Thar's from bloody Liverpool, tharl nee'r be a real pit mon." In an effort to counter this foul slur, I tried to tell him that Knotty Ash was in fact, in Lancashire, and to extol the cultural virtues of my fair city, I listed a few of its most notable attributes—ferries, trams, black buildings, chip butties, Arthur Askey, Z cars, Littlewoods Pools, Anfield, Yates's Wine Lodge, Chinatown, Cilla Black, Hartley's jam and bomb sites. Strangely, he seemed singularly unimpressed.

And then sometime later, the unthinkable happened: In 1974 someone, obviously from the south, decided it would be a good wheeze to make some small changes to the County boundaries. So as if by magic, St Helens, Clock Face, Collins Green and Haydock moved from Lancashire into—wait for it—Merseyside.

At the same time Wigan and Leigh disappeared into Greater Manchester and, as if that wasn't enough, Warrington and Widnes found themselves in Cheshire, a county noted for its rich farmers and 'ladies who lunch.' This also meant that for the first time in its genteel history, Cheshire now owned two great hairy rugby league teams.

These minor adjustments to people's heritage led to mass protests, picketing, marches on town halls, strong letters to Editors, heated debates in pubs, threats of suicide, refusals to acknowledge, incorrect addresses, street parties, fund raising, missing county boundary signs, renewed hatred of politicians, broken windows, petitions, protest songs and placards.

All of course, to no avail; after all a few broken windows in Wigan was hardly going to make the front page of the London Evening Standard.

The only group of people who seemed largely oblivious to these earthshattering events were Scousers. It's true to say that most Liverpudlians, believing they already occupied the cultural centre of the known universe, had no idea they'd been part of Lancashire in the first place.

I digress. We were talking about hobbies. Before entering this new world I had no idea that whippets and ferrets constituted a hobby. In fact, I had never set eyes on either of the species, let alone take delight in owning, grooming, breeding, showing, buying, selling or betting on the creatures.

I was however, wrong. I remember, the first time I saw a whippet, thinking, "Bloody hell someone should notify the RSPCA." It looked to me like an emaciated greyhound with severe anorexic problems, a sort of canine equivalent of Twiggy. I was chatting to Pat about my sighting one morning and he agreed with my observations; in fact, he said "One of my neighbours kept two of them and he maintained they were friendly, playful, intelligent and good with children. I guess that meant they wouldn't readily eat one. Mind you, compared to bloody ferrets, they're probably very desirable."

Once again, I found myself at a disadvantage. To my certain knowledge ferrets weren't on the 'must have' accessory list for the average scouser. Mongrels from the Dog's Home, yes, budgies from the Market, yes, cats saved from drowning, yes, rabbits from the pet shop, yes. But ferrets— definitely not.

I mentioned this gap in my zoological education and Pat said, "I wouldn't worry; unless that is, you want to own something that's born to kill and the only sign you'll get of affection is when they try to bite off your sodding fingers."

"If that's the case, why does anyone want to keep them?"

"They're mainly kept for hunting rabbits, which is a bit safer than gassing them with cyanide."

"Bloody hell Pat," I said, "So the ferret is the lesser of two evils?"

"You could say that," said Pat. "Once they're down the rabbit hole, they chase the rabbits out into nets over the entrances, so that our brave boys can club them to death."

"Sounds like a fun day out," I said.

"Aye, and it's not just the rabbits you have to contend with. You then have to grab the ferret by the scruff of the neck and stuff it into a sack before it bites you. Oh and by the way, the little bastards smell something awful. There's no doubt in my mind," said Pat, "You'd be better off keeping pigeons—but only just."

Continuing in what I fondly thought of as my David Attenborough mode—that of a friendly interrogator, I asked, "What's the attraction in pigeons?"

"Beats me," said Pat. "As a hobby it leaves a lot to be desired. For a start there's the outlay, you've got to build a loft for them, and some of the birds cost a fortune. All this just so that you can stuff them in a basket, drive for miles, let them go and hope to god they find their way back in a given time."

"So you're not that keen?" I said.

"Oh, I don't mind what some idiots spend their money on, as long as they're not too near to me. If you have the misfortune to live close-by, the little sods perch on your gutters and crap all over your windows. That's not too bad, but they also perch on the wife's washing line with the same disgusting results."

Possibly the greatest surprise I had regarding a hobby was when I made the acquaintance of a chap named Harold.

Harold worked solely in the two main tunnels and his job was to inspect the railway lines on which the manriding and coal hauling locomotives travelled to and from the pit bottom. This meant he walked slowly along the lines, checking for damage, floor heave, dislocated joints and sleeper ballast. It took him half the shift going in and the other half going out, after which he made out a status report, had a shower and went home. He never worked any overtime and other than when someone met him en route, was alone all through his shift. The notable thing was the fact that Harold was extremely well educated, had a classics degree, a wife who was a concert pianist—and his hobby was astronomy.

I once asked Harold why on earth a person of his learning did what was not perhaps the most intellectually stimulating job in the world. He said, "That's it exactly. Because of its routine nature, I can think about more esoteric things, I know I'll be free at two-fifteen every day and nobody bothers me with trivia." I realise this may make him out to be unfriendly, but nothing could be further from the truth. Harold was happy to chat, especially if you showed an interest in his hobby, and as if to prove the point, one day he mentioned he'd been the subject of an article in the local paper. "I'll bring a copy in if you like," he said; and true to his word, we met on our way in the next morning, and he passed me a cutting, saying, "Don't bother now, read it later when you have a minute, and let me know what you think."

Somewhat puzzled, I thanked him and stuffed the article into my snap bag.

Settling down for a well earned bite (as you do when you're knackered) I opened up the article and that's when I began to realise just how serious Harold was about his hobby. I'll extract some of the main bits, taken from the Evening Express of Monday July 26th 1954. See what you think.

On the evening of Thursday July 8th Mr Harold Hill, who is an amateur astronomer of 18 years standing and an experienced member of the British Astronomical Association, went out to the observatory at his home near Wigan.

The time: 9.25pm.

His intention: to close the dome of his observatory for the night.

It was usual for Mr Hill that he should scan the skies as he walked down his garden. But what was not usual was the object he saw in the southern skies. It was so unusual that it sent him running for his wife and a pair of binoculars.

And what he saw through the binoculars was so startling that he tore a small telescope in his observatory from its mountings in his almost frantic anxiety to focus his big 12 inch telescope on the object.

Mr Hill at first thought he had seen a super-nova—a temporary star that suddenly flames into brilliance and then dies away. But the object was not a super-nova. Mr Hill believes now that he saw—a flying saucer!

The article then goes on to describe Harold's report to the Astronomical Association and his somewhat frustrating conversations with the Air Ministry in London.

"I came up against such an utter conflict of opinion that at times I was utterly bewildered. I found desk-bound Air Ministry officials loftily dismissing flying saucer reports as 95% proved natural phenomenon and the other 5% also explained as natural phenomenon.

That sounded quite official, quite convincing and quite reassuring—but it hap-

pens to be the equivalent of saying that experienced RAF, BOAC and BEA pilots, trained anti-aircraft observers, radar operators and civilian astronomers don't know what they are talking about!

Indeed, when I pointed this out to the Air Ministry, they qualified their comments and instead of proof of natural phenomenon they began to talk of suggestions."

The article goes on at some length regarding other sightings and contains two telling comments from Harold.

"The assignment became one of the most fascinating I have ever undertaken. I started as a flying saucer sceptic. Now.........I am not so sure.

"I am driven, whether I like it or not, to the conclusion that what I saw was what has become known as a flying saucer."

You have to admit that Harold's hobby was a step up from keeping ferrets.

Three of us were chatting one afternoon about what we would do with a day off next week, when Les said, "Why don't we have a trip to Derbyshire. I've been there before and it's a grand county."

"Sounds fine," I said, "How are we to get there?"

Frank, the third member of our safari discussion group, then solved our problem by announcing, "I can borrow my dad's car if you like."

Perfect! All we needed to do was to arrange a pick-up point and trust Les to navigate our way across Lancashire, into Cheshire, over the Cat and Fiddle and into the heart of Derbyshire. Still, we mustn't get despondent just yet and at least we weren't going into Yorkshire.

Frank was a recent addition to our small underground team and worked with Les on days and with me on afternoons. He was a gangly, lugubrious lad with a nicely warped sense of humour whose main claim to fame was that he had once worked for Pilkington's Glass. We'd known each other for about six months when he announced he was about to get married. We felt that congratulations were in order, but I counselled him against confiding in Big Ernie, remembering the standard accusation that – "If thar's getting married, she must be in the club."

The upshot was that Frank invited us to his stag night, which was to be held in a pub just across the road from the Vulcan Foundry. Not wishing to pass up the chance to sample Greenhall Whitley's finest, we agreed. It was a great night, banter and insults were of a high standard, the beer was cold and plentiful, nobody hired a stripper (in fact they hadn't been invented at the time) and no one was hugged.

By comparison with the excesses of today's stag events, Frank's was a fairly low key event. We didn't hire a coach to Blackpool, fall about in the road, stab anyone, break shop windows, accost the landlady (a matter of taste rather than good behaviour,) leapfrog over gravestones, assault the police, or go out without our coats. What a lot of fun we must have missed.

We did put the world to rights, promise undying friendship, confirm the fact that we were the best Fitters in the pit, call one another 'mate' or 'mucker,' throw money in a kitty, spill beer, pee a good deal and inhale passive smoke.

Just before throwing-out time, Frank announced that we were all to go back to his Granny's house, where she had prepared a bit of supper. This sounded great, plans to raid the local chippy were abandoned and we all piled into Frank's dad's car. Frank then did his best to focus on the road while we, looking forward to a feed, were blissfully oblivious to the fact that he was totally ratted.

We arrived at Granny's to find it was one of those small two-up, two-down terraced house so beloved of Heritage Museums and hated by their occupants. We were introduced to Granny, who sat us down at the table in the tiny kitchen. Knives and forks appeared and without another word she opened the oven door in the cooking range and staggered across with a huge round enamel bowl. This was deposited in the centre of the table and, as Granny sagged back—we leaned forward and were treated to one of those sights that live on forever in the memory.

The bowl was about twenty inches diameter and some eight inches deep and was a type still popular as a means of soaking the feet. However, in this case, it wasn't feet we were confronted with; it was the sight of a thick crust of brown sliced potatoes with wisps of steam issuing from the occasional gap. And then there was the smell; our senses were now assaulted with the most glorious aroma of potatoes, meat and vegetables. I was immediately reminded of Desperate Dan's cow pie; such is the power of sensory overdose. But this wasn't cow pie; this was a classic example of that king of meals—Lancashire hot-pot.

Just as we were starting to drool, Granny recovered her strength and, grasping a huge ladle, drove it through the crust, lifted a huge steaming spoonful and asked, "Reet lads, pass thee plates and get stuck in 'afore it gets cold—who's first?"

As one body, a circle of plates were offered up at a speed which would have made the workhouse children in Oliver Twist seem disinterested.

Granny, whose dexterity with the ladle was awesome, filled each plate and then the real benefit of the giant bowl became apparent—there was plenty of lovely crust for everyone. As if that wasn't enough, she then produced a big jar of pickled cabbage, with more instructions to 'dig in.'

There are a small number of times in life when all is right with the world, nothing can be improved, it's good to be alive, all your prayers have been answered and becoming Doris Day's toy-boy doesn't seem to be entirely out of the question.

Well, let me tell you—the reality of that fabulous hot-pot feast certainly ranked alongside the ultimate DD fantasy.

Where was I?

Right, Les and I were early at the rendezvous, and as we waited for Frank to arrive, I asked Les how he came to know about the area. He said, "Ah well, me Auntie Maisie used to live in those parts and when I were a lad, I spent my school holidays with her. She were a grand lass but bloody hell she didn't half smell of mothballs."

I was about to ask if she suffered from moths, but just then Frank arrived with our transport.

His dad's car turned out to be a Sunbeam Rapier, which had seen better days; however, as we couldn't go by bus, we piled in. Les in the front to navigate and me sliding around on the bench seat in the back. The manufacturer of this vehicle, in a fit of commercial madness, had incorporated two interesting design innovations. The first was that the front seat was also of the bench variety, the result of which was that if the passenger adjusted the seat, the driver was either thrust into the steering wheel, or he couldn't reach the pedals. In addition, every time we went around a right hand bend, Les shot across and smashed into Frank, who then hit the offside door and drove the window-winder handle into his rib-cage.

The second 'good idea' was to have the gear-change lever mounted just under the steering wheel. This piece of engineering brilliance was known as a 'column change' and necessitated the use of extended linkages from the gearbox to the lever. Sadly, as the assorted linkages became worn, the gearbox didn't immediately respond to a corresponding movement of the lever. This made gear changing something of a lottery and it wasn't unusual for Frank, having, as he thought, changed into second, to find he had actually engaged third. This became particularly interesting as we approached the foot of the Cat and Fiddle. The other startling aspect of this design was watching the driver frantically searching for the gear lever when engaged in turning the steering wheel to the left.

Nothing daunted, on we went o'er hill and dale (as they say in proper books,) Les calling out directions, while sliding about like a metronome, Frank swearing at the gear shift and occasionally howling with pain as he made contact with the window mechanism, and me free as a bird in the back and trying to see where we were going, despite the bulky figure of

Les sliding across and blocking my view through the windscreen.

I suppose the other things to mention were the complete absence of seatbelts, airbags, side impact bars, ABS with EBFD (whatever the hell that is,) rear fog lights, air conditioning, electric windows, reclining seats, crumple zones (unless you include the complete car,) colour coded bumpers, heated rear windows, remote control central locking, alloy wheels, cruise control, spoilers, effective headlights, windscreen demisters (other than a potato,) and in-car entertainment (unless you count a radio with a reception range of about three miles from BBC Manchester.)

What we did have was leatherette seats (vinyl was an option,) a clock that ticked, cross-ply tyres, a plastic walnut dashboard, ashtrays, leaded petrol, rust spots, a three speed gearbox, peeling chrome, zero to sixty mph in twenty-two seconds, a Zenith carburettor, a two tone colour scheme and success in international rallies (but sadly not by me.)

However, considering that none of us had a car of our own, we were in seventh heaven, bowling along, nice and dry, warm as toast and resisting the very real temptation to sing. Despite some anxious moments when climbing hills on the road to Buxton, when the car began to slow down in an alarming manner, we made it, without mishap, to our destination.

This was a place called Castleton, which consisted largely of a main road, some gift shops and a large car park. However, in addition to these attractions it had spectacular scenery, a ruined castle, lots of geology and some caves.

This latter claim to fame by Castleton came as something of a surprise, as Les had sold the 'grand day out' on the promise of hills, dales, fresh air and a good pub. Frank and I were convinced there had been no mention of us venturing down more bloody holes in the ground when we set off—after all, we could have all the darkness we wanted every day of the week and get paid for so doing—we said.

After a while and despite recriminations, Les managed to convince us, by buying another round of John Smith's finest, that all would be well, we would enjoy the experience and be glad we came. (Again, I should point out that 'drink driving' hadn't been invented at the time.)

So, thirst quenched and butties consumed, we set off on our grand underground adventure. And although at first, Frank and I were loathe to admit it, Les had come up trumps. That day we were bowled over by some amazing natural wonders. As I recall, we did the complete tour, including Treak Cliff Cavern, Poole's Cavern, Blue John Cavern and finally Speedwell Cavern. Speedwell was somewhat different from the others, as it is a partially flooded lead mine, and visitors are taken through the workings by boat, uniquely propelled by a man lying on his back, pushing along the roof with his feet.

By about five o'clock we had overdosed on natural wonders and were becoming fed up with 'oohs' and 'aahs,' so we nipped back into Castleton for a well earned pint. As Frank so aptly put it, "It's bloody tiring is touring."

Les, still basking in our increasingly diminishing plaudits and determined to continue as the fount of all knowledge, was pleased to point out that Peak Cavern used to be known locally as the 'Devil's Arse,' but they changed it, as there were concerns this might put prospective visitors off.

Frank said he thought the title was much better suited to Bold Colliery and couldn't help but feel a tinge of jealousy as none of the caverns required hard hats, gas tests, roof supports, dust barriers, explosives, Deputies, Overmen, coal dust, conveyors, or a three thousand foot vertical shaft.

We all nodded in agreement that this caverning lark was a doddle compared to our sad lot, until that is, Les mentioned that none of the caverns sold pies. Sometimes you just need to be reminded of how very lucky you are.

Chapter Twenty-Three
More Fun in the Open Air

Sports Day—a phrase designed to strike terror into the majority of the nation's schoolchildren. Well, we were no different. It wasn't the open air part, it was the difficulty of trying to hide in the crowd from some organising idiot determined that you should enter the long-jump, pole-vault or (heaven forbid) a race up and down our slag heap.

No, the ideal sports day for us underground chaps was to lie in the long grass, soak up the sun, decide once and for all that Doris Day was infinitely more desirable than Barbara Stanwyck, and drink the odd can of beer.

However, as is often the way, I was persuaded otherwise and against my better judgement I found myself 'volunteering' for membership of the underground fitters' tug of war team. Now when I say volunteering, I use the word in its loosest sense. The choice was put to me by Bert our Chief Engineer who, having failed to woo me with talk of loyalty, sportsmanship, the good of the department, team spirit, letting the side down, finest hour, self esteem and 'its not the winning, it's the taking part,' then modified his approach and made what in mafia parlance is known as, 'an offer you can't refuse.' The details were somewhat vague, but the key element involved a veiled threat to my future overtime opportunities. Sometimes I find you just have to have the message spelled out concisely before you can decide what's best.

So on the appointed day, eight of us gathered on the field, while all around us children were engaged in various contests such as the three-legged race, the egg and spoon race, a skipping race and a diabolical thing requiring great dexterity called the hop-skip and jump. While all this assorted mayhem was going on, others were climbing up ropes fixed to poles with a vertical height of about ten feet. Having reached the top the objective was to swarm along the horizontal pole and climb down knotted ropes at the ends. As we watched, kids were climbing, falling, swinging and suffering rope burns to hands, legs and occasionally to chests. After a while, the scene at the base of the structure resembled a bad day on the Somme. There were bodies everywhere and kids were being scooped up by our Mines Rescue Team, acting as 'first aiders' for the day.

You have to remember that all this fun took place before the advent of the 'bouncy castle' and the 'elf & safety police. As we watched in growing unease, I couldn't help thinking that the last thing I needed was the tender ministrations of a hairy rescue man with a morbid fascination for bandages.

To say we were unprepared would be something of an understatement. What we did have in common was absolutely no idea about the finer points of the tug of war. We also were just beginning to realise the extent of Bert's con. As more and more teams joined us on the field, it dawned on us that the forthcoming contest was a lot bigger than we had been led to believe. Not only were there several teams from our pit, but groups of big, heavy guys from other pits in the area were beginning to arrive.

Any hope we had, that no one else would turn up, had now disappeared and another worry began to emerge. As the new arrivals started to discard coats and jackets we realised they were all kitted out in a sort of uniform. Shorts and matching rugby shirts were the favourite, whilst others preferred to be seen in rather fetching blue overalls. We, on the other hand, didn't so much resemble a team as a random assortment of refugees. Not realising there would be a dress code, we had turned up in various shirts, trousers and the odd jacket. The only saving grace, as it turned out, was the fact that we all were wearing boots. Don't ask me why, I guess it was collectively the first footwear that came to hand, or in this case—foot.

The other fairly important thing we had in common, was the fact that none of us had ever taken part in a tug of war before. And just as we were debating whether to make a run for it, a small tractor and trailer turned up and two guys flung the biggest rope we had ever seen at our feet. Frank said, "Bloody hell, the last time I saw anything like that it was wound around a ferry boat bollard." We approached the thing somewhat tentatively and Les gave it a sort of experimental kick, but it just lay there.

Just then and unbeknown to us, a minor miracle occurred. Bert, presumably mindful of our potential to embarrass him in front of everyone, had managed to persuade another Fitter to join our 'team.' Named Martin, he had recently completed his National Service and being of an athletic bent, had been a member of his battalion's tug of war team.

Still largely ignorant of the trauma to come, we gathered round and Martin gave us a quick lesson on the finer points. Well that's not quite true, we weren't really into 'finer points,' what we needed were basic principles which, thankfully, Martin began to spell out.

He laid out the rope in a straight line and allocated positions along the half which would be ours when the fun began. I was given the dubious honour of being the 'anchor man,' and so proceeded to wind the slack end around my waist. Tying a knot proved to be well nigh impossible, as it was very thick and being made of manila, difficult to bend into a small loop. Anyway I persevered until, that is, Martin, having spaced the lads out arrived to find I was firmly tied to the rope.

"What the bloody hell are you doing?" wasn't the greeting I had anticipated, thinking how I had used my initiative and was already prepared for the off.

"You're not supposed to fasten it around you, unless that is, you want to end up with a ruptured spleen, kidney failure, dire shortage of breath and the distinct risk of being pulled along the ground like a sack of spuds. Now undo the bloody knot and I'll show you how it should be held."

This was an altogether new type of Martin as far as I was concerned. Normally he was laid back with a nicely warped sense of humour and yet here he was doing a passable imitation of an SS Gruppenfuehrer. I began to realise that Bert must have also dropped some strong overtime hints to Martin as well.

He then began to explain how the rope should be held and it sounded to me as though the technique had been invented by some demented sailor. However, and this took numerous attempts on my part and an increasingly tight lipped effort on Martin's, the rope was finally put in place.

'In place', as far as Martin was concerned, meant that the rope now passed under one of my armpits, went diagonally across my back, over the opposite shoulder from the rear to the front, then backwards with the remaining slack hanging free on the opposite side to the armpit through which the rope had passed in the first place.

Nothing to it, as long as I didn't have to let go of the damned thing for the rest of the afternoon. It's also true that I had begun to hate Martin in the same way that I already hated Bert.

Finally, we were ready for combat. Our first encounter was with a team from one of our sister pits. We stood by the rope and waited.

Then as the judge received a signal from both coaches, he issued the immortal words, "Pick up the rope," followed by "Take the strain," then, "Steady," then—"Pull!"

And suddenly the pride of the Fitters' Department was at stake, so we pulled like persons possessed—and won. Round one to us, we were flushed with success and Les suggested a beer was in order. A good idea until SS Martin put a damper on the proceedings by citing another regulation, which stated that the interval between contests should not be more than six minutes.

Back to the field to await our next competition. The enemy soon appeared and this lot looked somewhat more formidable than the first, or perhaps it was just their matching shirts that gave that impression. Anyway, it was about now that things started to get serious. We began to see we were in for a long afternoon and we realised that Martin (the SS part had now gone) was a real asset and really did know his stuff.

Once we had started, he took up a position about midway along our rope, but instead of watching us as had we expected, his eyes were firmly fixed on the opposition.

We were now at the point where there is no movement, both teams were leaning back, taking the strain and other than the odd grunt, it is silent. Then suddenly Martin turned from watching the other team and shouted at us, "Lift, stamp, pull!"

This was our signal to lift one leg, stamp down with our boots on the outer edge and as soon as they dug into the ground, give an almighty backward heave. It worked a treat and the other team never recovered. It was now apparent that Martin was a superb tactician and, having noticed a tremor in the opposition, issued the order he had rehearsed with us. Congratulations all round and even a visit from Bert couldn't dampen our spirits. There were however, some growing signs of unease—the further we went in the competition, the more knackered we became, our hands began to look like red jellyfish, our right feet were in agony, my armpit was raw, there was no time for a beer and Bert was becoming distinctly emotional (not a pretty sight.)

Fortunately there was a brief interval while other contests were completed and we all collapsed on the grass. Martin, for some unaccountable reason, decided we were now ready to absorb some advanced tug of war strategies and proceeded to talk in guarded terms about the potential for good honest cheating. This seemed to consist of vague references to 'climbing,' 'propping,' and 'the grip,' but just as we collectively geared up to leap on his head, there was a tannoy announcement.

The gist of it was that hot pies were now available and we had reached the semi-final, which would take place forthwith. No time for pies then.

We were now in thrall to that old favourite 'mixed feelings;' on the one hand we were absolutely shattered, and on the other, we were rather chuffed that a scruffy bunch like us could have got so far. Just then, Bert arrived full of praise and offering useless advice such as, "Reet lads, don't thee forget—hang on and pull the bastards over, we're all rooting for thee."

I heard Les mutter something that sounded like, "Well at least the daft sod didn't mention the need for a girder." A bit cryptic, but we knew what he meant.

We now waited anxiously to find out who our semi-finalists would be and unfortunately, we didn't have long to wait, as I was greeted by a shout of, "Now Briun, 'art ready for a good thrashing then?"

And there, looming over the rise was the dreaded figure of Ernie, with a complete rope slung casually over his shoulder and looking horribly relaxed, as though he'd been lying in a deckchair all afternoon.

I turned to the team, "We're stuffed lads, this lot'll kill us."

Les said, "Why, do you know the guy carrying the rope?"

"Oh yes I know him, and what's more I've been wrist-wrestling the sod for the past year and have never even won a round. I'll tell you something else; Ernie could probably beat us on his own."

Before I could say any more, Ernie arrived, gave me a slap on the back which, I am convinced, dislocated half a dozen vertebrae and said, "Is this thee team then? They don't look up to much." And with that he gave the lads a terrible smile, followed by, "Reet, let's get going, I'm gasping for a pint."

So ended my first and last foray into the world of tug of war.

Just as I'd predicted, Ernie's team made mincemeat of us and not even Martin's best exhortations made any difference. We were dragged across the line twice in quick succession, after which Ernie again slapped me on the back again and said, "That were reet good—but I think your lads could do with a feed of pies."

Chapter Twenty-Four
Keeping Alive

This is the serious bit. You may have thought—and I don't know where you got the impression from—that life down a pit was just a bundle of laughs. Well in a way it was, but at the same time we did our best to stay alive. For example we engineering types never, ever, moved a roof support or re-set a pit prop—we always asked a collier to do this for us. By the same token, a collier wouldn't dream of delving into a hydraulic drive unit.

This self-imposed demarcation had nothing to do with 'jobsworth;' it was a recognition that we each had specific skills and an awareness of what was, and what was not, safe to meddle with.

So it's now time to get you involved with the dreaded Health and Safety. But let's get something clear before we start, we're not talking here about idiocy such as banning kids from playing conkers or climbing trees or from hugging one another, that's 'elf and safety and has no place in a sane society. Our regulations were of a more serious nature and were aimed at preventing us being buried, blown-up, gassed or asphyxiated.

It is a truism that all mining regulations were born out of disaster and there is little doubt that in the early days there were many tragic accidents, resulting in considerable loss of life. It's not my intention to deal with the social history of mining, as this has been documented by many people who are far better qualified than I.

When I joined the industry, the mines were already nationalised and the Mines and Quarries Act was in place. Our bible, which emanated from the Act, was 'The Law Relating to Safety and Health in Mines and Quarries,' a good deal of which I had to memorise. For instance did you know that before a horse can be taken down a pit, it has to be subject to an examination to ascertain whether it is suffering from 'glanders?'

In my opinion, the most important breakthrough in mine safety came about because of the curiosity of a great scientist named Sir Humphrey Davy.

In 1815, he received a letter from some Newcastle miners, which told of the dangers they faced from methane gas. They said the gas often filled the mines and could be sparked off by the candles they had fixed to their helmets to light their work. The resulting fires and explosions caused many deaths and they earnestly sought his advice on what could be done to reduce the risk.

Fortunately, this plea induced him to address the question of how to construct a miner's safety lamp. Can you imagine this direct approch succeeding today? It would take an army of civil servants three years to investigate the request, before rejecting it on the grounds that it wasn't Sir Humphrey's department. Fortunately for the lads, his experiments, with samples of methane sent from Newcastle, convinced him that "Explosive mixtures of mine-damp will not pass through small apertures or tubes;" and in several papers read before the Royal Society, he showed that wire gauze provided the perfect example of the small apertures he needed. Not only that, but it was also a good conductor of heat.

What Davy had done was to separate the flame from the gas so that the heat lost by contact with a large cooling surface (the gauze) brought the temperature of the gas which was ignited, below that required to cause an explosion outside the gauze.

I know this sounds convoluted, but I can give you a simple analogy. Remember when you were in school having a chemistry lesson, and while the teacher wasn't watching, you would try to set one another on fire with a bunsen burner?—of course you do.

Using the same piece of kit, we can devise an experiment which will recreate exactly what Sir Humphrey discovered. Gosh isn't this exciting—who needs the Open University? Well, actually I do, particularly if Kate Humble is the presenter.

Okay, this is what you do—take the bunsen burner, hold a piece of wire gauze an inch or two above it, and open the gas supply. Then, as the gas passes through the gauze, apply a light just above the gauze. Don't wait too long or the gas will fill the room and you could lose your eyebrows, most of the windows, all of your friends and the roof off the bike-shed.

What you will see, if you follow my instructions (trust me, I'm an engineer,) is a flame on top of the gauze but, as if by magic, no flame on the underside. This is because the gauze will dissipate heat so fast that the temperature of the gas beneath is unable to rise to the point of ignition.

And that, children, is exactly how the Davy Lamp works.

His discovery meant that our early mining comrades could do away with the candles (before they did away with them) and instead, could take this new miracle lamp down the pit. Although the light was still provided by a naked flame, it was safe from methane gas because it was surrounded by the metal gauze.

And we think we're clever just because we've invented the non-stick frying pan.

Sir Humphrey, being a true philanthropist, took out no patent for his invention so, in recognition of his modesty, the Newcastle <u>coal</u>-owners presented him with a dinner-service of silver plate. No expense spared there, then.

Early on in the development of the flame safety lamp, they realised it could also be used for gas measuring purposes; by observing differences in the shape, height and colour of the flame, the volume of methane present in the air sample being tested could be estimated.

Now, as I'm sure you know, methane, being chiefly made of hydrogen, is lighter than air, and so collects in cavities in the roof. By holding the lamp up into a cavity, the size of a blue cap over the flame will, to a practised eye, indicate the amount of gas present (i.e. the more gas the higher the cap.)

Another important safety attribute of the Davy lamp was that, if the flame went out, miners would be alerted to the fact that dangerously low levels of oxygen might be present. A bit like the canary falling off its perch again.

If we're talking about value for money, it's worth remembering that Sir Humphrey's wire gauze principle was used in almost every type of flame safety lamp for nearly two hundred years.

So now you know why every Overman and Deputy carried a Davy lamp with them at all times. However, even with this degree of vigilance, things could still go wrong.

Those charged with the enviable task of making sure we obeyed the regulations, were a group known collectively as 'Her Majesty's Inspectors of Mines.' These laugh-a-minute characters were invariably chosen from the ranks of Senior Mine Managers, so conning this bunch was virtually impossible, even if you had a sort of death wish and wanted to try.

They held ultimate sanction over every pit in the country and their word was quite literally law. When visiting a pit they gave no softy advance notice that they would pop along sometime next week; on the contrary, they would simply turn up, meet the Manager and announce their intended itinerary.

This meant that the only advance warning we ever had was a quick phone call from the surface, letting us know we had about an hour to make the place look wonderful. News of this nature would of course, be the catalyst for all sorts of tensions to emerge as we desperately tried to avoid the sack.

Such an announcement meant that Eric would immediately begin travelling around the district at about Mach One speed, and on the way he would poke at packing, hang up coats, tidy up cables and tell everyone about ten times to "Be on your guard lads, t'inspector's coming."

Bill and Pat would occupy themselves by checking their stock of explosives, re-winding detonator cables and playing with their batteries and firing keys.

In the meantime, Davvy would drag colliers off the face to shovel up coal that had fallen of the conveyor, re-stack spare props and arch girders, fill up dust barriers and re-hang coats (which Eric had already re-hung three times previously.)

Sadly none of this futile activity served to reduce Davvy's increasing frustration at seeing Kenny and I leaning nonchalantly against a transformer. In the end he could stand it no longer.

"Nar then you two, I want thee both on the face 'afore the Inspector comes in bye. I'm not havin' him see thee lying around doin' nowt, so get thee arses up on the face and if he comes past, just bloody well look busy—now sod off, the pair of thee."

We looked at one another and at the retreating back of Davvy, but realising that further discussion was futile, we crawled onto the face and wriggled down just by Ernie's pack.

"Bloody hell," said Ernie, "Something must be up; we never see both the Fitter and the Electrician on the face at the same time."

Kenny summed up our hurt feelings. "Sod off, Ernie."

Some time later we were aware that our visitor was about to arrive and consumed with curiosity to see the great man, we sidled into the main gate again. In an effort to look busy I was clutching a pair of ring spanners and Kenny was staring at the dials on his Megger, although quite what we were supposed to be doing was beyond me.

Anyway, just then we saw lights coming up the tunnel towards us. They would stop for a short time, lights would be waved around and then move on again. Finally they arrived at the transformers where Kenny and I were pretending to be busy. Looking round as you do when pretending to be surprised, we saw the Great Man, the Deputy Manager, Davvy and Eric, who was hopping from one foot to the other (in Eric terms this was the equivalent of standing stock-still.)

At this point, HM Inspector announced that before going onto the coalface, he would climb up on the scaffolding, which stretched across the end of the tunnel, to carry out an examination. The scaffolding was in place ready for the afternoon tunnel gang to drill into the rock, blast about six feet down and set new ring girders in order to keep pace with the advancing coal seam.

Without further ado he climbed the ladder, walked to the centre of the plank, turned to the assembly and said, "Lights out, gentlemen, if you please."

This could mean only one thing—he was going to test for gas.

Lights were duly extinguished and a sort of hush descended on the watchers, all staring up to where our man was holding his Davy lamp in various places across the face of the rock. And then the unthinkable happened.

"Lights on, please, gentlemen," intoned the Insector, then as he reached the ground he turned to the Deputy Manager and said, "I'm afraid there is clear evidence of gas in your main level."

Even as the gasps of disbelief were still being heard, he turned in our direction and said, "Good morning gentlemen, which one of you is the Electrician?"

Kenny, thinking he was about to be sacked said, "Er, I am."

"Thank you. I want you to isolate the electrical supply to the cutter and face conveyor, lock the switchgear off securely and hand the keys to your Deputy Manager, please."

Kenny, still in fear of his job, complied. The only sound now was the sharp clunk of the switchgear contacts being broken and the snap of Yale locks as Kenny hurried to obey.

I couldn't help noticing that although the assembled watchers were silent, every time the isolating lever clanged, Eric jumped as though he'd been shot. The keys were duly handed over and our man turned to the Officials and said,

"Well, gentlemen, here we are at the entrance to the coalface and gas has been discovered at the top of the main gateway. As you are aware, this is an untenable situation and so I have closed the face until you can assure me that all necessary steps have been taken to eliminate the problem. As such, it is not my intention to carry on with my inspection and have, therefore, no intention of travelling up the coal face. Mr Deputy, I am instructing you to bring all the workers off the face until I can be satisfied that all is well. Thank you gentlemen, and good day to you."

He then turned to the Deputy Manager and said, "Perhaps we could travel out and meet again on the surface."

Eric, feeling he had been unleashed, dove onto the face and started herding the bemused colliers into the main gate; bear in mind that all they knew about the recent dramatic events was a sudden lack of power. Obviously, one of the first off was Ernie, who, ever mindful of protocol, yelled to no one in particular, "What the bloody hell's going on? I can't be doin' with this, I've a sodding living to earn."

At this point there was a sort of low moaning sound from just behind Ernie, which turned out to be coming from Eric, who had just arrived back at base.

"Now Ernie, just thee calm down while we sort things out," said Eric, in a futile attempt to put himself between Ernie and Senior Management.

Kenny and I looked at one another, realising in the same instant that this was not what Ernie wanted to hear, and sure enough, he reared up to his full height, bent down so that his coal-dust covered face was level with and about an inch away from Eric's and shouted, "Calm effing down? What does't effing mean 'calm down,' don't thee be calming me down, Eric you little bastard, it's not my bloody fault there's gas in the effing tunnel! All I want to know is when are you going to switch the bloody power on again?"

Eric, despite being the recipient of this tirade, was still in placatory mode, "Now then Ernie, there's no call for language like that, just settle down till we figure out what's best."

We held our collective breath and waited for the next explosion, but amazingly it seemed that Eric's suicidal approach had worked. Ernie shook himself like a big yard dog, turned to me and said, "Well Briun, we might as well have a wrist wrestle, while the clever 'uns decide what's to be done."

I thought, "Bloody marvellous, the Inspector's found gas, shut down the coal face, stopped the colliers pay, frightened Kenny to death, embarrassed management and worst of all, is about to cause me a lot of pain."

On the third day (a bit biblical, but factually correct) the Great Man duly returned, tested for gas all over the place, pronounced himself satisfied and left us with a final instruction. "Thank you, gentlemen. Mr Electrician, you may now re-energise the machinery."

This episode was my first real experience of absolute power, administered under the auspices of Health and Safety, and mightily impressive it was too. I suppose that although we were dismayed at what had happened, no one thought to challenge the decision. We knew that not only was he correct, he was acting in our best interests. I remember chatting to Ernie about the episode, in between having my arm dislocated, and it was significant that he too was in no doubt, when he confided that, "Aye, yon man knows what he's on about." Praise indeed!

Recently I had cause to wonder what Her Majesty's Inspector of Mines would have made of an article in the Daily Telegraph in May 1997, which said:

"Wellington boots now come with a twenty-four page user's manual in accordance with an EU Directive for Personal Protective Equipment. The booklet is printed in ten languages and gives advice on risk assessment, storage conditions, life expectancy, washing in a mild detergent and resistance to electricity, cold weather and oil—but not water! Users are advised to try each boot for fitting before use."

I think it's called progress.

Chapter Twenty-Five
Being Kept Alive

But what, I hear you ask, do we do if it all goes wrong? Well, once a feeling that the wrong career choice has been made, coupled with abject fear and a tendency to panic, have been overcome, we sit and wait for the Mines Rescue Service to arrive. This is a dedicated group of miners who are prepared to put their lives in jeopardy to save others.

In this section, I want to try and give you an insight into the role and devotion of these guys and I suppose we need to be serious for a minute— if only to remind us that working in a pit wasn't all just 'beer and skittles,' as they say.

Injuries to workers down a coal mine could be due to a number of reasons, such as a roof fall, being caught in machinery in cramped conditions or as the result of an explosion. A badly injured man or someone trapped by a roof fall had to rely on the skill and bravery of fellow miners to come to the rescue.

What follows is an attempt to provide a brief understanding of how the Service evolved, how it was managed and how it operated under emergency conditions.

Everybody is aware of our three main emergency services, the Police, Fire and Ambulance, but much less is known about others such as the Mountain Rescue Service or the Mines Rescue Service. There is a significant difference between these two. The mountain rescue teams are mostly (but not always) involved with people who get into difficulties whilst engaged in recreational activities, whereas the Mines Rescue Service was always involved with victims who had suffered whilst trying to earn a living.

In 1931, the Lancashire and Cheshire Coal Owners' Association decided that the formation of a 'Permanent Corps' System in the style of the Fire Service, where a full team was always ready for immediate turn out, would provide an efficient service. Accordingly, they built a Mines Rescue Station in Boothstown. The site offered sufficient space for the Rescue Station itself, accommodation for the Members of the Permanent Corps, the Instructors and the Station Superintendent. The main factor that influenced the choice of site was that the village of Boothstown was more or less in the centre of the Lancashire coalfield.

The prime purpose of the Mines Rescue Station was to have fully trained rescuemen, suitable vehicles and appropriate rescue equipment, available for immediate response in the event of an emergency incident occurring underground. The aim was to render the skilled assistance necessary to save life and preserve property, whenever an emergency situation occurred, that produced an irrespirable atmosphere.

The operative word here is 'irrespirable.' In our context it's taken to mean a gas or vapour incapable of being inhaled because it's either poisonous or contains insufficient oxygen. An underground incident occurring in fresh air would usually be dealt with by the miners, who were there at the time, but if breathing apparatus was required, the involvement of the Mines Rescue Station was unavoidable. Their Services would always be sought whenever the following incidents occurred: gas and coal-dust explosions, open fires and serious outbursts of gas. For inrushes of water and roof falls to involve the Rescue Service, would depend on the severity of the incident. However, if in either case, the ventilation was impaired, causing potentially dangerous conditions due to the build-up of gas, then breathing apparatus would be required and that would certainly involve the Rescue Service. As soon as the Colliery Manager was alerted to an emergency situation below ground, he would set an Emergency Plan into action. All underground workmen, not involved with the incident, would be withdrawn to the surface without delay. An Incident Control Room would be organised and a Senior Official would be appointed as 'Controller.' From that moment, all activities and procedures would go through him. A Rescue Station Official would be in charge of the Rescue Room and would be in contact with the Controller and the Fresh Air Base underground. As soon as a doctor arrived, all rescue men would be medically examined before going underground. However, the first few teams would be sent underground without delay (particularly if lives were at risk) without a medical examination. After this, it was usual for teams to be rotated on a two-hourly basis and would continue in this way, until the incident had been successfully dealt with.

There were no set rules in Mines Rescue Work, because there were never two incidents alike. Teams would be despatched from, and would always return to, the same base. Rescue personnel had to be prepared to make decisions on the spot, depending on the circumstances they were confronted with. There were three guiding principles, however, that applied to every underground emergency.

The first was the recovery of survivors and this was given priority over all other considerations. This may seem obvious, but the emphasis was on 'survivors,' and any dead personnel were left until the end of the incident. This placed an enormous responsibility on the team captain, who in some cases had to decide between life and death. On the surface, only a Medical Doctor is qualified to make such a decision, but underground, wearing breathing apparatus in irrespirable atmosphere, the team captain hadn't the luxury of a doctor at his side to make it. If he wasted time recovering a person who was obviously dead, he could be criticised later. Nothing can be done for a person who is already dead, but an awful lot can be done for someone who is injured, but still alive.

Bear in mind that cap lamps, under normal conditions, will only effectively illuminate about ten yards ahead under ideal conditions, whereas under emergency conditions, with the presence of smoke and fumes, this distance could be reduced to a couple of feet. The team would normally press on until all survivors had been recovered. When this moment arrived, the rescue teams would then move on to the second task, which was to extinguish fires. An open fire underground, of any size, was a potential danger to men and property. In the Lancashire Coalfield, there was an abundance of methane, which, in certain mixtures with air, will explode. Explosions had to be prevented at all costs, so all active flame had to be extinguished. Very often, when exploring after an explosion, it was only minor fires that were found to be alight. These would be quickly dealt with before moving forward. It's bad enough going into an area after an explosion; it would be horrendous to be there if a second one occurred.

When all fires had been dealt with, the team could then move on to the third task, which was to restore ventilation. The rescue teams would now attempt to put the affected parts of the mine back to normal fresh air conditions. Repairs would be carried out, so that the ventilating air could travel around the district in as near to normal speed and volume as possible. If this could be achieved, the involvement of the Rescue Service would be very much reduced. The use of breathing apparatus would no longer be required and the vast majority of the rescue workers could be stood down.

In practice, however, a rescue team would normally accompany colliery workmen who were brought in to act as stretcher bearers to remove any dead personnel. The exact location of these would be clearly noted before removal. The bodies would be taken to the surface, where they would become police property. A suitable place would be designated so that the bodies could be laid out for identification.

There have been many occasions underground when men have been trapped by large pieces of debris, in such a way that they were unable to be moved. This would be serious enough in itself, but usually there were other factors which threatened the life of the casualty and also, the lives of the rescuers who, in most cases, were the victims' own workmates. Roof falls could cause serious obstructions, thus reducing the airflow. This, in turn would cause the percentage of methane in the atmosphere to increase. In addition, there was always the obvious danger of further roof falls. The collapse of the roof on a coalface or an underground roadway is difficult enough to deal with safely, but when there is an injured person, buried or partially buried beneath the fallen debris, the clearing operation is even more difficult. Generally, it was only possible to attempt it from one side of the fall (usually the air intake side.) Some of the larger pieces of rock could weigh several tons and be positioned so they are helping to support the rest of the roof above the casualty.

In some instances, casualties have been almost completely dug out, only for the rescuers to find that a large rock was trapping one of the casualty's limbs. Similar situations on the surface would be difficult enough to deal with, but there the trapped person could be kept alive and free of pain by medical personnel until some mechanical lifting device was brought to the scene.

In an underground situation, morphine would be given to the trapped man to ease pain, but the rescuers were faced with huge risks to all concerned and time was never on their side.

Towards the end of the 1950's, the NCB Medical Department came up with a novel solution and devised an Emergency Amputation Kit that could be carried underground. The kit contained all the necessary tools and equipment to allow a doctor to perform the amputation of a limb in an emergency situation. There was also an adequate supply of anaesthetic for those of a sensitive nature. All the items were kept in sealed, sterile containers packed into a steel box. Whenever a doctor was required underground, the Amputation Kit was carried by two members of the rescue team, who were also there to assist in the operation. On many occasions it was opened at the site ready for use, but fortunately, was never needed, as the trapped men were freed in the conventional way. When it was realised that the Kit wouldn't be needed, it was difficult to say who was the more relieved, the doctor or his two assistants.

Whenever fire occurred underground, men not required for fire fighting were instructed to travel outbye to the pit bottom. Sometimes men have mistakenly or by force of circumstance chosen to travel outbye via the return airway, which quickly became contaminated with smoke and fumes. Those fumes always contained the deadly poisonous gas carbon monoxide. In many cases, during underground fire incidents, otherwise fit and healthy men have lost their lives from exposure to this gas when, had they had protection in the form of a respirator, a large proportion of them would have successfully made their escape into fresh air.

Although the need for protection against carbon monoxide was widely recognised, there was little interest for the underground workforce to carry a respirator. In 1950, an open fire occurred at Cresswell Colliery in Derbyshire where eighty men were forced to retreat via the contaminated return airway and all eighty died from carbon monoxide poisoning. It was seen later that a significant number were only a short distance from fresh air when they were overcome. After this incident, half-hearted attempts, in the form of voluntary carrying trials, were made to introduce a self-rescue respirator. None of them were successful and the project was unofficially shelved.

However, in 1959, an underground fire occurred at Auchengeich Colliery in Scotland at a time when forty-eight men were travelling on a man-rider at the start of the morning shift. The man-rider was situated in the return air roadway (which was common practice) and the men were promptly exposed to the smoke and fumes. Again, all the men died from carbon monoxide poisoning.

Following this, there was a renewed campaign for self-rescuers, and after a slow start, underground trials were successfully carried out and finally, by the end of 1968, every NCB Colliery was equipped with self-rescuers. After that time, it was compulsory for everyone to have a self-rescuer on their belts before being allowed to go underground.

Well here we are—at the end of the 'serious' bit and you can perhaps see why we used to say that all mining legislation was born out of disaster. But I like to think that by learning from our mistakes, we kept many more people alive for the future.

I would like to finish by telling you a story that I first came across one day when, having left the pit to become a Lecturer, I found myself faced with a problem. I was given the enviable task of teaching mining legislation to a bunch of sixteen-year old apprentices who, having joined the NCB for fun and adventure, found themselves back in a classroom. As you might imagine, they weren't exactly turned on by the exciting prospect of committing chunks of the law to memory, and it's no exaggeration to say I was struggling for their attention.

Then, quite by accident (no pun intended!) I came across a report of a mine disaster and having read it, found myself captivated by the contents. So, taking my life in my hands one morning, I said I would tell them a story. One which I would like to share with you now.

It is a superb illustration of the extraordinary lengths to which ordinary people will go in order to save the lives of their companions and is probably one of the most dramatic uses of breathing apparatus in the annals of mining disasters.

It concerned an incident which occurred at Knockshinnock Castle Colliery in Ayrshire, Scotland at about seven-thirty pm on Thursday the seventh of September 1950, when without warning, a large volume of liquid peat and moss broke through from the surface into the main coal seam. Hundreds of tons of material disappeared into the mine and the crater which it left in the field extended for nearly two acres. The visible hole was forty-five feet deep and over three hundred feet long.

As a result of this catastrophe, a hundred and sixteen men on the afternoon shift were trapped in an underground district about two miles inbye and thirteen more were missing. Although the trapped men were in a fresh air zone, the roadways leading to the shafts were blocked, making escape impossible. In fact over the next twenty-four hours or so, the sludge continued to flow into the mine and having filled the main tunnels, it rose some sixteen feet up the winding shaft.

A Rescue Headquarters was established on the surface at Knockshinnock and an Operational Base was established at Bank No 6 Mine, a disused colliery nearby. This base consisted of Senior Officials, HM Inspectors and the Mines Rescue Superintendent. In the meantime rescue apparatus had been made available from nearby rescue stations and calls were sent out for all the rescue brigade men to report for duty. The central rescue station at Coatbridge had also been warned to stand by in readiness.

In view of the distance inbye (a word used by miners to denote inward travel) and the lack of haulage facilities, volunteers were asked to stand by and act as carriers to the rescue teams. At eleven-thirty pm on the seventh, senior officials, together with two local brigades equipped with breathing apparatus, descended the disused Bank Mine to make a preliminary inspection of the abandoned workings. At two-thirty am on the eighth, the party returned to report that it was possible to travel the two miles along the old road inbye, to the point where the connection to Knockshinnock would have to be made. Unfortunately, they also discovered that some nine hundred yards of this road was full of methane.

Numerous investigations were then carried out to establish the true extent of the disaster. Having received reports and examined all the options, it became obvious that the only way in which the imprisoned men could be rescued would be to enter the disused mine and dig a connection to the trapped men at the end of the blocked tunnel identified by the investigation party.

The first task was to try and remove the gas and as electricians, engineers and voluntary workers were now available, arrangements were made for the installation of several large auxiliary fans in the tunnel. These fans were not lightweight; the first one was capable of moving twelve thousand cubic feet of air per minute, while the other two transmitted eight thousand cubic feet each. By midday on Friday the eighth, the gas had been removed for about three hundred feet up one roadway and the hope of clearing the rest appeared good. Stupendous efforts to improve the ventilation continued over the next four or five hours, but it became obvious that more urgent measures would have to be adopted if the gas from the Bank Mine was to be cleared in time. With this in view, one fan was replaced by a larger version and another fan was installed. In addition, all the air available from the Bank Mine surface fan was directed into the operational area. However, despite these incredible attempts, no further progress was made in removing the gas. Following an inspection and a review of all the circumstances in the early hours of Saturday the ninth, the fact had to be accepted that despite all efforts, there was no immediate prospect of substantial progress.

It was now apparent to those in charge of the rescue operations that clearing the gas from the workings was impossible in the time available and consideration was now given to the possibility of the trapped men having to be brought through the irrespirable zone by means of a self contained breathing apparatus, known as a 'Salvus.'

With this in view, instructions were given to collect as many sets of Salvus breathing apparatus as possible. This apparatus, like the 'Proto' used by the rescue brigades, is of the regenerative type and works on the principle that the same air can be breathed over and over again if, after each breath, the carbon dioxide is extracted and the requisite amount of oxygen is restored from a pressurised cylinder. A significant disadvantage in this case was that the Salvus was only intended to be used for half an hour, unlike the Proto, which was designed for two hour use.

Fortunately, as there was telephone communication with the trapped men, the rescuers were able to inform the man in charge, an Overman named Andrew Houston, of the position. He was instructed to explore the end of the blocked tunnel from his side, which he did and confirmed that the roadway was open to the point of the blockage.

At about four pm on Friday the eighth, the telephone to the imprisoned men began to show signs of weakening, so the trapped men were instructed to start making a passage through the barrier on their side. They were told to halt just short of the old road in case the methane should foul their atmosphere and, in order to test the air flow, they were instructed to make a small hole in advance and to watch the direction of the air. If the air came towards them they were to immediately plug the hole and await further instructions. Fortunately it was found that the air travelled outwards from their side and so instructions were given for the hole to be enlarged. The flow of air outwards didn't persist, however, and after a while it died away.

This physical breakthrough enabled a team of rescue men to pass through the gap and bring food and drink to the trapped men. Naturally, with their arrival, they thought their hour of rescue had come and they now had nothing to do but walk out with the rescue team. Andrew then had to explain to them that the gas had not been cleared from the old tunnel and that it might be some considerable time before they could be rescued.

Recognising there were no longer any other options, a plan was devised to use a series of rescue teams to escort the trapped men out, all of whom would be wearing the Salvus apparatus. It was also recognised that this would be a risky venture, since none of the trapped men were accustomed to wearing rescue apparatus of any kind. Word was also coming back from Andrew Houston that a number of them were becoming restless and puzzled about the delay in their release. This was more prevalent among the younger men and some were even talking about making a suicidal dash for safety through the gas filled roadways.

At this juncture, David Park, the Deputy Labour Director, who had just arrived, suggested it might be a good idea for someone senior to put on a Proto apparatus and go through to the trapped men. This would enable him to explain the position to them, the difficulties being encountered and what was being done to effect their release.

He then volunteered to undertake this task, as he had, at one time, been the captain of his local Rescue Brigade. In addition, he also knew many of the men personally, including Andrew Houston, whom he felt could help him to calm the men.

His offer was accepted on condition that he came back after talking to the men (an instruction which he subsequently ignored.) He then joined a rescue team and entered the workings at about three-forty am on Saturday the ninth. It took about twenty-five minutes to travel through the old roadway and his appearance was warmly welcomed by the trapped men. He told them what was being done to rescue them, calmed their fears and generally restored their morale. It later became clear that his action was, in large measure, responsible for the ultimate safe rescue of everyone.

After addressing the men, he had a look around and found that the methane level near the connection was rising. He now believed that unless something was done very quickly it would be too late. He therefore sent a rescue man out to relay the substance of his concerns to those in charge of operations, whilst at the same time being careful not to alarm the trapped men.

Drastic measures were now put into place and at about twelve-thirty pm it was decided to send a rescue team in to bring out an injured miner on a stretcher. They believed it would also give the other men confidence if they could see their injured colleague using the Salvus. And so at about two-firty-five pm the rescued man was brought out safely by the team.

Following an earlier instruction, eighty-seven Salvus sets from all readily available sources had now arrived. This enabled the rescue men to form a 'chain' along the whole length of the gas filled roadway in order to pass the sets of Salvus apparatus through to the trapped men. It's worth remembering that throughout this exercise the rescue men were standing in an old, disused tunnel which was completely filled by a deadly gas.

A major operation now commenced and a final rescue team was instructed to travel in to the trapped men. On arrival, they were to disconnect their own breathing apparatus and do all they could to build up morale. They were able to explain the general plan of action and use of the Salvus before fitting it to each man and sending him out. This team were also instructed to remain on the job without relief if possible, while further supplies of Salvus sets would passed to them along the 'chain.'

As the sets arrived, David Park took the precaution of examining them before they were fitted and discarded quite a number for various reasons. Had he not taken this precaution it is more than likely that there would have been several casualties among the escaping men.

All the tunnel teams were briefed before entry regarding their own relief as their own Proto breathing sets diminished. Stretcher cases were not to be attempted unless authorised and definite instructions were given that, if a man wearing Salvus apparatus collapsed, they were not to do anything to impede the evacuation.

Meanwhile, Andrew Houston drew up a rota regulating the order in which the men were to be brought out. He had decided that the older men should go first, but as the strain of waiting began to tell on some of the younger members, many were allowed to go before the older men.

And so the rescue plan was put into operation, men were fitted with the Salvus, given instructions on its use and sent on their way along the 'chain,' then, as each rescued man arrived at the underground fresh-air base, they were medically examined before being allowed to proceed to the surface.

At about eight-twenty-five pm, Andrew Houston was instructed to come out, leaving David Park to establish, as far as possible, the last known positions of the missing men.

The last of the trapped men reached the fresh-air base just after twelve am on Sunday the tenth, the complete evacuation having taken some eight hours.

Twenty rescue brigades were used in the operation. Excluding the brigade which remained inbye throughout the whole operation, six brigades were constantly maintained in the danger zone which extended over a distance of eight hundred and eighty yards, the rescue men being spaced out at intervals of twenty yards or so.

Afterwards it became obvious that the emergency use of the Salvus apparatus at the Knockshinnock incident could not be ignored. It was a tough assignment and remains one of the greatest triumphs in the history of the Scottish Mines Rescue Service.

David Park and the inbye Rescue Team also performed heroically—by training one hundred and sixteen trapped men to use a totally unfamiliar rescue kit and to wear it with confidence while travelling along a disused, gas-filled tunnel.

It is also important to remember that despite these magnificent efforts, thirteen men were killed due to the inrush itself.

I would like to end with a quote from Sir Andrew Bryan's Official Report of the Accident (which, incidentally, makes compulsive reading.) Although he paid fulsome tribute to the many brave personnel involved in the rescue, I feel this particular comment encapsulates the selfless devotion of ordinary people when faced with the need to save lives.

When the last of the men had been rescued, Mr Park organized a search with a rescue brigade to make sure that no one had been left behind. He was the last man to leave. There is no doubt that his action in joining the trapped men and his courage, calm demeanour and initiative in the face of a very ugly situation largely contributed to the success of the rescue operations. By voluntarily joining the trapped men, David Park deliberately took a very serious risk. Had the atmospheric conditions inside the Knockshinnock workings deteriorated faster than was actually the case—and it was always a possibility—he would have found it morally impossible to put on his breathing apparatus and leave the men.

I couldn't help thinking that had this accident occurred in the USA, Stephen Spielberg would have made a film of the epic rescue.

Now, having made this clever remark, a most amazing coincidence occurred which forces me to retract my implied criticism of the British film industry. Elizabeth, a good friend of ours, asked me when my mining book would be ready, as she hailed from a mining family and would be interested in reading about the subject.

I then mentioned I had included an extract from a rescue that took place in 1950, and finished by repeating my remark about a missed opportunity to capture the rescue on film.

She then completely flummoxed me by saying, "Oh but I think they did. In 1952 they made a film about a mining disaster near where we lived and my mother was employed as a 'stand-in' for one of the actors." It then became even more surreal when she said she had a copy of the film and would be happy to lend it to me so that I could see whether in fact it was a dramatisation of the Knockshinnock incident.

The film was made in Scotland and starred many of the well known actors of the day and, as the story unfolded, there was no doubt about it, the film was indeed based on the actual events that took place in Knockshinnock. The epic was called The Brave Don't Cry and starred John Gregson in a role loosely based on David Park; and John Rae who played the part of the Overman Andrew Houston. Sometimes you just can't believe your luck!

Oh, I nearly forgot—the apprentices were spellbound!

Chapter Twenty-Six
An Uphill Struggle

Imagine for a moment, it's winter 1961. You've saved hard, cancelled Christmas, ignored overdue bills, held several car-boot sales and worked overtime. But you've made it—it's a fine sunny January day, the sky is azure blue and the mountain is pure, dazzling white. This is the life, all the sacrifices were worth it, we're in the Alps and we're going skiing. The woolly hat is firmly in place, the padded ski suit (obtained from a well known mail order catalogue) fits like a glove and the day-glo pink stands out beautifully against the snow. Perfect.

Pausing only to adjust your goggles, you gaze upwards—this is it—the piste beckons. Although you're not absolutely sure what a piste is, you're certain you'll like it.

Just then, you hear a strange, low rumble. It can't be thunder, there's not a cloud in the sky and there are no trains halfway up the mountain. What the hell is it?

And then, just as you gaze once more up the steep slope, you see a great cloud of white powder crashing down the mountainside straight towards you. The rumble becomes louder, the cloud becomes bigger and the speed seems to be increasing exponentially and what's more the damn thing's coming your way.

Where to run? How to run? You're wearing a funny suit, big boots, a daft hat and you're carrying skis. You now remember last night in the bar, the fortified wine was flowing and there were lots of clever jokes about avalanches. Well now you're about to be in one.

Now change the scene slightly. You're at the bottom of a tunnel, peering up a steep slope by the light of your cap-lamp and you hear an awful rumbling sound. As it becomes louder, you see a wall of coal rushing towards you. It's falling off the conveyor and appears to be unstoppable. Visibility is now down to a few feet as the dust cloud arrives. It's now time to take evasive action, a view shared by your five colleagues, and as one body, you all dive into the only refuge which turns out to be a small manhole cut into the side of the tunnel.

Please don't get confused here thinking, "Ah yes, I know what he means. I've seen these manholes in the London Underground, they're brick-lined refuges where people can stand in safety when a train comes past."

Well no—actually our cut-out was crude in the extreme, it was hacked out of the rock in between the tunnel girders, it had no nice brickwork, it was very small and the only concession to comfort was a bit of sawn-off scaffolding wedged into the sides to make a seat.

The fact that when we arrive en masse it is already occupied by a wee man whose job it is to sit there all day and switch the conveyor on and off makes no difference. By now the damned stuff is rapidly filling up the tunnel, our tool bags, the conveyor drive, the transfer chute and is flattening our snap tins.

What we had, in technical terms, was a radical shortage of frictional resistance—a bit like an avalanche really.

How did this minor problem come about, I hear you ask?

Well somebody, probably safe and sound in the area offices, had a good idea. Why don't we join numbers one and three pits together, they said. This means we could send lots of lovely coal out of number one, the small pit, into number three, our bigger pit and alleviate the bottleneck at their small winder by using our giant three-deck winder. (Remember the bungee episode.)

So, without further ado, a team of displaced persons who specialised in tunnelling, set to and drove a connection. Now, in view of the adventures to come, the key dimensions of said tunnel are worth bearing in mind.

The cross-section was fifteen feet wide by eleven feet high, the gradient was 1:2.8 and the overall length was eight hundred and seventy yards. And at the risk of boring you, I want you to keep the figure of 1 in 2.8 in mind because on looking upwards, the view closely resembled the north face of the Eiger and looking downwards – it was like peering over the top of the Cresta Run.

So, having connected the two pits, all we had to do was install a forty-two inch wide belt conveyor, build two transfer chutes and rig up a signalling system.

A word here about signalling. The normal method was to stretch a length of wire from one end of the tunnel to the other. Each end was then connected to a sophisticated bit of kit consisting of a five pound hammer hinged at the handle and mounted on a loose steel plate. As you pulled sharply down on the wire, the hammer lifted off the plate, then, as you let go, the hammer would crash down on the plate, giving off an audible signal. All you had to do then was devise a code—so that for instance, three hammer blows meant start the conveyor and two blows meant stop.

However, in our case, there was a major flaw with this set-up. Due to the length of the tunnel, there was a tendency for the wire to stretch to such an extent that the puller was left with a great loop of loose wire, whilst at the other end the hammer remained exactly where it was. Something had to be done.

Cleverly, we ran two galvanised iron wires, separated by small insulators mounted at about three foot intervals, along one wall. A low voltage current was passed along the wires, but as they were separated, the circuit was broken. A bell was connected to the wires at each end, which rang whenever the circuit was connected.

Now for the clever part; in order for the man in control of the conveyor to be able to signal to his counterpart at the other end, we designed a piece of hi-tech equipment. This consisted of a foot long piece of copper pipe screwed at right angles to a short length of brush pole for the handle. Now whenever he wanted to make a signal, all he had to do was touch both wires with his copper pipe and - hey presto - a circuit was made and the bells rang. Brilliant or what?

All that remained was to devise a cunning set of coded signals, which I am now at liberty to share with you. One long ring meant stop, two short rings meant start, three rings meant put coal on, four rings meant stop sending coal and most important of all—six rings meant snap time.

So having finally completed the conveyor installation, staggered up and down the length of the tunnel checking the belt alignment, set the correct tension, tightened the rope supports, adjusted the drive rollers and had a snurch, we were ready to start.

The appropriate rings were given and the wee man turned the switch, the belt began to run and after a short time we said "Right, make three rings."

This meant that some eight hundred yards up the steep slope, another wee man was about to start his conveyor, which was already full of coal, and start to deliver it through a 'Billy and Jimmy' chute and onto our belt.

We peered hopefully up the tunnel shining our lamps on the conveyor as it swept past. Then within a short space of time, we saw the result of all our efforts—a belt full of coal trundling towards us. The more emotional among us let out yells of triumph; we've done it, look at that lot coming down the slope, time for a celebratory drink of lukewarm water. Then, just as the first load shot into our transfer chute, Neddy, always one to spoil our moment of glory said, "Reet lads, let's shut off the conveyor and see if it's all in good order."

Les, seeing the futility of arguing, nipped across to the switch and turned it off. This meant that electrical power to the motor was stopped, the 'fail-safe' brake was automatically applied and the conveyor came to a halt. Except that in this case, the 'fail-safe' brake screamed in protest and with an almighty bang disintegrated. The belt, now in the grip of our old friend gravity and not having to worry about speed control—started to accelerate.

We need now to consider a number of important statistics. The belt, now under 'free-fall' conditions is coming down a 1 in 2.8 slope (I told you to remember this figure). It's forty-two inches wide and carries an average of six hundredweight of coal every yard. This equates to about two hundred and forty tons of coal lying on the belt at any one time. And it's all coming towards us at an increasing rate of knots.

In the meantime, we're frantically sending four rings up to the other end, with a tendency to repeat the signal as things became more hairy. This mysterious onset of multiple signalling meant that those at the top were now thoroughly confused and could no longer interpret our commands. Fortunately (for us) they decided to err on the side of caution and stopped sending coal.

As I mentioned earlier, we were now all crammed in a disgusting heap on top of the wee man, trying to filter out the worst of the dust, hoping we weren't about to be buried and wishing we'd gone into the army.

The newly arrived coal, having piled up in the chute and filled up the tunnel to about half-way, squashed the belt to such an extent that it started to slow the avalanche down. After which, the whole sorry lot gave up and came to a shuddering halt.

Cautiously, we emerged from the man-hole (to the relief of the wee man) and for once we were speechless, until Les, gazing about him, summed up our feelings with the immortal words—"Bloody hell."

At this point 'management' arrived and even they seemed stunned by the carnage. I think it was Frank who suggested that as the tunnel was now half blocked, why didn't we just seal it off and let Number One pit carry their own coal out. Sadly, this wasn't too well received and we realised that if things were to be fixed, we would first have to dig out the conveyor drive. I won't bore you with the details, but it took four shifts of colliers to remove the stuff and reveal the awful mess to our drive system.

We met with the belt manufacturer whose opening gambit was to blame us for the maltreating their equipment in such a cavalier fashion. After which, and no doubt feeling better, they went back, as they say, to the drawing board. Their task, at least as we saw it, was simple—we needed to be able to stop the belt without destroying everything in the vicinity and we needed to avoid burying the wee man.

Some weeks later we were once again ready to try out their revolutionary solution to our dilemma. Peering under the structure we were taken aback to see that the drive shaft had been modified and a huge steel disc had been mounted between the motor and gearbox. There was a sort of clamp affair fixed around the top of the disc and a proud conveyor engineer told us it was a 'disc brake.' Apparently this mysterious bit of kit had been tried out on some high speed motor-cars with great success and was capable of stopping a rapidly moving object in no time at all. Being largely simpletons and having only recently graduated from throwing a metal bar into the spokes of a moving mine car as the favoured means of stopping it, we were all very impressed. One person not quite sharing this adulation was the wee man. Sadly, he hadn't quite recovered from being buried under five hairy fitters and wasn't fully convinced this new-fangled disc thing would prevent it happening again.

Once again the magic signals were sent, the conveyor started, coal was fed onto the belt, cap-lamps were shone up into the darkness, snap tins were moved to higher ground, and then with a deepening rumble the coal arrived.

Neddy, once again casting himself in the role of chief tester said, "Reet lads, let's switch the bugger off'"

Les, somewhat nervously, switched off the power and we waited for the belt to stop. At this point we heard a terrible scraping sound as the brake calliper closed around the disc. Within seconds, as the scraping turned to a banshee type wail, a couple of fairly alarming events began to unfold. One was that, despite the awful noise, the belt continued to deliver coal at the same rapid pace; and the other was that the brake disc began to glow. As we watched, it went rapidly through the complete temperature spectrum, until it became white hot. At this fascinating point in mechanical mayhem, the brake pads disintegrated, which in turn, led to a sudden increase in momentum. And even without the benefit of hindsight we knew the conveyor was about to self-destruct—again.

It was time to join the wee man in his shelter.

Meanwhile Les, in a sort of blind panic, had grabbed the copper device and was desperately sending all kinds of incomprehensible signals to the guys at the top of the tunnel. In a futile effort, as he said later, "To stop the bastards putting more coal on the conveyor."

Finally, with a terrible inevitability, the weight of coal won the day. The conveyor ground to a halt, there was dust everywhere; the tunnel was once again full of coal, we were no longer advocates of the disc-brake solution and the wee man was moaning gently whilst doing his best to stand upright.

It's not that we were blasé, you understand, but when you've been buried once, being buried the second time doesn't have the same impact (other than by the odd lump of flying coal, that is.)

I could go on, but this is supposed to be a mildly entertaining book, so I'll just say we finally solved the problem by installing two conveyor drives in tandem. We located the second one at the top of the tunnel, leaving the original at the bottom. The thinking behind this was based on the theory that, as the conveyor was now being driven by a two motors, there was less strain on the belt and we also had the benefit of a braking system at each end.

We did, however, have one more minor setback during initial testing— life can be like that, I find. What happened was that we filled the belt with coal (again) and decided (again) to switch off in order to see how the new system behaved.

Sadly, we couldn't have synchronised the brakes properly, because the top conveyor brake came on marginally before the bottom one. This had an unfortunate effect on the belt, which was stretched by the bottom conveyor and then snapped about six hundred yards up the tunnel.

The wee man, who by now was acting on auto-pilot, leaped into his shelter, curled himself into a ball and awaited the arrival of us lot. I guess the whole debacle was summed up by the same guy, when asked later if he was okay, said, "Bloody fitters, we never had this trouble with pit ponies."

Chapter Twenty-Seven
An Offer You Can't Refuse.

I once had a narrow escape from being charged with assault; hard to believe I know, but it could have lead to a possible sacking, almost certain suspension, loss of dignity, social unacceptability, ostracisation, letters to The Times, protest marches, picketing, and hate mail. Well, maybe not all at the same time.

But, I hear you ask, how could our hero possibly be guilty of such a heinous crime? There must be some mistake, surely?

Well, possibly—but first we must set the scene, as they say in all good novels. It all came about when I found a message tied to my lamp asking me to pop along to the Technical College, as Geoff wanted a word. Cryptic in the extreme I thought. What did he want, was I to be forgiven for making him present me with a Churchill book? Only one way to find out, so I 'popped along,' knocked on his door and was ushered in to the presence.

Greetings were made and I was asked to sit down, still uneasy, wondering what I had done wrong. Was it because I had completed my studies at Wigan instead of St Helens? You can't be too sensitive about what might be construed as going over to the enemy.

However, Geoff's next question really did throw me off balance.

"How would you like to be a Lecturer?"

I must have stared at him with a look resembling that of a half-witted gargoyle, as he stared back at me for a minute and then repeated the question.

"I said, how would you like to be a Lecturer?"

Now as questions go it was perfectly reasonable, clear and concise. Unfortunately, it was just about the last thing I'd been expecting. Suddenly I was about to make a decision which would either maintain the status quo—working underground, snap, mice, snuff, dark, wet, cold, hot, dust, roof falls, bent double, heavy lifting, wrist wrestling, overtime, concessionary coal, towels, soap, walking for miles, good mates, turkeys and erudite conversation. All this had to be instantly weighed against the need to buy a Harris Tweed jacket with leather elbow patches, a tie, a briefcase, shiny shoes, a haircut, a gabardine mac, several pens and pencils, text-books and a clean handkerchief. On the other hand, I told myself, there would be daylight, free weekends, no overtime, a salary instead of wages, members of staff instead of mates, mental stimulus, no wrist wrestling, and no swearing. However, this latter benefit turned out to be somewhat inaccurate—as we shall see later.

So I said "Yes, please,"—and that's how I became a member of the professional classes (or so I fondly thought.)

I won't bore you with the nitty-gritty aspects of joining the academic ranks, but suffice it to say that, as the first flush of euphoria faded, a number of hitherto carefully hidden facts began to emerge.

Firstly, the Education Authority had hit on an economic wheeze whereby they paid salaried staff monthly in arrears. For some reason, I wasn't fully aware of the implications of this strategy when I signed up. It was, therefore, something of a shock to find that, having drawn my final week's wages from the pit, I then had four more weeks to go before I saw any more money. Remember, working on less than £20 per week didn't leave an awful lot over for savings. In fact, it left sod all. So there we were, faced with the prospect of having nothing to eat for a month, a tank three quarters full of petrol, text-books to pay for and on top of all that, I had to put five shillings a week into the staffroom tea fund. Mind you, despite bordering on starvation, I was now a man with a briefcase.

Funnily enough, I have, at various times, found myself a little short of the 'readies' so to speak. Providing a temporary solution to this problem has involved me in a number of surreal activities including that of a TV salesman, an assistant master in a secure unit, but none more so than the month I spent de-greasing Fiat cars.

It was a chance to earn an extra £15 per week while on holiday from my new job at the Technical College. Someone, who was obviously as strapped for cash as I was, put me onto a casual job in Fiat's main warehouse in Warrington, where the cars, newly arrived from the docks, were stored prior to distribution throughout the UK. The job involved a team of chaps, decked out in waterproof clothing, de-greasing each car as it arrived from storage. The system operated on an endless belt principle whereby the car moved slowly through a bay where two lucky guys, one on each side, washed the car, using a mixture of high pressure paraffin and hot water forced through huge lances. You couldn't hang about, as the car was delivered into an adjacent bay, where a team of ladies dried it off and applied polish. Obviously, if we hadn't cleaned the grease off properly the ladies would go mad, shout nasty things through the doors, report us to the foreman and have to send the vehicle through the system again. And you thought nuclear physics was difficult.

Due to the fumes generated by the evil mixture, the caring company decided that we should be limited to ffiteen minutes inside the booth at any one time. This meant we worked on a rotation system whereby at the end of your stint, you were relieved by a bloke looking like an overdressed arctic fisherman. Now, as there were two bays at any one time, we had four on spray duty and five (don't ask me why) sitting outside on a bench. Making nine in all – are you still following this?

Anyway, as I became familiar with the set-up, I noticed a common thread running through the day. There were continual, bitter, recriminatory, fatuous, pointless, accusatory arguments about whose turn it was to don the gear and claim their fifteen minutes of fame in the wash-bay. It had to be seen to be believed—there was denial, name calling and finger-pointing; there were veiled threats, excuses and pathetic lies. In the meantime, based on the mistaken belief that we were all there to work, I tried to remain aloof from the claims and counter-claims. Sadly, this didn't always work, as one or other of the gang would turn to me (in my reluctant role as an unbiased observer) and seek support for their contention that everyone, except he, was a lazy sod. It was about this time I first properly understood what Joseph Heller was on about when he wrote Catch 22.

We have to understand here that although the lads were friendly, they didn't really understand me any more than I understood them. It was nothing to do with a language barrier; rather it was the fact that they were working at the limit of their intellectual capabilities whereas I, being considered clever, was viewed with a mixture of both suspicion and envy. However, once they realised I posed no threat to their activities, random acts of kindness prevailed. I was offered a copy of the Sun, asked if there was anything I wanted stolen off a car (wing mirror, radio, petrol cap, etc.) and shown how to open the door on a top of the range car, so I could eat my sandwiches in comfort.

Fridays were the worst, as heated debates about whose turn it was to relieve one another in the steamy inferno reached a crescendo. Interestingly, during the course of these pointless arguments, there was never any sign of the Foreman. Well that's not quite true; you could just about see him through the glass panel, paying what seemed to be an inordinate amount of attention to one of the polishing ladies.

And then, after one particularly virulent row, I fell, as they say, for the 'three card trick.' I was approached somewhat hesitantly by one of the lads, who plied me with flattery—citing my education, lectureship, ability to read The Times, willingness to work and non-involvement in their political wrangling. Apparently, they had held a discussion and decided I could 'do them a favour.' Stressing again my academic capabilities, they believed I was just the chap to develop a duty rota system. This, he said, would stop the arguments, as everyone would know when it was their turn. Peace would return and I would have their undying gratitude. Not only that, but I was encouraged to choose a set of tyres from any model in the yard and they would be delivered to an address of my choosing.

Thinking, mistakenly, it was a good idea (the rota, not the tyres,) I agreed and said I would see what I could do over the weekend. Catching the eye of our womanising Foreman, I mentioned my plan to bring peace and tranquillity, but he just shook his head and gave me a very funny look.

That weekend, instead of cleaning the windows, I joined a number of sheets of paper together, divided the resulting strip into five days, then eight hours, then fifteen minutes before entering nine names in rotation, and ended up with a five foot long complex chart of which I was very proud. I really should have known better, but that's self-aggrandisement for you.

On Monday morning, the lads were all eagerly waiting for the answer to their prayers and there were gasps of amazement as I unrolled the chart and pinned it to the wall under the clock. There was a buzz of excitement as everyone stared at the chart, found their name, checked their times then, accompanied by much back-slapping and mutual congratulations, we went to work. A bit like the seven dwarfs, but scruffier.

The euphoria lasted until Wednesday afternoon. It was at about this time that the awful truth began to dawn on the lads—having to strictly adhere to a timetable meant there was no room for manoeuvre, ability to go missing, cheat, lie, argue, spend time in the bog, nip out for a bet or arrive late in the morning. In other words, hard won freedoms had been taken away—and by none other than yours truly.

How fickle is adoration! By Thursday morning it was as though I had contacted Lhasa fever, the Sun was no longer available, offers of wing mirrors had been withdrawn and my waterproof hat had mysteriously disappeared. And then, just before finishing time, one of my erstwhile pals grabbed the chart, ripped it to shreds and without a word, flung it in the bin.

Happily, by the following Monday, things were all back to normal, football matches were dissected, pub fights were recounted, sexual exploits were graphically described, losing bets were itemised, and they were all speaking to me again. Just as I was about to settle down for my break, the Foreman made a rare appearance. Staring for a moment at the space on the wall, he gave me an awful grin and said, "I could 'ave bloody told you it were a waste of time—and to think, you're supposed to be the clever one."

And with that he trundled off to meet his polishing lady.

Back to the plot......

Another small, but fairly important issue when being a lecturer was the need, at all costs, to appear intellectually superior to your students. This involved a bluff similar in scale to the one which convinced Hitler that the D-day landings were going to take place at Calais (I'll bet the guy who thought that one up had been a lecturer.)

Firstly, you had a year's syllabus to divide into weekly chunks; you then had to prepare a one or two hour lecture covering the subject in question, develop notes, prepare worked examples, set calculations, answer tricky questions and exude confidence—whilst pretending to know everything. The only difficulty with this dreamworld was the fact that you were far from being prepared a year in advance. In fact, in the majority of cases, you were just about half an hour in front of the students with regard to knowledge of the subject. Dealing with questions which you had absolutely no idea how to answer, meant replying with enthusiasm along the lines of, "I'm really glad you asked me that. Now, I could delay things today by answering, but what I would prefer to do is bank the question and answer it fully when we come to the part of the syllabus which deals with your particular query. In that way, the whole class can gain full benefit from the explanation."

This, of course, was complete rubbish; it really meant that I hadn't a clue and would need to swot it up before the following week's lecture. I think it's called lying with impunity.

Fortunately, my guide and mentor during the early days was a great chap called Jack. He was ten years older than me and we quickly became good friends. He was at his happiest in the workshops where he masterfully introduced groups of reluctant apprentices to the fine arts of turning, milling, grinding, shaping, welding, brazing, screw-cutting, blacksmithing and the odd dirty joke.

I recall trying to follow in his footsteps and on one occasion, when doing a stint in the workshop, I had given the students something to make. Towards the end of the lesson I had to examine the finished product in order to pass judgement on its accuracy, finish, etc. As confidence grew, I decided to emulate Jack's rapport with the students and tried my own version on a lad called Churnside, who had offered up his work for comment. Overcome with keenness and a totally false sense of my own importance, I decided it wasn't up to the required standard. Sending him back to improve the article, I again rejected it on his return. The third time he arrived, I decided to become demonstrative and so, with a flourish I flung his work onto a nearby bench. At this point Churnside stared at me with something approaching hatred and very quietly said, "Mr Page?"

"Yes?"

"You make me sick."

A year or two later, 'the powers that be' decided the College was becoming overcrowded and so looked around for a department who could most readily move out. This, we believed, was education speak for—"Let's get rid of these awful mining people."

The upshot of these political manoeuvrings was that we were shifted, lock, stock and barrel, to a recently vacated Convent about fifteen minutes walk from the main campus.

I know what you're thinking, what are they doing, letting a bunch of hairy miners loose in a convent? Well interestingly, at least for the first few weeks, even the most cynical blokes (including the staff) were somewhat overawed by the premises. The building had been run as a preparatory school for many years and was late Victorian with large stained glass windows. However, the greatest distinction between the college and our new premises was to be found inside the rooms, along the corridors and up the stairs. There was highly polished wood everywhere, the walls gleamed, the desks looked as though they had glass tops and the banisters were as slippery as a cresta run. It was obviously the result of the sisters' having no television, together with an overwhelming urge to do penance.

We soon got used to the polish, but what took a little longer to get used to was the fact that being a Catholic establishment, there had been saintly reminders everywhere. Obviously, these had been removed when the nuns vacated, but what remained were the distinct outlines on the walls, showing where they had been. For instance, at the top of the stairs we were faced with the outline of a huge crucifix; each classroom had the outlines of holy pictures along the walls, our staffroom had a similar crucifix looking down on our tea-making facilities and there were outlines of various saints, which had stood on plinths, along the corridors.

But the most disconcerting reminder of the previous tenants was to be found in the staff toilets. Again, there was polished wood everywhere and even as you shut the cubicle door, the clear outline of Saint Catherine could be seen staring down, in what many took to be disapproval. The WC's were also Victorian and the bowls were extremely ornate, having wreaths of flowers painted around the inside. The toilet seats were mahogany and polished to a mirror-like finish, but it was Jack who summed up our discomfort by remarking that, every time he sat there, he couldn't help thinking he was occupying the same seat as generations of nuns' bums.

I digress. I was about to tell you of my narrow escape from arrest for violence. It all came about when I had a class of second year apprentices and was gamely trying to enthuse them with a riveting subject called 'Mechanical technology applied to steam winders.' You can see how it would really grip them, especially when you realise that the class started at five pm and went on until seven pm. Anyway, it was just my luck to have, seated at the front, a budding criminal who made it very clear that he didn't rate either me or the subject and would therefore, prefer to read the Daily Mirror, or better still, engage his nearest colleague in loud conversation.

Appealing to his better nature turned out to be a waste of time (he didn't have one.) Slowly the class, and me, wore on whilst he continued to cause mayhem, modelled, I suppose, on the behaviour of the average rock group in a four star hotel. Eventually I snapped and moving to within about six inches of his face, I ordered him out of the room and, as he moved to do so, I followed. Once in the corridor, he still wouldn't shut up, and then said something deeply personal to which I took great exception.

Within a millisecond, his neck had somehow fastened itself in my hand and he had leaped backwards to hit the corridor wall with some considerable force. At this point he had at last stopped talking, but I did notice that his face was turning a sort of dark maroon colour. Fortunately, (for both of us—as it turned out,) his head had somehow made a loud bang on the wall of a room which happened to be occupied by Jack. Coming out to see what had caused the noise, he was surprised to see a lad with a funny coloured face hanging from my arm, with no sign that he was about to be released in the near future.

Acting with commendable speed, Jack freed me from the lad's neck, checked his breathing, told him to get off home, nipped in to both classes and dismissed them, took me into the staffroom for a cup of tea and then asked, "What the hell happened?"

So I told my story, during the course of which I began to realise I may have overstepped the mark—so to speak.

"Too bloody right you have," said Jack, neglecting to adopt a comforting mode. "We'll need to report this, because as sure as hell you can bet he will."

Anyway, to cut a long story short, I was given dire warnings of the possible consequences (sacking, fining, jailing, hanging, disgrace to the profession, etc.) I must say however, my unilateral action had a salutary effect on my students and a produced a degree of covert admiration from fellow staff members. In the meantime I tried to adopt a low profile, while waiting to see what might be the outcome.

This occurred one afternoon when I was summoned to Geoff's office to find that a National Union of Mineworkers official had arrived in order to represent the assaulted victim. I was able to invite Jack along as a 'friend' and, as evidence of my ruthless attack on an innocent lad was revealed, I have to say it didn't look good apropos of a long and successful career in further education.

The Union man was a bluff looking chap who reminded me of Charlie Drake, a diminutive comedian who had his own TV show. Getting down to business, our man reeled off a list of more and more damning facts—the lad was traumatised, his mum could testify to the fact that, even several days later, you could still see finger marks on his neck, he had a permanent headache due to having his head banged on the wall and wasn't eating properly.

Jack looked at Geoff, I looked at Jack, Geoff looked at me and our man looked pleased. What it definitely didn't look—was good.

Geoff tried to intervene, "Are you sure the lad suffered from all these symptoms?"

"Aye, it looks that way. His mum says he can't touch her best steak and kidney pie, but what I can't understand is what made you attack him like that?"

"He swore at me," I said.

'He what?'

"I said, he swore at me and, speaking as an ordinary citizen, not as a lecturer, I'm not prepared to put up with an ignorant kid like that swearing at me in front of his mates, so I ordered him out and when we got in the corridor, he swore at me again."

"I didn't know that," said our man. "What exactly did he say?"

"He told me to f-off several times, then he said I was a stupid effer for being in this job and that all my children must be effing bastards."

"What? You're telling me he swore at you and was rude about your family? I didn't know that. Well, that puts a different light on matters. I can't condone that sort of thing. I wouldn't like it myself and he can't just come here at great cost to the NCB and start effing and blinding at your good selves, no indeed. I'm not having that."

Once again we looked at one another; could this be my saviour?

He was.

"Just thee leave it with me. I'll have a strong word with yon git, swearing at a lecturer indeed! No—it's not on. I'll see to that, he wants a bloody good hiding, that's what he wants and I'm just the chap to see he gets it."

And with that, he stood up, apologised, shook me by the hand, said he was sorry to have bothered us and went off muttering something about sacking.

"Bloody hell," said Jack, "Tha's had a bloody lucky escape and no mistake, bloody hell."

I said, "Jack, stop swearing at me, you know what might happen if I get upset." And with that, the three of us made a nice fresh brew.

Chapter Twenty-Eight
And Finally.…..

First of all, let me say, by way of a disclaimer, that all of the foregoing consists of my own reminiscences and as such, some parts may contain inaccuracies with regard to the more technical aspects of mining. Sadly, this can't be helped, because while I'm good on broad statements, my grasp of detail has long since disappeared.

If you think I am merely being evasive or worse still, lazy, just test your own memories for a moment. For instance, how many people can remember the formula for calculating a quadratic function? And yet we all learned it at one time or another—I think.

Anyway, enough of the apologies, should you wish to learn more about coal mining in Britain, there are hundreds of books on the topic. In a similar way, I have tried to steer clear of politics, as once again, enough has already been written about this thorny subject and by people far better qualified to do so than me.

What I would like to do by way of a social comment is to pay tribute to a band of men who were a privilege to know (although I have to confess I didn't always realise it at the time!) They represented comradeship in its finest sense and a way of life that has now, sadly, all but disappeared. They allowed you no delusions of grandeur and were quick to point out the error of your ways. However, in turn, I found my underground colleagues to be kind, helpful, patient, supportive, cynical, loyal, funny, blunt and highly skilled. I met colliers who were fantasists, crude, religious, romantic, incredibly strong and cruel to mice.

I worked with a Shotfirer who could complete The Times 'Mephisto' crossword quicker than Inspector Morse. And I could also hold erudite discussions on geology, astronomy, sex, thermodynamics, rugby, gardening and the relative merits of Maureen O'Hara when compared to Anna Magnani (On the one hand—Irish, passionate, a red headed beauty, figure to die for; on the other hand—Italian, black hair, sultry accent, voluptuous, figure to die for.) Obviously, not a decision you could make in haste.

But perhaps above all, they were patient with me when it mattered and collectively they kept me safe when I hadn't a clue about working in the most awful conditions it was possible to imagine. Thanks lads.

For the record—mining at Bold Colliery ceased in 1985, followed by the closure of Bold Power Station in 1991, leaving what was now one hundred and thirty hectares of derelict land.

Fortunately, in 1986 a Groundwork Initiative known as 'Waste into Woodland' began work on the site, resulting in the creation of 'Colliers Moss Common.' Utilising the spoil and waste, they have created a diverse landscape with water features (including lagoons, streams, wetland areas and fishery.) There are focal points, artworks, seating areas and an amphitheatre, which serve to make the whole site a beautiful and peaceful place to explore as well as an important habitat for wildlife.

The remnants of mossland around the fringes of the site have been restored and areas of sphagnum moss are expanding. The site supports a range of notable species including water vole, common lizard and various species of dragonfly including Blacktailed Skimmer and Emperor.

The design of the entrance gates was inspired by the power station cooling towers; new paths have been introduced with signs and visitor information. As a result of these developments half of the site has now been designated as a Local Nature Reserve.

I can't help but wonder, as people stop to quietly enjoy the reserve, whether they might just hear distant echo of laughter from Davvy, Pat, Bill, Ernie, Joe, Les, Frank, Colin, Kenny, Harold, Billy, Jimmy, Little Eric, Andy and the Wee Man.

Or perhaps it's just time I had a lie down.

THE END

In the 1950's Brian decided to make a daring career move based on almost total ignorance of the facts. This was to work underground in one of the deepest coal-mines in Lancashire. Like a number of things in life, it seemed to be a good idea at the time. Sadly, he had failed to consider the implications of working in pitch darkness among folk who spoke a language unheard of in Knotty Ash and whose pet of choice was a thing called a Whippet.

What he did learn was that miners were keen to stay alive, loved beer, rugby, assorted lasses and considered dynamite to be a labour saving device.

Having spent some nine years underground he arrived, blinking in the light, to lecture other unfortunates in the art of mining engineering. He utterly refutes accusations that his leaving in any way hastened the demise of what was once a great British industry.

Also from PlashMill Press

A Boy's Own Offshore Adventure
by Brian Page

Price: £11.99   ISBN: 978-0-9554535-1-9

Silver Threads
by TOM RALSTON

Price: £9.99   ISBN: 978-0-9554535-5-7

Poaching the River
by Rod Fleming

Price: £11.99   ISBN: 978-0-9554535-0-2

THE TOBACCONIST
by JENNIFER DALMAINE

Price: £9.99   ISBN: 978-0-9554535-2-6

Free Carriage!

Carriage anywhere in the world is free when you order direct from PlashMill Press. Please see our website for terms and conditions.

www.plashmillpress.com